The Furniture
of Old Ontario

Philip Shackleton

The Furniture of Old Ontario

Macmillan of Canada
Toronto

ISBN 0-7705-1665-3

First edition, 1973
Second printing, October 1973
Third printing, 1974
First paperback edition, 1978

Designed by Robert Burgess Garbutt

Printed in the United States of America for
The Macmillan Company of Canada
70 Bond Street
Toronto, Ontario M5B 1X3

In memory of
Marge Shackleton

This book had its beginnings in her keen enthusiasm for the craft traditions of Canada's settlement period. The work was begun in partnership and she completed the first of the photographs, principally at Upper Canada Village and Black Creek Pioneer Village, before her death in 1967.

Contents

Acknowledgements

No one person, least of all the author, can be given credit for the making of this book. I expect to shoulder full responsibility for its failings, its errors, and its omissions, but the credit for whatever may be good in this work I must share with those many generous persons who have given readily of their time, their counsel, and their research findings.

In the classic words of an author's acknowledgements, it is impossible to mention here every person who has helped me in this study of early Ontario furniture. I would, however, find it equally impossible to conclude without recognizing in print my particular debts to some few of them.

Mrs. Jeanne Minhinnick, who enjoys nothing so much as debating the virtues of local period furniture, has shared most generously of her knowledge and insight into the traditions of Upper Canada. Mr. W. N. Minhinnick, who affects to deplore the cult of the antique, has been a kindly and constructive critic. My sincere thanks to them both.

I have enjoyed the greatest possible help and co-operation from the staff of Upper Canada Village, from its Director, Mr. William J. Patterson, from Miss Marjorie Dissette, Curator of Furniture and Furnishings, and from Miss Barbara Snyder, Registrar and Librarian. I received similar kind assistance from the staff of Black Creek Pioneer Village and from its Administrator, Mr. Russell Cooper.

I am grateful to the Sigmund Samuel Canadiana Gallery of the Royal Ontario Museum and, for their particular help, to the Curator, Mr. Donald B. Webster, and Miss Janet Holmes. I have found museum and gallery curators prepared, without exception, to upset their schedules and delay their own work in order to help me. Among them, I must make special mention of Mrs. Alix Gronau at Dundurn Castle, Miss Margaret Home at the Jordan Historical Museum of the Twenty, Mr. R. Alan Douglas at the Hiram Walker Museum, and Miss Margaret Machell at The Grange, Art Gallery of Ontario.

I have enjoyed very much a lengthy and happy association with many members of the staff of the National Historic Sites Service and I have been particularly privileged to have ready access to their research library in Ottawa.

To special friends, who share in quite different ways a very real interest in the household furnishings of an age past, I am most grateful for the many different kinds of help that they have given so freely — to Ruth and Blake McKendry, Elginburg, to Mrs. Elizabeth Ingolfsrud, Toronto, to Mrs. Dorothy Duncan, Toronto, to Mr. Charles McKenzie, Ottawa, and to Mr. Edgar McLean, Prescott.

I have been constantly amazed at the long-suffering patience and the generosity of private collectors and museum curators who have allowed me to disrupt the calm of their homes and their galleries with my intrusive cameras and lights. I wish to thank them each and all, for without their sufferance there could be no book at all.

I have photographed many hundreds of pieces of furniture during the course of this work but I must acknowledge with gratitude additional illustrations that have been provided by the Royal Ontario Museum, the National Gallery of Canada, the Metropolitan Toronto Library Board, the Archives of Ontario, the Public Archives of Canada, the London Public Library, the Ministry of Industry and Tourism for Ontario, Mr. Henry Dobson, Mr. M. F. Feheley, and Mr. Duncan Cameron.

To the Canada Council, whose grant has helped so much to lighten the burden of travelling and photographic costs during the years in which I have pursued my research and my recording of the furniture of old Ontario, I offer my very sincere gratitude.

PHILIP SHACKLETON

Introduction

ONLY WITHIN recent years has there developed in Canada any truly widespread interest in our domestic past. Only within the last thirty years has the collecting of "Canadian antiques" changed from a quaintly eccentric pursuit to a popularly approved pastime.

Within our own day, a particular appreciation and affection has developed for the furniture of early Ontario. We like it. We collect it. We use it to furnish our twentieth-century homes. The new demand for domestic furniture of a past century is sufficient to guarantee that whatever has survived to this date, be it good or bad according to universal design standards, will probably be preserved, even cherished, for a good many years to come.

Within the period of a single generation, there has matured in Canada some genuine sense of national identity, and it is within that same period that a large number of individuals have for the first time spent a great deal of time and energy seeking tangible cultural roots, material evidence of local and national history that they can see and handle and even come to own. For some, the household effects of our forebears provide some of that material evidence. Scuffed and worn but mellowed with time, the chairs and chests of a century gone are cultural roots of a kind that many of us are quick to recognize. As vital, perhaps, to our sense of history as school-book stories of General Brock's last battle and Lord Durham's last report.

The furniture illustrated in this book will not be mistaken for the furniture of princes and barons. It is the furniture of a people in a down-to-earth society, and for its greater part it reflects the solid values of a peasantry and a newly important middle class.

With our democratic sensibilities, it is perhaps easy for us to identify its qualities with our present-day values. But whatever there be of philosophical explanation, it is not difficult to accept that many of us who like this furniture of our local past like it because it is ours. It belongs to us. Its story and the larger story of the province belong to us, the people who live in Ontario.

Just as we are a people now largely of European origin, so it follows that our historic furniture is largely and primarily of European tradition. The basic forms, the structural and ornamental characteristics of our locally made furniture, are derived from models originating in other parts of the world.

The truth is, there appears to be nothing radically different about the chairs and tables and chests made and used by our ancestors in the relatively short history of this small part of the world. Our forebears evidently devised no new forms of furniture and there is insufficient evidence to suggest that they originated here any peculiarly new style or fashion.

Priority values were clearly understood in Ontario's pioneer communities. Our great-great-grandparents were too busy clearing bush, building houses and barns and forts, hacking out roads, contriving schools, even rebelling against or defending the political *status quo* of the colony, to have given much time or effort to modifying the furniture concepts of western civilization.

The frontier society, of course, is not the place to look for the finest expression in the arts and crafts. The patronage of established wealth and culture provides the essential encouragement in societies where artists and artisans thrive. To reach for high style in old Ontario, wealthy citizens had either to import the fashionable furniture of the period or to accept that which local cabinet-makers produced to emulate it.

All of this is not to suggest that the furniture of our provincial past has no value. A sampling of the examples illustrated in this book will reveal well chosen materials, quality craftsmanship, and design of some ingenuous charm. It is possible even that some viewers, after seeing all the pictures, may conclude that there is something just a little different that sets apart some of the historic furniture of the province.

A complete survey of that old furniture will include at the one extreme the improvised frontier variety, quickly and crudely shaped by shanty dwellers from whatever materials were available, and at the other, the most sophisticated cabinet-work, the refined products made of choice materials by skilled craftsmen who were most closely attuned to fashion's whim.

The major concern of this book is with the many varieties and grades of furniture that fall between these extremes.

The tradition of crude, home-made furniture from the period of shanty life in Ontario is much revered by some present-day collectors. But for those who made it and those who used it, it was makeshift. It was chopped or whittled or otherwise fashioned from sticks or boards or tree trunks to serve basic needs for a limited time. As far as the old-time owners were concerned, the shorter that time the better.

There are collectors today who find the greatest appeal in the very crudest furniture from early days, but those who lived in the early days generally waited no longer than absolutely necessary to replace it with more serviceable, more efficient, more comfortable, and more elegant furniture.

One must conclude, on the other hand, that relatively little of what might be called extremely fine furniture was made here in times past. Those with particularly sophisticated tastes appear often to have indulged those tastes with the help of suppliers outside this colony. Fashion's direction within the colony seems generally to have been tempered by a spirit of provincial sturdiness.

The flowering of eighteenth-century taste was on the wane by the time the first English-speaking settlers set to work with axes in the all-but-virgin forest. While there is evidence to show the survival of Georgian design in many provincial forms, one does not expect to find here native furniture of the most exotic orders.

Cabinet-makers and joiners and carpenters during Ontario's first hundred years made a great deal of furniture in both native and imported woods. But they made it for the farmers and the townsmen of a new and raw colony, not for the members of some European court. Within its period it was not intended that it be compared to the work of older and richer societies.

The photographs and the period pictures which illustrate this book provide a view of what it seems most fitting to call the provincial furniture of old Ontario. Some of us are quite fond of it.

The People

Tʜɪs sᴛᴜᴅʏ concerns the furniture made and used by those people who came in the eighteenth and nineteenth centuries to occupy the lands immediately north of Lake Erie, Lake Ontario, and the upper St. Lawrence River.

The Indians of this land had been a nomadic people. Their values were different from those of the Europeans, and in their own culture they produced little that history calls furniture. Whether or not the late-comers of white skin brought or evolved a superior culture is quite another matter.

By the mid-eighteenth century, the French had established several military or trading outposts across present-day southern Ontario; Fort Frontenac, on the site of contemporary Kingston, and Fort Rouillé, the first white settlement to suggest that Toronto had a future, were the best known. But the forts decayed or were destroyed and no identifiable furniture from these posts remains for study today.

Still in the days of New France, there grew along the Detroit River, in the general area of today's Amherstburg and Sandwich, a small farming community based on the traditional French seigniorial system of land tenure. It was part of the larger community which straddled the river and survived under the protection of the key post of Fort Pontchartrain, on the site of the present-day city of Detroit.

Some simple furniture survives from this French-speaking community on the Ontario side of the Detroit River. There is probably little, if any, remaining from the eighteenth century, and the nineteenth-century pieces to be seen in museum displays differ in no appreciable degree from the simplest of Quebec furniture traditions.

By including the odd isolated fur post in the north, one can claim there were English-speaking residents in Ontario before the fateful Battle of Quebec in 1759. Such residents, however, were as nomadic as the Indian people with whom they came to trade and we have little trace of their furniture today.

Even the conquest did not bring immediate British settlement to this part of the world. King Louis's wild bushlands along the Great Lakes became King George's wild bushlands. There was transfer of title but no actual change in condition.

It was the American Revolution that brought Ontario into being. The displaced persons after that uprising, those who chose continuing loyalty to the Crown, those whose lands and homes had been confiscated by rebels, sought new homes in lands that remained British. Many were re-settled in already established parts of British North America, but some thousands came to the wilderness that was to become Upper Canada. As refugees, and hence a problem to administrators, they appeared a large group, but as settlers establishing a new colony, they were stronger in tradition than in numbers.

It was a ready-made population and a good one. They were North Americans, familiar with the character of the land, accustomed to making a livelihood in the new world, accomplished in what later became to be called American know-how. This continent was home to them. The new lands to the north held many hardships but few surprises. No group of people could have been better qualified to pioneer Ontario.

The refugees were known from the beginning as Loyalists, United Empire Loyalists in the cumbersome designation conferred by Governor Sir Guy Carleton on all those who arrived before 1783. For a generation and more, Upper Canada was almost exclusively theirs. Some had escaped the revolution with appreciable wealth; they carried away money, household goods, even a few slaves. Others brought little more than the clothing they wore. They represented every level of society and the widest range of trades and professions from the revolting thirteen colonies. Among those tradesmen were carpenters, joiners, and cabinet-makers.

Allegiance to the Crown was held in common by Loyalists and those who followed, but there was cultural diversity among the settlers even in the earliest years.

Palatine Loyalists brought German traditions to new communities along the St. Lawrence River and the Bay of Quinte. There were Loyalist Scots who spoke little English. There were Quakers who did speak English but whose standards and manners set them distinctly apart from their neighbours. Mennonites who came from Pennsylvania shared pacifist views with the Quakers, but their language and traditions were provincial German.

Iroquois Loyalists, allies of the British cause during the revolution, came north in appreciable numbers. Mohawks largely, they moved from northern New York State to the Grand River Valley and the Bay of Quinte shore.

Another group of Germans, after a brief stopover in New York, came to Markham Township, north-east of Toronto, in 1794. And for years after the revolution, there was a steady migration from the new republic of those who came to be known as late loyalists. There remains some suggestion that the particularly attractive land-grant terms that came with the actual political establishment of Upper Canada in 1791 may have had something to do with settling certain cases of wavering allegiance.

Still, in those first few years, it scarcely seemed a boom colony. At mid-eighteenth century there may have been a hundred French-speaking families in the entire area. At the outbreak of the War of 1812, thirty years after the American Revolution, there were probably no more than 100,000 persons in the colony of Upper Canada.

The American influx was greatly reduced even before 1812, and the end of that war brought the first large-scale immigration direct from Britain and Ireland. Their numbers varied from year to year, seldom more than 20,000 in any one year, but immigration from the old world continued throughout the rest of the century.

Upper Canada had been established as a primarily English-speaking reserve for Loyalist refugees. It continued to serve as such for refugees of a new kind. These were the thousands of British families displaced in the old land by the rapidly changing social and economic conditions of the nineteenth century.

The enclosure movement that removed countless small farmers in Britain from their lands, the turmoil of the industrial revolution itself, and the postwar depression following Waterloo in 1815 combined to throw thousands of working families into the most hopeless economic distress. Emigration was a frightening prospect, the more so under assisted programs that made it clear there would be no return tickets for those dissatisfied in the new world. Frightening it was, but for those trapped by economic forces they could not begin to understand, it appeared the one hope for some improvement.

The post-war waves of home seekers, the shiploads of poor from Ireland, Scotland, and England, really began to tame the Ontario hinterland. The pre-1812 settlers had scarcely penetrated the bush;

their villages and farms hugged the Great Lakes and St. Lawrence watercourse, few of their communities more than out of sight of the United States.

The Loyalist generation had seen the founding of Kingston, Cobourg, York, Niagara, and Amherstburg, each of them on the southern border of the colony. It was only after the 1812 war that the new groups of settlers broke land where the communities of Perth and Bytown, Peterborough and Goderich were to grow.

Farmers and labourers speaking French moved inevitably from the Lower to the Upper Canada side of the Ottawa Valley. More German-language groups contributed to the growing population. Some Americans still thought they saw greener grass north of the Lakes. Some old-world colonists moved on when they were convinced it must be greener south of the Lakes.

The distinct traditions of different homelands explains in part the variety in home-furnishing styles in the settlement period. Equally important were the considerable class distinction and the contrast in wealth among those pioneers. There were affluent Loyalists from Virginia and there were ground-down poor from Highland crofts. There were gentlefolk whose pride was their only wealth and there were opportunists whose sharp eyes and sharper manners guaranteed their survival.

From perhaps 50,000 persons in 1800, the population grew to about 100,000 by 1812. By 1825 the total was scarcely more than 150,000. In another ten years it had doubled. By 1840 it had passed 400,000 and by 1850 it had reached 800,000.

It was not a large colony either in population or in area, and it is dwarfed by contrast to the Ontario of today. The position of Upper Canada's northern border always seemed a little uncertain, and Canada West, as the colony became known after the 1841 Act of Union, included no territory beyond that recognized today as the southern and smaller part of the province.

Today's Ontario is a huge mass, a thousand miles across in any direction. Yesterday's Ontario was only a few hundred miles in breadth. The furniture illustrated in this book was found within that few hundred miles, and scarcely any of it originated any farther north than a line drawn roughly from Arnprior to Goderich.

Style Background

S OME VERY general acquaintance with changing furniture fashions in Britain and the United States is essential to understand the apparently mixed up and overlapping styles to be seen in the furniture of Ontario's first one hundred years. Since the colonists here had no contact of consequence with other parts of the world, it is to these two countries that one must look for the influences that most affected our forebears' tastes.

In the mid-eighteenth century the making of furniture was everywhere still a craft and the standards of craft were still high. When the Loyalists came to Canada, the Rococo style was just giving way to the Classic in the most up-to-date British architecture and interior furnishings.

The graceful curves and asymmetrical character beloved of Chippendale and his school were losing favour to the more sober straight lines of a revived Classic period. And the genius of the period was Robert Adam.

The ancient worlds of Greece and Rome had been rediscovered. Excavations at Pompeii and Herculaneum excited widespread interest. Books about classical ruins were immensely popular and amateur archeology became a very proper hobby for British gentlemen.

For architect Robert Adam and his partner brothers, the wealth of classical tradition left by Greek and Roman builders provided richly varied inspiration for a new classical age in Britain. The Adams built palaces and furnished them with matching furniture, also of their design; their clients were very wealthy.

The next well-known name in the sequence of British style is George Hepplewhite. He followed the Adam lead in the classical tradition, making furniture adapted for the affluent, not just the extremely wealthy. His well-known book, *The Cabinet-Maker and Upholsterer's Guide*, is a collection of furniture designs probably representing the work of his fellow fashionable London craftsmen and not Hepplewhite's alone.

Published in 1788, just after his death, it was a popular reference for British cabinet-makers and a source of furniture patterns widely copied as far away as North America. Even better known perhaps is the name of Thomas Sheraton, who published in London between 1791 and 1794 his now famous work, *The Cabinetmaker and Upholsterer's Drawing Book*. It illustrates a further reworking of the Adam style supplemented with borrowings in detail from the works of other designers and craftsmen, principally the contemporary French. Sheraton was neither cabinet-maker nor designer, and even as a publisher he was a failure in his own lifetime. But whether borrowed or stolen, the styles illustrated in his several works are today firmly linked to his name.

These and other pattern books of the period apparently came even to Canada; certainly it appears they were consulted in the cabinet shops of Quebec and Montreal. The late-eighteenth-century classical lines from these source books can be seen reflected in the museum examples of furniture which came from those relatively sophisticated Canadian centres of the period.

Furniture whose inspiration came at least in part from Hepplewhite or Sheraton publications is found in some quantity in Ontario. Most of it is countrified in character. While some craftsmen here no doubt studied the actual *Guide* or *Drawing Book*, our provincials' debt to Georgian period design is more often through older pieces of furniture used as models.

The Directoire style was a French version of the Greco-Roman school and its principal designer was the renowned Louis David, France's leading artist of the time. It is a style of concern to the Ontario story because it was taken up enthusiastically by furniture men in the United States. From there, pieces of furniture and the inspiration drifted north. American cabinet-makers after the revolution were happier to adopt French than British designs. The slightly modified treatment developed there has since been designated the American Federal style, and New York's Duncan Phyfe was the outstanding cabinet-maker to work in that style.

The heavier-yet neo-classical style known as Empire superseded Directoire when Napoleon decreed that a style be created to mark suitably the era that began with his coronation in 1804. There were fresh borrowings of Roman devices of military flavour and of Egyptian motifs which were intended to memorialize Bonaparte's campaign in that country, but Empire remained another rendering of the classical revival.

Napoleon appointed as his official architects and decorators Charles Percier and Pierre Fontaine, and it is their book, *Recueil de Décorations In-*

térieures, which catalogues the furniture of the Empire style.

This was evidently the work whose designs had the greatest influence, considerably delayed because the Directoire remained popular there, on furniture-makers in the United States after 1820. And the major influence of the Empire style in Upper Canada was clearly that filtered through and adapted by cabinet shops in the States.

Empire from France was also a factor in the development of what is now called the Regency style in England. The British, even when at war with their cross-Channel neighbours, still looked to the French as reliable style-setters. Still, it's quite possible that the same Egyptian motifs which recalled to the French Napoleon's glorious campaigns, commemorated for the British Nelson's victory at the Nile in 1798.

A. This Ontario-made chair is a virtual reproduction of an ancient Greek chair called a *klismos*. The sabre-shaped legs and the gracefully swept rear stiles, joined by rails which guarantee both comfort and security, are features designed more than 2,500 years ago. The Grecian model was restored to fashion about the year 1800. The chair illustrated, made of birch and stained to simulate mahogany, was probably made here between 1820 and 1840.
Upper Canada Village, Morrisburg

Regency, in fact, was at times called English Empire. And the work of George Smith, as seen in *Designs for Household Furniture and Internal Decoration*, published in London in 1808, is an interesting reworking of the classic inspiration in close association with the spirit of new French fashions.

Ornamental features used in Empire furniture, and so it follows in Regency, were eagles, dolphins, swans, harps and lyres, acanthus and anthemion leaves, cornucopiae, and a very strange winged foot. Inlay in metal was high style and it became the inspiration for gilding and decorative painting in more modest furniture that followed.

English Regency has a solid look about it. Simple outline and an emphasis on straight lines, together with a chaste use of classical ornament, mark the best examples of the furniture. Like other period terms relating fashion to duration of reign, the word itself is something less than completely satisfactory. In practice Regency is generally used to cover the British period from about 1790 until Victoria came to the throne in 1837.

It was still part of the continuing classical revival, and the classical revival was based almost entirely on architectural traditions. Little was known of the furniture of the ancients, and so their architectural devices were generally added

B. An ambitious design for a wardrobe complex appears among the illustrations of George Smith's 1826 publication *The Cabinet-Maker and Upholsterer's Guide*. It is representative of high-style furniture of the period. The decorative carving was derived from ancient Greek motifs.

Metropolitan Toronto Library Board

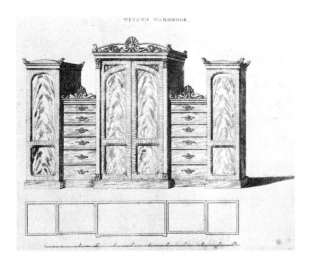

C. The cabinet-maker who produced this wardrobe adapted his design quite obviously from the George Smith illustration (Plate B). While it does not have the flanking units of the original plate, and although the panel pattern of the full-length doors has been simplified, its outline and elaboration are so similar to the 1826 illustration as to make the source of inspiration unmistakable. The wardrobe was evidently acquired when new for The Grange, D'Arcy Boulton's Toronto home built in 1817. The Grange, long since part of the Art Gallery of Ontario, has latterly been restored as a period exhibition house. Walnut and figured walnut veneer are the main woods of this piece. The manner of veneer use is similar to that of two sideboards (Plate 402) which appear to have been specially designed for the house.

The Grange, Art Gallery of Ontario, Toronto

to or adapted to the contemporary forms of western furniture. But the *klismos*, a chair which appears well detailed in Greek vase paintings as early as 500 B.C., was successfully revived shortly after 1800. Thomas Hope, in his *Household Furniture and Interior Decoration*, published in 1807, offers several designs which are near duplicates of ancient Greek models. They show a chair style with legs of a single sabre-like curve and a back which suggests the Greeks understood the value of both grace and comfort.

The new *klismos* of the nineteenth century was soon much modified but the debt to antiquity was clear in both imported and locally made chairs popular in contemporary Upper Canada. The term "Grecian chair" was familiar here, as in much of the western world, for more than fifty years.

Hope, however, cannot be given sole credit for the successful revival. The sabre leg is standard equipment for chairs of the Directoire. And Greek models appear frequently among the illustrations in Rudolph Ackerman's *The Repository of the Arts*, a British periodical appearing from 1809 to 1828, and a reference that likely was consulted in Canadian workshops.

The English George Smith published a new work in 1826, *The Cabinet-Maker and Up-holsterer's Guide*, in which he wrote that his 1808 work had been made obsolete by the rapid changes in taste. Smith's new designs foreshadowed the heavier early Victorian fashions, and he observed that chairs of the period suffered from mixing all the different styles together, a comment that meets pretty general agreement today.

Smith's emphasis on more massive forms appears to have had considerable influence in North America. Preserved today in The Grange, a fashionable house built in Toronto in 1817 for the younger D'Arcy Boulton, is a walnut wardrobe of local manufacture which is among the furniture known to have been in use there from early to mid nineteenth century. The wardrobe is so similar to one of Smith's 1826 illustrations as to deny any possible doubt of its design source.

The craftsmen of Upper Canada may not have been familiar with the works of all the British authors who originated or recorded fashions in furniture of their day. One who certainly was familiar to furniture-makers here was John Claudius Loudon, whose *Encyclopaedia of Cottage, Farm and Villa Architecture and Furniture* was first published in London in 1833. It was probably the first book of its kind catering primarily to the rapidly increasing middle class.

While Loudon's more than two thousand illustrations include Gothic and Elizabethan revival as well, his work is largely of a late provincial Regency flavour. The book was immensely popular and was revised and re-issued again and again, even as late as 1867.

Loudon's *Encyclopaedia* was published at a time when a considerable number of colonists here had graduated from the rough pioneering period and were sufficiently prosperous to demand furniture closer to contemporary fashion's ideals. His wealth of line illustrations appeared also when some considerable furniture production was under way. Whether or not Loudon was the direct inspiration for particular pieces, he did produce the primary most popular work illustrating furniture of a type that investigation reveals was generally familiar in Upper Canada.

Loudon's terminology also reflects something of the long-lasting importance of the classical revival in western society. Recalling that his work was still being printed in 1867, it is significant to understand that he used the terms "Grecian" and "modern" as virtually synonymous words.

By this period, scarcely anyone could have remained unaware of the relentless changes being brought about by the industrial revolution. Country furniture-makers for many years to come still were to preserve traditions which put utility and structure ahead of ornament, but in the larger markets it was the work of the machines and their clever masters that was favoured. Decoration and not structure became the first concern.

Elaborate carving became increasingly important. Rich carving suggested the furniture's owner was affluent; that the carving became coarse and was eventually effected by machines was not important to the newly affluent middle-class buyers. There was no way to avoid a decline in the quality of craft. The increasingly capable machine, the growth in wealth with the growth of machine manufactures, the increase in demand for all sorts of products formerly within reach only of the more affluent and the more cultured—these were basic among the factors that reduced product quality.

Traditional training, the kind of thing typified by the apprentice system, which was governed by conservative craft guilds, was not entirely doomed as yet; it just couldn't control the machine or the appetites of consumers who were newly rich.

Changed conditions in old-world industrial society were at variance with those which had produced the traditional system of craft manufacture. Among the important factors were a rapid growth in population, increased and more widely distributed wealth, and improved methods of

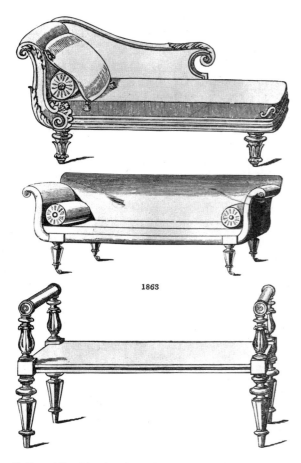

1863

D, E, and F.   Line drawings of three pieces of furniture illustrated in the *Encyclopaedia of Cottage, Farm and Villa Architecture and Furniture* by John Claudius Loudon. The book appeared in London first in 1833 but was so perennially popular that it was still being reprinted as late as 1867. These sketches are representative of furniture designs published in England which were widely imitated in old Ontario in the second and third quarters of the century. The drawing in Plate D was offered by Loudon as a Grecian couch suitable for a villa drawing-room. The sofa in Plate E was described as one "which we hope will come within the reach of many cottagers." The drawing in Plate F is of a bench for a porch or hall and is very similar to a great many country pieces made and used in Ontario after 1850.

transport. The decline of craft and the widespread distribution of style and pattern books also worked to reduce regional differences in furniture character.

No longer did craftsmen strive to make the best possible quality for a relatively small clientele of the privileged and the cultured. Many turned to making, at necessarily lesser cost and quality, furniture for middle-class householders clamouring for the means to display their new affluence.

New woodworking machinery was the key to greatly increased production. When output volume became such an important factor, the craftsman also lost direct contact with his customer. The merchant came between them.

Rapidly changing economic forces caused great distress for many families, but over-all conditions in society did appear to improve. Although workers in factories frequently lived under the most appalling conditions, at the same time there were many more British families owning their own

G.   This selection of English chair designs comes from Loudon's *Encyclopaedia*, a book of designs that probably was consulted by many furniture-makers in old Ontario. The six uppermost are described as plain Grecian chairs suited for cottage parlour use; all but one have caned seats. The three lower are "Grecian elbow chairs with stuffed seats". Armchairs would be the term used today. The chair at the lower right was intended for a woman because it comes with a sewing work box on a sliding frame. Most of the design details represented in this plate were used by Ontario chair-makers.

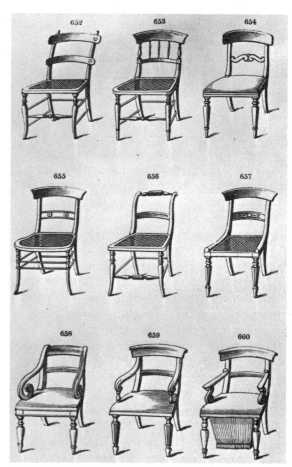

homes in the nineteenth century than in the eighteenth.

The cultured clientele of the earlier period had sought elegance in its furnishings. The newly prosperous of the industrial era made comfort a higher consideration. Mechanical inventiveness responded as readily as design, and one of the greatest advances of the period was the innovation of the metal coil spring, the key to deep and luxuriously comfortable upholstering.

The last phase of the classic revival, and one that strongly influenced Ontario work, originated in the United States. It was probably the first furniture style designed specifically for machine manufacturing. It followed the accepted trend of increasing weight and mass and its most famiiliar feature was the use of scroll supports. It owes some debt to the French Restoration style but much more to the band-saw, which was found to be ideally suited for producing the C- and S-shaped scrolls that dominated much North American furniture towards the middle of the century.

The first illustrations of the style appeared in a lithographed advertisement from the New York furniture factory of Joseph Meeks and Sons. The date was 1833 and Meeks at the time was the leading middle-class furniture supplier in the United States.

In 1840 the style was more effectively offered to other furniture-makers with the publication of *The Cabinet Maker's Assistant* by Baltimore architect John Hall. This, the first furniture pattern book to be produced in the United States, illustrates a style that present-day commentators call debased. Hall's patterns and labour-saving methods, however, were extremely popular here. The considerable quantities of furniture in this heavy-handed style still to be seen in Ontario provide the proof.

Upper Canada, or Canada West as it was properly called after the Act of Union of 1841, was experiencing the industrial revolution while not yet out of the frontier pioneering period. The population had grown and there were many furniture-makers active by the 1840s. Ontario antique shops today are very well stocked with their work, which can be recognized by its flaring curves and scrolls and with much crotch mahogany veneer over pine and whitewood. The patterns come straight from John Hall's book.

The American counterpart to Britain's Loudon appeared in print in 1850. This was Andrew Jackson Downing whose *The Architecture of Country Houses* catered to the same kind of middle-class consumers as Loudon's *Encyclopaedia*. He recommended the "Grecian" style, which turned out to be the style of John Hall. But he also reported on other contemporary trends, the Gothic revival for one and another called Elizabethan.

This latter was something of a provincial rendering of Jacobean lines, and bore scarcely any relationship to the earlier Elizabethan character. In practice, it was typified by much ball-and-spool turning. Its greatest popularity was reserved for mass-produced cottage bedroom furniture, most of it in cheap but attractively painted wood. Its most familiar piece is what came to be called the spool bed. Because its popularity coincided with that of the great Swedish singer, it was more

H. Andrew Downing called this piece of furniture a moving sideboard; it was usually mounted on castors and was recommended as a great convenience in busy dining-rooms. With respect to style it was described as being "in the French taste" in Downing's 1850 book, *The Architecture of Country Houses*, published in New York.

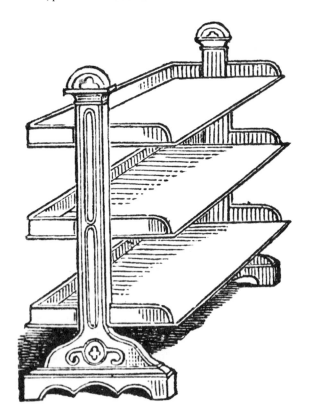

I. A number of walnut "moving sideboards" are still to be seen in Government House, residence of the Governor General, in Ottawa. Design inspiration may possibly have come from Downing's book, published some years before the vice-regal residence was furnished by the Government of Canada.

Government House, Ottawa

many of them were all that widely adopted, but style books did appear to guide any who perhaps wished to build Hindu pavilions, Saracen villas, Egyptian chairs, Tudor bedsteads, Burmese assembly halls, or Persian baths.

The style that was most enthusiastically taken up throughout the western world at mid-century was the rococo revival. It was the movement that finally was to replace warmed-over neo-classic as fashion's favourite. The balloon-back chair, which came to be the most familiar expression of the style, was introduced in the 1830s. It appears in Loudon's *Encyclopaedia*. Downing favoured it too and called it "antique French".

In our own time it's the style most often understood when the term Victorian is used. It represented a reaction to the sober classical tradition, a return to an old romantic favourite in a new machine-age character. The period terminology offers antiquarians some choice: the French style, antique revival, and Louis XV revival. The most precise is probably rococo revival.

Straight lines were largely replaced by curves. The asymmetrical character of the old rococo was expressed in lavish carving, the more the better, and the work of carving was in due time taken over and interpreted rather heavily by machines.

In 1845 T. B. Jordan was ready in England to patent the first really practical wood-carving machine. The popularity of the rococo revival, more particularly that of the balloon-back chair, lasted till the end of the century. In the latter half of the century, Jordan's machine, with others that followed, helped immensely to meet the huge demand for carved furniture.

Furniture of the Gothic revival also lent itself to machine production. The crockets, finials, tracery, and other ornamental devices which characterize nineteenth-century Gothic were often produced by means other than human hands. Just as Gothic devices were only tacked on to buildings of the period, so the basic structure of furniture was not touched. The forms remained the same; only the ornamental icing was changed.

In 1851 the first of all the great international exhibitions was held at London's Crystal Palace. The extensively illustrated catalogue of the Great Exhibition displays the rich variety of industrialized craft production from Europe and North America.

romantically known in its period as the Jenny Lind bed.

The Gothic revival was not new with Downing. By 1840 its influence was strong enough that even some country furniture was ornamented with pointed arches. The movement is much associated with the romantic novels of Sir Walter Scott and it perhaps owed some of its revived popularity to its reputation as a properly British style.

Even for the very early years of the nineteenth century it is difficult to place successive fashions in any kind of neat time sequence. For the greater part of the century it is quite impossible. The demand for novelty brought forth a bewildering presentation of romantic historic revivals. Not too

J and K.   Two plates from Downing's *The Architecture of Country Houses* illustrate the kind of low-cost painted pieces

that became popularly known as "cottage furniture". Those in Plate K preserve some of the style characteristics generally called Empire, particularly the provincial version of a French "sleigh" bed. The furniture in Plate J exhibits the so-called spool turning characteristic of what was then called the Elizabethan style. Many pieces of furniture similar in style to those illustrated were made and used in post-1850 Ontario.

It also reveals a complete absence of any original contemporary design. The complete collection of pictures testifies only to a grandly ambitious striving after novelty. Never before had there been such a display of products made bigger, richer, and more elaborate for the sake of impressing by their conspicuousness.

Scarcely any antique romantic tradition had been overlooked by the exhibitors of furniture. Many elaborate pieces were made, no doubt, specially for display at the Great Exhibition, and the ambitious and ornate standards revealed in the catalogue were probably far removed from those of real-life home furnishings in any of the participating nations.

The display products revealed, at least in time's perspective, not just a dearth of design talent at a time when machinery was vastly increasing the production of material things, but a failure to understand that the newly arrived technology required a new approach to product design.

After 1850 there was a period when the design of fashionable furniture was very much an eclectic matter. Further schools of the revival sort brought forth such styles as Victorian Renaissance and even a kind of erroneously conceived Turkish in the waning years of the century.

The machine had evidently defeated the designer. Reaction came, but at first it was expressed as a return to ideals of the craft tradition, and as such it had no long-lasting effect. It wasn't until the Art Nouveau, a movement whose roots can be traced to the early years of the century, but which actually came only to bloom fully in the 1890–1900 period, that designers turned away from established historic traditions to work in a genuinely original manner.

In old Ontario it wasn't every household that responded constantly to changing winds in world furniture fashions. Some of those winds, of course, were reduced to light breezes by the time they reached the bush frontier. In some households there was no concern for current fashion, in others no awareness. Even in the tiny cities of the colony, in reasonably close contact with the outside world, the importance of new modes was much less than in the fashion-setting centres.

There remained in all parts of the world districts where provincial ways and peasant arts continued to flourish in the machine age. The industrial revolution didn't immediately overcome provincial craftsmen everywhere. Upper Canada was such a district, an agricultural colony, slow to react to bewildering changes in what was becoming an industrial world.

Despite the efforts of merchants to bring the latest benefits from London and New York to Brockville and Niagara, older styles prevailed to a great extent among all levels of society. There was, of course, great discrepancy in conditions between colonial metropolis and colonial backwoods, but even in the little capital, impressions varied with the observer.

L.   This elaborate rococo-revival parlour table comes from the illustrated catalogue of the Great Exhibition in London in 1851. As the beaver motif suggest, this heavily carved black walnut piece was among the Canadian exhibits. It was made by a Montreal firm; while Ontario makers at the time were producing similar work, none reached the world's first big international fair.

In *The Emigrant's Guide*, writing of York in 1831, George Henry reported: "bootmakers from Hoby's, tailors from Bond Street, milliners and dress makers from the West End; in fact, here is a London in miniature."

The capital had a new name when Anna Jameson wrote her *Winter Studies and Summer Rambles in Canada* five or six years later. "Toronto," she said, "is like a fourth or fifth rate provincial town, with the pretensions of a capital city. . . . It is curious enough to see how quickly a new fashion, or a new folly, is imported from the old country, and with what difficulty and delay a new idea finds its way into the heads of the people, or a new book into their hands."

There are homes today in many countries where one finds old pieces of furniture in current use, not because they are valued as antiques but because "they've always been there", or because they serve the owners as well as modern replacements might. Standardized home interiors, in which all the furnishings conform to a particular period style, are found only in the pages of professional decorators' publications.

In real-life homes, the rising popularity of one fashion did not and still does not require the discarding of another. Current favour in the nineteenth century was shared by different brands of exotic novelty during the succession of revived historical styles. While the occasional appeal of something new may have helped send some old pieces to attics and others to the shops of second-hand merchants, there were many households where much of the old was preserved in daily use long, long after its acknowledged period.

The nineteenth century was a time when an almost frantic search for the novel made acceptable period taste a matter of confusion even in those countries which led the march into a new technological age. In Upper Canada, some colonists were always ready to adopt the very latest furniture styles imported from abroad. The larger number were equally ready to live with yesterday's styles and those of the days before yesterday.

Furniture in Ontario

FROM THE very beginnings of settlement in Ontario, the period testimony makes it clear that there has been great variety and contrast in the quality and elegance of her people's furniture. The tradition of hardship and makeshift among settlers is familiar to those who have read anything of the province's early history. At worst the narratives of bush pioneers record the greatest possible privation. At best, they read like the diaries of jolly campers, learning to use tree stumps for tables and shipping boxes for chairs.

Stories of triumph over hardship in the wilderness provide a firm foundation for a proud folk history. Once safely in the past, frontier life has been romanticized to suggest that each newcomer fashioned a home, with all its fittings and furnishings, using little more than the raw materials supplied by the bush. The fuzzy folklore tradition has it that for perhaps fifty years or so, everyone in the newly opened colony huddled in cheerless shanties, suffering complete isolation from and denied all the comforts and refinements of the civilized world.

The truth about life in early Ontario is somewhat different. There are records in great number to substantiate the picture of bush life with log shanties and a generally primitive way of living for many. The records also testify to formality, sophistication, wealth, and elegance to some considerable degree in the living styles of others even from the very earliest period.

Considerable disparity in relative wealth and education and contrast in class and national backgrounds make it clear that tastes and standards and the means to express them varied tremendously among the early citizens.

Differences in privilege and opportunity were major but certainly not the only factors bearing on the degree of success and good cheer with which immigrants adjusted to the new life. Some individuals were better suited physically or mentally to the lot of the settler. Some enjoyed the convenience of well-stocked merchants near by; others knew years of inconvenience and frustration because there was no supply market within easy reach.

The narratives and diaries of settlers and their visitors, as well as the reminiscences in later years of writers who recalled the pioneer period, tell varied stories of home life in the early years. So

M. This primitive chair is representative of makeshift furniture that settlers improvised for their own use. Axe, adze, knife, and auger were tools available on every farm and the only tools required for making chairs like this. The seat is a slab of basswood; the other parts are hardwood pieces whittled to shape. Found in Waterloo County, it is the kind of chair settlers made for limited use, to be replaced by something better in due time.

Mr. & Mrs. Horace Dahmer, Guelph

also do the advertisements from early periodicals and data from old commercial records.

The written records, as well as the variety of furniture to survive for our present-day inspection, make it apparent that it was a colony in which there were mansions as well as hovels. There were homes where conditions ranged from helpless squalor through modest comfort to fashionable luxury. There were also some aristocrats living in shanties and some peasant immigrants whose new homes were palatial if contrasted to those they had forsaken in the old world.

Pioneer commentators, among them some who found themselves reduced in station, and travellers who sometimes found their creature comforts not adequately waited upon, made occasional unflattering judgements of the domestic scene. The

literature of the frontier leads one to suspect that reports at times were coloured by prejudice or frustration or by that dyspepsia which transients must have suffered at the tables of provincial inn keepers.

It was the novel picture of makeshift furniture that was most frequently remarked by visitors and new settlers alike. References to more formal varieties of furniture are less frequent and written very much in taken-for-granted terms. But literate and cultivated observers on the frontier were intrigued by the novelty of settlers' home-made comforts, probably much in the way that observers today can be charmed by the homely conveniences contrived by Boy Scouts in camp.

To recall only the shanty tradition is to forget that a goodly number of our first residents were

N. Another primitive chair was shaped directly from a section of pine tree trunk. The seat and vertical face below it are of sawn boards nailed to the trunk section. The arms have a reinforcing edge facing of thin sections of pliable hardwood. It is unlikely that the crude forest chair was intended originally for rocking; the present rockers appear late both in style and in fact.

Black Creek Pioneer Village, Toronto

persons of some little wealth, or taste, or both. Poverty at home was the reason that brought many later settlers to the Canadas; it had nothing at all to do with the arrival of the Loyalists. No ordinary refugees, there were among them some with the determination, if not always the means, to live in some elegance. There were also some who managed to bring a few pieces of treasured furniture from their old homes to their new.

The wealthy and the privileged who joined the Loyalist trek established here a cultivated tradition on a level not normally expected in a colonizing period. Some of them in the first tiny settlements set up housekeeping with fine and formal Georgian-style furniture. Many pieces, which according to family tradition were brought north by Loyalist ancestors, disappoint the researcher by betraying, through style, a later origin. A sufficient number of pieces, however, appear to satisfy pedigree claims and do bear witness to a genuine although perhaps sparse tradition of the use of American eighteenth-century furniture in some of those early homes.

It is probable that a fairly large amount of fine English furniture was imported by administrators and military officers serving here as well as by some permanent settlers. Continuous immigration from the United States up until the War of 1812, as well as a fairly busy trade between citizens on each side of the new international border, also indicates that furniture of American origin continued to enter Upper Canada.

Cabinet-makers in post-conquest Montreal, some by then working in current English styles, helped to supply the demands of the Upper Canada gentry. Montreal was for many years the chief wholesale source for Ontario merchants, supplying them with merchandise both of local and of British origin. The occasional reference made in the period to certain items being supplied "from below" indicated simply that they had come from Lower Canada, from down-river.

Attribution of an eighteenth-century Ontario origin to particular pieces of furniture remains a matter not entirely proven by documentary evidence. The precise kind of record-keeping that links names to trades and to specific products was not the first priority of Loyalist settlers. It is possible, nevertheless, to name a few individuals who followed the cabinet-making trade in Upper

Canada before 1800; the difficulty is to identify precisely the furniture they produced.

The wife of our first Lieutenant-Governor, Mrs. John Graves Simcoe, was one of those who particularly enjoyed the adventuresome camping character of life in the early days of the colony. Although among the most excellent of diarists, she made only slight reference to furniture in her writings of the period 1792–96, but she does describe at Queenston and Newark (the present-day Niagara-on-the-Lake) newly built houses of such impressively elegant period standards that it is impossible to think of them as having been furnished with anything but comparably impressive cabinet-work.

The worldly and aristocratic La Rochefoucauld was another who remarked favourably on buildings in Newark; he wrote in 1795 of the home built by Surveyor-General David William Smith: "In point of size and elegance, the house is much distinguished. It consists of joiners' work, but is constructed, embellished and painted in the best style."

Mrs. Simcoe's sketch of the house, as well as its plans which survive in the Public Archives of Canada, shows it to be a distinguished Georgian building; many would call it a mansion. It was a show-piece in its day, and had it survived the burning of Niagara in 1813 it would remain a show-piece today. That it was intended to be furnished with anything but fine furniture in walnut and mahogany or rosewood is scarcely to be questioned.

The narrative of Patrick Campbell provides an interesting reference to the standards maintained by Chief Joseph Brant, leader of the Iroquois Loyalists. On visiting Brant's home in the Mohawk village three miles below Brantford, he wrote in 1792: "Tea was on the table when we came in, served up in the handsomest china plate and every other furniture in proportion. After tea was over, we were entertained with the music of an elegant hand organ, on which a young Indian gentleman and Mr. Clinch played alternately."

Campbell also contributed a household vignette after a stopover in a private home near Kingston: "We arrived about nightfall and after refreshing ourselves with some tea, some glasses of port and madeira wines, two card tables were produced, on which we played till supper-time."

An inventory of household goods in a home of some comfort in 1794 lists among the furniture three cupboards, a double table, three chairs, benches, a large looking-glass, and three bedsteads. One of the beds evidently stood in the kitchen.

According to the *Upper Canada Gazette*, first published at Niagara, later at York, an occasional exotic item appeared here before the end of the eighteenth century. In an advertisement among its columns in 1797, R. Clench offered for sale one billiard table.

In the same year, commission agents W. & J. Crooks advertised a "complete set of tables, consisting of two large dining and two ends, one sofa, one elegant mahogany liquor case, one large black walnut writing desk".

Since black walnut is a North American wood, it is quite conceivable that the desk may have been the product of some Niagara district cabinet-maker.

Another eighteenth-century document, this one listing furniture of a provincial and almost certainly of a French tradition, is the inventory in 1781 of the effects of the late Father Pierre Potier, Jesuit missionary for the previous thirty-seven years to the Assumption parish on the Detroit River.

The dining-room furniture consisted of one clock, one sideboard, one table, and ten chairs. In the kitchen, only one table and three kneading troughs were mentioned. His furniture was completed by one cot and a bookcase holding about a hundred books.

There was appreciable growth and development in the colony during the first decade of the new century. Between 1800 and the outbreak of the War of 1812, the population doubled to reach 100,000. Tradesmen and merchants increased in numbers and their advertisements in the few periodicals of the day contribute significant details to our picture of early home life.

One of the most ambitious and successful of Upper Canada tradesmen was the merchant whose most distinctive name was Quetton St. George. His main shop was in York (now Toronto), which had officially become the colonial capital in 1797, but St. George also did business through merchant-agents in Kingston and Amherstburg, and operated what was probably a kind of frontier trading post north of York on Lake Couchiching.

As early as 1803 his regular and frequent advertisements listed an encyclopaedic selection of merchandise. He did not stock what we might describe as a general selection of furniture because it was the common practice at that period for clients to deal directly with the furniture-makers.

His shops, however, did stock in considerable quantity small imported items that properly should be classed as furniture; mahogany shaving-cases and looking-glasses in many styles were typical examples.

Of greater significance to the story of furniture in Upper Canada are his advertisements offering hardware and fittings that would have been of use only to furniture-makers. Most of the hardware, it appears, came from England—brass and iron hinges, commode handles, H and H-L hinges, chest locks, and brass locks.

Cabinet hardware of American origin is probably indicated by St. George's 1810 advertisement in the *York Gazette* in which he offered "bureau mountings and soffa castors just received by the sloop Marianne from Niagara". Another advertisement includes a considerable choice of stylish looking-glasses and basic cabinet hardware "just arrived from England and New York".

Furniture-makers themselves were less likely to indulge in newspaper advertising. The frequency with which the general merchants of York and other communities offered desk fittings, ring latches, wood bed castors, brass drawer handles, case locks, commode knobs, and clock-case trimmings suggests, however, that the cabinet trade here was not an idle one.

Montreal merchants also advertised in the first periodicals of the young colony. They advertised a great variety of goods and among that stock was cabinet ware, clock faces and fittings, and hair seating, that long-lasting chair-seat covering woven of horsehair. The Montreal dealers' target was generally the merchant class of Upper Canada, but the eventual client for the wares mentioned above was the local furniture-maker.

Blacksmiths, who no doubt were in greater demand than cabinet-makers in the very early days, contributed to the supply of wrought-iron hardware. Local smiths produced hand-made hinges, hooks, and latches, more particularly for the work of country furniture-makers. But the advertisements, early and late, indicate that Eng-

I.   Ontario country furniture of the early nineteenth century period was usually given a paint finish. This group of pieces indicates that a wide variety of colours was available. The red chest is of the lift-top type; it only appears to have drawers. The open dresser from Wellington County has a single stencilled fruit design applied to each end board. The Windsor side chair is basically of American design but one that occurred here with some frequency in the 1800–20 period. The small dome-topped chest comes from the Niagara Peninsula and exhibits an excellent non-objective painted and grained finish.

Dr. & Mrs. Peter Bell, Sharbot Lake

lish and American hardware, ready made and therefore convenient, was the more often used by most cabinet-makers.

Auction sales, at which privately owned estates were dispersed, were frequently advertised. The *York Gazette* in 1811 announced a particularly noteworthy sale at Holyrood House, owned by William Firth. Among the fine furniture knocked down were "elegant mahogany four-post bed-steads on castors, with chintz and dimity furniture, tent bedsteads, dining, card and pembroke tables, presses, wardrobes, capital 8 day clock in black walnut case, fine-toned, double key'd harpsichord and pianoforte, inlaid with satinwood".

There can be little doubt that most of this furniture was of English manufacture, although the clock case listed, being of black walnut, is probably American or Canadian.

By auction or by private sale, British army officers frequently disposed of their old-country furniture before returning home. The *Kingston Gazette* in 1813 gave notice of an auction of tables, chairs, stoves, carpets, and other "furniture belonging to Capt. Enright, 10th, R.V.R." Again and again, sale advertisements identified furniture as the property of a gentleman or an officer "about to leave the province".

Even vice-regal representatives followed the practice, as is indicated in a letter from York dated November 23, 1817. Commenting on the resignation of Lieutenant-Governor Francis Gore, Mrs. William Dummer Powell wrote, "their rich and expensive furniture is now selling, few articles are in my means to purchase, you may judge of the rest when I tell you that a Library Table of Rosewood left with us to take care of is 48 Guineas. The dining tables are 72 Guineas and everything in proportion. It gives Dr. Strachan an opportunity of furnishing his most elegant Mansion which is the handsomest in the Province."

Dr. Strachan, of course, was then rector of York and later to become the first Bishop of Toronto.

Among the earliest of Upper Canada craftsmen to use newspaper advertising was the one who published this statement in the *Upper Canada Gazette*:

> The Subscriber returns his sincere thanks to his Friends and the Public, for the great encouragement he has hitherto met with, and begs leave to inform them, that he now intends carrying on his business

in all its branches; and those who wish can be served with Chairs of every sort in his branch without delay—armed Chairs, Sittees [*sic*], and dining ditto, fan-back and brace-back Chairs. He very shortly expects a quantity of different paints; it will then be in his power to finish his Chairs in the best manner, and by his great attention to perform his promises, hopes to merit protection and support.

DANIEL TEIRS.

York, January 23, 1802.

N.B. He also expects a quantity of common chairs from below, which he will dispose of on reasonable terms.

It is not likely that Mr. Teirs labelled or marked the chairs that he manufactured. If there are in private collections today any chairs which are claimed to have come from his shop, they are not generally known to furniture researchers.

But the terms "fan-back" and "brace-back" in that single advertisement make it clear that Teirs was making Windsor chairs in eighteenth-century American patterns. These words are still used by antiquarians to describe certain Windsor chair styles.

The reference to paints is one of many in the early years of the century which prove that a reasonable variety of colours were available for finishing and decorating furniture. His postscript regarding "common chairs from below" suggests that he had ordered a shipment of low-cost chairs, probably simple ladderbacks and possibly of French-Canadian tradition, from Lower Canada.

Since newspaper publishing was a trade also in its infancy, there were in the early days very few periodicals in which other tradespeople might advertise. The town of Kingston, whose leading citizens hoped it might replace York as the capital, didn't have a local paper till about 1810.

Throughout that year, the *Kingston Gazette* printed a simple advertisement for cabinet-maker Abia B. Sayre, who notified readers that he was prepared to make "clock cases, sideboards, desks, bookcases, bureaus, dining tables, bedsteads, etc.".

In the columns of the same periodical, Kingston residents were notified in 1811 of the plans of one business man to branch out. In the discreet commercial language of the period, they read that Samuel Howe, "builder of houses and barns, 22 years experience, will keep on hand, or furnish at short notice at his shop at Fredericksburg, all kinds of cabinet work—also fanning mills."

Local furniture-makers did not make a general practice of continuous advertising. It was common for them, however, to publish a notice when commencing business or when setting up in a new location. Typical was the Kingston notice in 1812 of William Baker, who "intends commencing the joiner and cabinet business at Point Frederick".

The military had some occasion to call on provincial furniture suppliers as is indicated by the *York Gazette* in 1815. The Commissariat Office advertised then that it required:

> "150 chairs
> 50 tables with drawers, for officers
> 20 tables without drawers for soldiers."

They were "wanted for the service of the Barracks Department", possibly to replace barracks furniture lost when the Americans burned York's public buildings and its fort in 1813.

In this first period of Upper Canada's history, one that it is convenient to end with the American war of 1812–14, furniture-makers in the province had no exotic woods with which to work. The mahogany and rosewood pieces mentioned in sale advertisements were almost certainly imported. There was, of course, no dearth of trees here, and with the coming of sawmills, the immediate forest provided most of the raw material for its new furniture.

There were bush homes, of course, put together without the use of sawn lumber. There was doubtless some limited use of pit-sawn boards for furniture, but by the time cabinet-makers had set up their work-benches there were water-powered mills with vertical saws producing an ample supply of lumber for their use.

The greater demand in sawn lumber was for the soft woods, more easily worked in timber framing and for use as siding in frame construction. But the value of local hardwoods was familiar to Loyalists and they were evidently put to early use. Among the Simcoe papers of the last decade of the eighteenth century is a list of "some of the earliest articles of exportation from Upper Canada". Included in the list are curled maple, black birch, and cherry wood.

The 1791–2 diary of Patrick Campbell, whose principal concern in touring Upper Canada was to investigate the prospects for Scottish emigrants, reported on the quality of local cabinet woods:

"Black walnut of Upper Canada, will admit of as fine a polish and gloss, and is equal for household finishing and furniture, to any perhaps in the world." He appears to have made his assessment on the basis of locally produced furniture because he went on to remark that the wood was not familiar in Europe.

The interesting qualities of native hardwoods were also commented upon by Lord Selkirk during his visit in 1804. From York he wrote, "There are some beautiful species of Timber made use of in furniture & ornamental house furnishing—Black Walnut, Curled Maple, and Cherry." He appears to have suggested that these woods were the more often used locally although he added, "these are sometimes sent down St. Lawrence for exportation."

These three—walnut, maple and cherry—have ever since been the most highly regarded of native cabinet woods. Birch was also used in great quantity; it is a hardwood of excelling working character and one that accepts staining very well, being used most frequently with a walnut or mahogany finish. Hickory, which can be bent without splitting, was of particular value to the chair-makers.

Pine as well as whitewood, the common trade name for basswood and poplar, was used as a secondary wood in fine work and for vast quantities of common furniture intended to be painted or stained. Butternut, which is a relative of walnut, but whose wood is lighter in colour, does not appear to have been used frequently for furniture in the early years. By the 1820s, however, its value as a walnut substitute, particularly since walnut did not thrive in the cooler parts of the province, was well recognized.

Ash was another wood much used in common chair making generally and later in cheaper case furniture meant to be painted or stained. Chestnut too was used for cheap furniture in the later years of the nineteenth century. Oak, although in good supply, was very little used for furniture, possibly because it was not in fashion during that century.

Although there must have been delays and frustrations from time to time in acquiring stains, varnishes, paints, and other products used in furniture finishing, the records indicate that the accepted finishes of the time were generally available from merchants in principal centres by 1810.

In Kingston, for instance, in 1811 one shopkeeper could supply paints in blue, black, white, carmine, Indian red, ivory black, yellow ochre, rose pink, and other colours.

Pigments such as Spanish brown and vermillion, which provided in blend much of the basic red paint finishes which survive on common furniture to this day, were also on the market by that date, as were pumice-stone and rotten-stone, used to polish dried paint surfaces. Litharge, a forerunner of today's Japan dryer, was a paint-drying agent used to hasten the oxidizing and hence the drying quality of paint bodies.

Anyone familiar with present-day dealers or collectors of the more primitive of old Ontario furniture will have been exposed to the persistent tradition of "buttermilk paint", a concoction of earth pigment, usually red, with buttermilk, making a crude kind of casein paint which pioneers are said to have lavished on furniture and wood-work trim alike.

Since pigments ground in oil and linseed oil itself, as well as drying agents, were acknowledged as superior and were known to be generally available, it is unlikely that the dairy substitute was very often used except as a frontier exigency. Most of the pieces which well-meaning enthusiasts today suggest were coated with buttermilk paint were, in truth, given an oil-base paint finish.

A system by which individual Canadians were provided with some government compensation for personal property losses sustained during the War of 1812 is one of the most valuable sources for historians concerned with the domestic scene of that time.

Citizens hoping for recompense had keen recollections of property gone, and the war claims taken as a whole make a rich documentary midden, contributing a great deal to what we know of their homes and, more particularly, of their furnishings. One prominent and wealthy citizen submitted a lengthy and detailed list that even included five bottles of ketchup.

Since household inventories of the period were rare, the war claim documents, now in the Public Archives of Canada, shed probably more light on furniture in use than any other reference source up to that date. Even so, only when woods are mentioned can one guess as to the origin of specific pieces.

A Mr. McKee of Sandwich claimed after the war for the loss of a large sofa, six mahogany chairs, a sideboard, one mahogany and one cherry chest of drawers, and one "elegant" mahogany table. It's pretty certain that the cherry chest was made here; one must be dubious about the rest.

At Niagara, however, Mr. Kirby provided a list that suggests he patronized local makers. He reported the loss of three cherry and walnut tables, a dozen Windsor chairs, and two feather beds. The word bed meant bedding or mattress in our present terminology; bedstead is the word that would have been used if the wooden framework had been intended.

One claim from Cornwall included a cherry tea chest, another a portable mahogany desk. Many of the documents identify furniture only in very general terms, but one in which detail of description is the rule is the claim of Niagara's wealthy William Dickson.

There's little doubt that the greater part of his furniture had been imported; one can read of his nineteen neat gilt chairs, a parlour looking-glass, a large brass-clamped liquor case, and a mahogany bedstead that he had purchased from the Count de Puisaye. The inventory also includes items which very possibly were made in the Niagara region, among them a neat new bookcase of cherry with glass slides, one pine and one walnut cupboard, a neat cherry cradle, a cherry office desk for four persons, three walnut and cherry pigeon-hole cases with brass locks.

One cannot discount the possibility that such furniture of native woods might well have been made in the new United States, but in the period prior to the War of 1812, there is every likelihood that those pieces of cherry and walnut were custom made for the reasonably affluent by cabinet craftsmen who were new Canadians.

Both grist-mills and sawmills appeared early along the front where the Loyalists had taken up lands. The simple mill with its vertical saw (the faster circular saw was not common till after 1840) could be set up on almost any little stream because it required only a slight head of water to run. According to returns made to the Government of Upper Canada, there were 429 such mills operating in 1831.

In the back country, however, during the second period of settlement, there was often some lag in services and supplies. The 1817 narrative of William Bell, Presbyterian parson and one of the founders of the town of Perth in Lanark County, reports conditions that probably were familiar in many of the new communities: "The house was nothing more than bare walls and a roof. . . . Mechanics were scarce and their wages high, and even boards were not to be had as the saw mill was not yet in operation. . . . From Dr. Thom I got two boards, out of one of which I made a table."

Though lumber was afterwards available from the new mill, the shortage of craftsmen evidently continued and Bell wrote from time to time of turning his own pious hands to the making of bookshelves for himself, and benches and a temporary communion table for his congregation.

The military settlements like Perth and Richmond were begun right after the War of 1812; their first citizens were demobilized British army men. They were the first of many thousands of newcomers from Britain and Ireland, strangers to the continent as already pointed out. It was this period of immigration that produced the wealth of literature reflecting on the crude quality of homes and furnishings in Upper Canada.

Edward Talbot, who arrived in 1818, wrote a few years later of his impressions of the homes of other settlers:

> His furniture is never of the most costly description, and is seldom cumbersome. A bedstead, roughly hewn with a felling-axe; the sides, posts, and ends held together in screeching trepidation by strips of Bass-wood bark; a bed of fine feathers; a table, that might be taken for a victualler's chopping block; four or five benches of the same rude mechanism; and the indispensable apparatus for cooking and eating, compose the "tout ensemble" of a Canadian's household furniture. He seems to have no idea of cottage comfort and seldom evinces any inclination to make his hut even tolerably pleasant.

It's plain, however, that one's viewpoint at the time might have been coloured by the kind of comfort and elegance to which one had been accustomed. Rustic charm and unaffected happiness are apparent in the report of a young couple who set up housekeeping in Norfolk County in 1825:

> In the old log-house there were three old rickety, broken-down chairs and an old square table. Well, the first thing Job did was to buy six cups and saucers, six plates, six knives and forks and a teapot. A bedstead was made by fitting small poles into auger-holes bored into the logs. These poles were about six feet long, and were small enough to have a good spring. The lower ends of these spring poles lay on a cross piece, one end of which was inserted in an auger-hole in the wall and the other supported by an upright. Job got a feather bed and some bedding from a man who owed him for work done, and being a carpenter he soon got things in livable shape. . . .

The stability of early furniture could never have been a matter of complaint for Lyman Judson of Yonge Township in Leeds County. In later years, a reminiscer wrote: "In the centre of the log cabin which he built stood a stump which was used as a hand-mill when occasion required, and also as the support for some basswood slabs serving as the top of a table."

There were some who scorned complaints about crude furnishings. Writing of settlement days in Dundas County, James Croil had this to say: "The total absence of furniture of any kind whatever, was not to be named as an inconvenience, by those who had lately passed through the severest of hardships. Stern necessity . . . soon brought into play the ingenuity of the old soldier, who, in his own rough and ready way, knocked together such tables and benches as were necessary for household use."

As the years passed some veterans of the bush-clearing days were less inclined to romanticize the good old times. From the Long Point district of the Lake Erie shore came the judgement of an anonymous farmer: "The old cord bed-frame was a veritable trough, and the only thing that made the squeaking old thing endurable was a plethoric straw tick."

Period travellers have also left us their frequent comments on the calibre of furnishings in the wayside inns of Upper Canada. Edward Talbot, writing in 1823, made a rather more detailed than average report of Dogge's Tavern in Oxford County:

> The furniture of a bar-room, excepting its characteristic accompaniments, consists of nothing more than a plain cherry-table, two or three pine benches, and a fire-poker. . . . The bed-chamber commonly contains four or five beds, clean and plain, with cotton sheets and linsey-woolsey coverlets, but having neither posts nor curtains. The other accoutrements of this apartment are two or three chairs, and a portable looking-glass, so small that a Lilliputian might put it in his waistcoat pocket; and,

so far from returning a correct representation of the objects which it reflects, that if you look at yourself in it lengthwise, it will double the longitude of your visage, and if breadthwise, it will equally augment the latitude. Such is the furniture of a Canadian bed-room! Sans wash-hand-stand, sans dressing table, sans bureau, sans pot de chambre, sans everything!

Talbot was kinder than some commentators but the impression comes down to us that rural inns were not particularly attractive. Hoteliers in the towns, however, were much more likely to cater to transients' needs and tastes, as is suggested by an 1837 advertisement for the Wellington Hotel at the corner of Church and Wellington streets in Toronto: "The parlours are spacious and elegantly furnished with bedrooms attached, airy and pleasant. The beds are large and double. . . . A splendid pianoforte with a choice selection of music for the use of ladies or gentlemen."

A prolific recorder of reminiscences was Canniff Haight, who, beginning about 1880, wrote magazine articles, pamphlets, and books about life in the Bay of Quinte area fifty years and more earlier. This district had seen its first permanent settlers by 1780, and the period of which Haight wrote was one in which a reasonable degree of comfort and prosperity had been attained. Haight reads rather like a patient grandfather recalling stories of the sturdy pioneers for the moral benefit of forgetful young readers of later years:

> Every kitchen had one or more spacious cupboards. . . . The furniture made no pretensions to artistic design or elegance. It was plain and strong, and bore unmistakable evidence of having originated either at the carpenter's bench or at the hands of some member of the family. . . . I have a clear recollection of the pine tables, with their strong square legs tapering to the floor, and of how carefully they were scrubbed. Table covers were seldom used, and only when there was company, and then the cherry table with its folding leaves was brought out. . . . In the hall stood the tall old-fashioned house clock, with its long pendulum swinging to and fro with slow and measured beat. . . . The furniture was plain and substantial, more attention being given to durability than to style or ornament. Easy chairs—save the spacious rocking-chair for old women—and lounges were not seen. There was no time for lolling on well-stuffed cushions.

Haight provided what is possibly the most lyrical commentary on the ladderback chairs that were so popular everywhere in Upper Canada:

> The old chairs, which, in point of comfort, modern times have in no way improved upon, were also of home make, with thin round legs and splint-bottomed seats, or, what was more common, elm bark evenly cut and plaited. Many a time have I gone to the woods in the spring, when the willow catkins in the swamp and along the side of the creek turned from silver to gold, and when the clusters of linwort nodded above the purple-green leaves in the April wind, and taken the bark in long strips from the elm trees to reseat the dilapidated chairs.

A graphic picture of the old-time beds was also provided by Haight:

> The old high-posted bedsteads, which almost required a ladder to get into, went to the lumber heap long ago, and low, sumptuous couches take their places. The great feather tick has been converted into the more healthy mattress, and the straw tick and cords have been replaced by spring bottoms. It used to be quite an arduous undertaking, I remember, to put up one of those old beds. One person took a wrench, kept for that purpose, and drew up the cord with it as tight as he could at every hole, and another followed with a hammer and pin, which was driven into the hole through which the end passed to hold it; and so you went on round the bed, until the cord was all drawn as tight as it could possibly be.

A scene of some contrast is contributed by reminiscences of "Gairbraid", the home of William "Tiger" Dunlop in the Canada Company's Huron Tract. Dr. Dunlop had come to Canada in 1826, his second trip, this time as an official of the company, and the references quoted probably concern the early 1830s:

> At Gairbraid the two rooms most characteristic of the times and of the occupants were the dining-room and the kitchen. In the former stood a large, round dining-table of solid mahogany, fitted to seat twelve persons; and ranged round the room were twelve most solid chairs to match, upholstered in Brussels carpet. . . . The huge fireplace in the end of the room was flanked by large walnut presses, wherein a wealth of china, silver and glass, was stored, and beside them a napery chest which testified to Scotch thrift and the spinning wheel. In front of the fire was an apparatus, in appearance something like a fender stool, where plates and hot meats were placed for warmth; for the Dunlopian sense of comfort was well developed. In the centre hollow of the sideboard stood a huge liquors-stand made of mahogany, brass bound, with large brass handles. It measured seventeen and one-half inches

high by thirty-three in length and twenty-three in width. It was simply a monster "traveller" on wheels, built to hold twelve gallons of liquid, containing a dozen large bottles from a converted military chest, each carrying a new label and measuring a good sixteen inches by nine, with a half-pound stopper, in itself a handful . . . they went the rounds of the room in pilgrimages suitable to the disposition of the company.

Henry Hyndman was one of those British gentlemen of some means enticed to the wilderness by the promotions of the Canada Company. Although he and his family spent an initiation period in bark shanties not far from Goderich, he shortly built a commodious house "fitted comfortably throughout with Old Country furniture, big four-posters and roomy arm-chairs". Hyndman made 1835 a memorable year locally by installing in that new home what was said to be the first piano in the district.

Even among affluent settlers, furnishings were not always in overly good supply, and in that same

O. William "Tiger" Dunlop is shown in an illustration published in *Fraser's Magazine*, a British periodical, in 1833. The chair in which he is seated may possibly be one of the "twelve most solid chairs" of mahogany, upholstered in Brussels carpet and used at Gairbraid, Dunlop's home not far from Goderich. The line sketch is taken from a painting of the period by Daniel Maclise.

neighbourhood it was not unusual to expect a guest to bring an extra chair or plate or some cutlery to help fill out the setting for an occasional festive dinner.

Shanty life in Upper Canada was much the same in character whether early or late, and contentment or better depended very much on the attitudes of the occupants. One who found considerable contentment was Thomas Need, whose experiences in rude frontier living on Sturgeon Lake were published in 1838. Referring to his home variously as shanty, rude hut, and mansion, he described it as "one apartment, 14 feet by 12 feet in the clear, and contained in the way of furniture, a camp bedstead, a chest of drawers, and a well-filled bookcase; it had also the somewhat unusual luxury of a chimney, pegs for the suspension of guns and fishing complements, and shelves for my scanty kitchen utensils, a hole in the planks served to admit light, and air found free entrance through numberless cracks and crevices; such as it was, however, it served my purpose well, and when the evening closed, I used to light my lamp and sit down to my books with a great feeling of comfort."

As well as such tales of travel and settlement experience, there were published in the earlier part of the century, principally in Britain, a considerable number of pamphlets directed specifically to emigrants from the British Isles, advising them of the "true" conditions in the Canadas and of how they might best prepare themselves to live there.

Emigrant guides were aimed usually at working-class emigrants, those with limited capital. That they were popular publications is proven by the great number written by a considerable variety of "experts" during a period of over fifty years. The advice was much the same from beginning to end; for once we can see a group of authors, some of them not averse to abstracting from their peers, generally agreed upon their subject matter.

Perhaps the earliest was *Advice to settlers in Canada*, published in Glasgow in 1815 and written by a "British traveller in America". The author recommended what was repeated by his imitators for years afterward: "Do not take a chair or table; if you have them, sell them and strengthen your labour; construct rude articles of that kind in the woods, and bye and bye you will be in a condition to purchase better."

Cattermole urged in 1831 that the only heavy

articles emigrants were justified in taking to Canada were books and clocks. John Howison wrote in 1821, "No one should take household furniture . . . everything that is necessary for the interior of a log hut can be procured in the settlements. Good furniture is not at all fit for the rude abodes that must first be occupied."

Writers of emigrant guides agreed that those sailing for the colonies should take with them smaller articles and those difficult to acquire here, but again and again the advice to forsake furniture was repeated. Reporting on the town of York in 1831, George Henry wrote of the arrival of newcomers by the frequent steam packets:

> You will see, probably, a few old chairs not worth half a dollar each, which have been brought nearly or quite five thousand miles; with old bedsteads, and other pieces of common furniture, that could have been disposed of at home for nearly as much as new would cost here; for wood being so very abundant in Canada, these common articles of furniture are very cheap in most parts of the Province; very good common chairs, quite new, are to be bought for four or five shillings each, and sometimes less; but the people at home imagine there are no persons here who can manufacture these kind of things. In this they are much mistaken; for such is the accumulation of furniture for sale in the Upper Province, that the body of cabinet makers of York, during the last session of the Assembly, petitioned the House to pass an act prohibiting the importation of furniture from the United States; therefore, emigrants should not bring any lumbering heavy furniture with them to this country.

Complaints by craftsmen, furniture-makers among them, over excessive patronage by affluent York householders of their American competitors were heard at least as early as 1827. A letter signed by "A British Mechanic" and published in the *Canadian Freeman* that year was caustically critical of the local gentry for "sending large sums of money out of the Province for the purchase of various articles of mechanism, such as carriages, saddlery, cabinet-ware, boots, &c. while our own mechanics who pay the taxes for the support of these same officials, are left to struggle with difficulty and distress, and our domestic manufactures, instead of exhibiting a spirit of improvement and enterprize are languishing into the most torpid inactivity. It is a well known fact, Sir, that a large proportion of the articles of mechanism required by the officials of this town, are purchased in New York, Buffalo, and Rochester."

The editor contributed some amplification to the subject and joined the letter-writer in naming offending officials, a cross-section of those who were to become known as the Family Compact. He opened with disparaging reference to the loyal British officials who entertained on "Yankee tables made in Buffalo". He continued with a sober examination of the economics of local trade:

> Certain articles of furniture can be had in the United States much cheaper, and better too, than in Upper Canada. We admit all this—but what is the reason? Because sufficient encouragement has not, as yet, been afforded the manufacturers in the colony, to enable them to compete with those on the other side of the lines. A cabinet-maker for instance, has but little encouragement, and does not create a market for that kind of lumber; consequently, he has to pay 10 to $12 per 1000 feet, when the man in Buffalo can have it for 3 or $4.— Neither will the article, perhaps, be so well finished —and why? Because the Canadian manufacturer has not sufficient encouragement to employ masterly hands in each department, but is obliged to make a man who may be skilled in one department slobber over the work of another, of which he knows little or nothing.

The only direct action, however, was limited to the petitions mentioned by Henry. In 1830 and in 1831, a group of York mechanics petitioned the House of Assembly to raise customs duties on timber and furniture imported from the United States. The House dealt with them in a manner still popular with some legislators—the petitions were referred to committees, which evidently forgot them.

Guide writers did advise artisans to bring their tools to Canada in the early years. While evidently readily available in the United States, tools were expensive here and, like so many other materials then, in short supply or obtainable only in a few major market towns.

Certainly after the War of 1812, judging by newspaper advertisements, the tools required by a cabinet-maker were not all that difficult to acquire. Tools suitable for carpenters, joiners, and furniture-makers have survived in some quantity, of both English and American make. For the most part, the basic forms of woodworking tools have changed little in the intervening years. The fine moulding planes of that day, each one designed to cut a different moulding profile, make one group, however, whose function has since been taken over by the power saw.

For the turner, who was a specialist supplying parts to chair- and cabinet-makers, the foot-powered treadle lathe was the essential piece of machinery from the earliest time. The same kind of lathe was frequently standard equipment in chair and cabinet shops.

A hand-operated device for the speedy cutting of mortise joints was used by some furniture-makers by the second quarter of the century, but it wasn't until the 1840s that steam power was adapted to some of the larger furniture factories. After 1850, the use of steam power in most larger operations was general, running lathes and saws, boosting production, and lowering both the price and quality of Ontario furniture.

Newspaper advertisements indicate that furniture hardware from Britain and the United States was first available from general merchants of a few major towns. After 1820, advertisements make

P. Hardware used by Ontario furniture-makers was largely imported from Britain and the United States. An 1830 advertisement from a business directory in Birmingham, England, illustrates a variety of wrought-iron hinges of types used in old Ontario for both house and furniture finishing.

it plain that brass and iron hinges, casters, drawer pulls and locks, latches, and the like, as well as tools for craftsmen, were on sale in every town of consequence.

Particularly with respect to country furniture, the availability of hardware, rather than strict matching of fashion to period, frequently determined what kind of drawer pulls were used. Brasses of Georgian tradition were used only to a very limited extent. Hardwood pulls, supplied by turners in stock patterns, were often applied to the finer cabinet products as well as simple country pieces.

Mushroom-shaped brass pulls were probably shipped from the United States, but pressed-glass drawer pulls, today more frequently thought to have come from American glass factories, were also imported from Britain. Ceramic drawer pulls, the brown knobs of flint-enamel ware and the glossy white "porcelain" kind that were so commonly used on Ontario furniture after 1850, probably originated entirely in the United States. The earliest record of the making of white ceramic pulls there is in the late forties but they were widely produced by American potteries from 1850 to 1870.

Since furniture hardware was sold by hardware and general merchants, householders themselves frequently applied new and more fashionable drawer pulls to old pieces of furniture. The earlier brass pulls were vulnerable to damage and, if broken or lost, were often replaced with any style of pull available. Case pieces thus may survive to the present day bearing hardware quite unsuited to its period character, but most drawer pulls leave distinctive scars and the story of hardware succession is usually easy to decipher.

Inventories of household goods are not all that frequent in Ontario records; those that are available have been preserved largely by chance. One of the more valuable of its kind is the inventory for sale by auction of the household effects of Daniel Haight at Adolphustown on the Bay of Quinte.

The date was 1829 and the brief descriptions of furniture pieces suggest that most, possibly all, were made in Upper Canada. Foremost in the listing was a black walnut desk, a cherry bedstead with cords, and a clock and case. Two other bed-steads were listed, as well as two sets of bedstead curtains and "Teaster sheet". That cherry bedstead was, no doubt, a high-poster, and it's likely that one set of curtains was for summer use, the other for winter. "Teaster", of course, means tester, the canopy above the high-post bedstead.

Six Windsor chairs were sold for forty-five shillings. As well as several tables listed without any particular description, there was also a pair of "half rounds" and one called a "combus" table. This just possibly may have been a misspelling of compass, familiar to builders at that period as a term meaning semi-circular.

Among other common furniture, two "waggon chairs" also appeared on Haight's list. These were chairs or seats of the ladderback type, with splint or bark seats, wide enough to hold two persons, and used in a farm waggon when that vehicle became, as on Sundays, a conveyance for family passengers.

Just as informative as an estate inventory was the occasional listing of prices of provincial merchandise. When Lt. Charles Rubidge wrote his advice for emigrants in 1838, he was specific in his description of furniture available. He wrote that Windsor chairs cost four to five shillings. What he called rush-bottomed bamboo were eight shillings and ninepence, while cane-seated chairs were ten shillings and more.

For the more prosperous he reported that "very handsome chairs of walnut, horse-hair bottoms and brass bands" were twenty to twenty-five shillings each. A set of cherry-wood dining-tables, which means the three-section set of a drop-leaf table with movable half-round ends to be added when needed, cost as little as six pounds, but the same table in black walnut cost ten.

His most graphic description was of "circular drawing room tables, very handsomely constructed [of] black walnut, mahogany, or birds' eye maple, carved pillars and claw feet", which were priced at from seven and a half to ten pounds. Four-post bedsteads with "carved pillars" might have been purchased for two pounds ten shillings.

According to Rubidge, "bookcases, sideboards, sofas and all kinds of furniture of modern patterns, all of the finest wood, may be procured at almost every town in Upper Canada, and as cheap, or cheaper, than in England."

A household inventory of simple descriptions is that of Andrew O'Keefe of Brockville in 1821.

This listing, now in the Archives of Ontario, includes one cherry table, one pine table, one wash-hand-stand, three benches, one desk, one chest, and two chairs. His home, like those of many other Upper Canadians, apparently was not cluttered with furniture.

Adam Fergusson was a Scot who travelled in Canada and the United States, published a book of his observations in 1831, and later returned to Upper Canada, where he founded the town of Fergus. In his book he incorporated further descriptions and prices of furniture in the province. The more impressive products included a sideboard with two doors and five drawers for fifteen pounds, a secretary or writing-table for ten pounds, sofas from twelve to fifteen pounds, and three-section dining-tables at seven pounds.

He also assured prospective settlers that they could buy such locally made pieces as breakfast tables, black walnut chairs with hair-bottoms, bureaus (chests of drawers) of various sizes, high-post bedsteads, washstands, and ladies' work tables. The price of a plain drawing-room table was four and a half pounds, of one with claw feet, seven and a half. Windsor chairs were priced at five shillings each.

Fergusson concluded: "These articles are handsomely and substantially finished; and the native woods, such as bird's eye maple, black walnut, birch, elm, oak, cherry, etc., supply excellent and beautiful materials."

An inventory of the effects of Capt. John Walden Meyers in 1821 is particularly worthwhile because the prosperous Meyers built in Belleville, possibly as early as 1794, one of the old colony's more impressive homes. Items of respectable value include a cherry table at one pound and five shillings, a desk at three pounds, and ten Windsor chairs which total two pounds ten shillings. Looking-glasses were apparently more expensive because four of them were appraised together at eight pounds. A clock, no doubt a long-case model, was valued at ten pounds.

Repeated mention in documentary records emphasizes the universal popularity of Windsor chairs. Some of them, no doubt, originated in neighbouring New York State but others, as indicated by advertisements, were made in the province. They were also acquired from Lower Canada; even Charles Ermatinger, fur-trading merchant at what is now Sault Ste. Marie, in 1828 ordered Windsors at four shillings fourpence direct from Montreal.

The frequently quoted Catherine Parr Traill was an English-born settler of gentle breeding. Her keen interest in natural history and in the outdoor life generally helped her, no doubt, to a sympathetic view of the style of living in the near wilderness of Douro Township, not far from Peterborough, where the Traills settled.

Her first book based on her own experiences in Upper Canada was published in 1836, and in it she reported her impressions on first seeing the interior of a log house: "Its furniture was of corresponding rudeness; a few stools, rough and unplaned; a deal table, which, from being manufactured from unseasoned wood, was divided by three wide open seams, and was only held together by its ill-shaped legs; two or three blocks of grey granite placed beside the hearth served for seats for the children. . . ."

Such apparently was the all too common rude quality of furnishings in the homes of the less fortunate. The Traill home, although rustic, was much more comfortable and the lady of the house took obvious pleasure in describing it: "Our furniture consists of a brass-railed sofa, which serves upon occasion as a bed, Canadian painted chairs, a stained pine table, green and white curtains, and a handsome Indian mat that covers the floor. One side of the room is filled up with our books. . . . We do not . . . lack comfort in our humble home. . . ."

Her advice to British emigrants was much like that of other writers of the period: "With respect to furniture and heavy goods of any kind, I would recommend little to be brought. . . . you may now buy goods of all kinds nearly as cheap as in England."

Mrs. Traill's works were more popular than most commentaries on backwoods life in old Ontario, and she certainly never had a serious rival in providing practical directions for living with some degree of comfort and grace on the bush frontier. For newcomers arriving in the 1860s, late editions of her books were still offering the kind of advice that had been suitable for settlers a generation or two earlier: "In furnishing a Canadian log-house, the main study should be to unite simplicity with cheapness and comfort. It

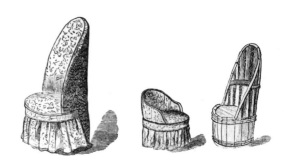

Q. One of Catherine Parr Traill's later books provided directions for making an easy chair from a flour barrel. Andrew Downing's American book *The Architecture of Country Houses* provided in 1850 several illustrations for the same do-it-yourself project. Mrs. Traill in her text provided the more detailed instructions, but the two writers agreed that the padded barrel chair frame should be covered in chintz.

would be strangely out of character to introduce gay, showy, or rich and costly articles of furniture into so rough and homely a dwelling. A log house is better to be simply furnished."

She recommended "painted Canadian chairs", probably meaning that Windsor style of the stencil-decorated arrowback class. She allowed that cherry and walnut tables were available but suggested that stained pine would serve just as well. She recommended bypassing the furniture-makers to the extent of urging husbands or sons to build from pine boards the frameworks for couches and sofas.

For an upholstered chair, Mrs. Traill had specific do-it-yourself directions: "A delightful easy-chair can be made out of a very rough material—nothing better than a common flour barrel."

She described how the flour barrel should be cut away at one side, how auger holes might be bored and ropes passed through the holes and laced together to form a secure and springy seat. She wrote that to complete the chair it should be "stuffed with cotton-wool, soft hay, or sheep's wool, and then a chintz cover over the whole, and well-filled cushions for the seat. . . ."

Susanna Moodie, a sister to Mrs. Traill, also became a new Upper Canadian. She and her husband settled first in Cobourg in 1832 and later in Belleville. Unlike her sister, she was not at first charmed by life in the colony.

She found the typical settler's log house cramped

and uncomfortable. One such she described as half taken up by its huge fireplace hearth, the other half almost filled by a bed. Somehow the single-room dwelling also had space for "a small home-made deal table, of the rudest workmanship, two basswood-bottomed chairs, stained red, one of which was a rocking-chair . . . and a spinning wheel. . . ."

Deal is a long familiar British term for an inferior or common wood, usually pine. Basswood-bottomed probably indicated ladderback chairs with seats woven of bark from that tree.

The Langton family is another of genteel British tradition whose experiences in the Sturgeon Lake area, not far from the Traill home, are familiar to us through letters written to relatives who remained in England. Of a visit to Peterborough made in 1837, Anne Langton wrote, "Painted wooden chairs are the most frequent, rush-bottomed ones being in the more elegant drawing-rooms."

R.   The genteel Langton family had furniture shipped out from England. This sketch by Anne Langton, done about 1840, shows some of that furniture in a cosy sitting-room

At the Peterborough inn at which she stayed, she revealed that seating accommodation was not liberally supplied; she wrote that at meal time, "We used always to take our chairs with us to the dining room." And referring to the bush home in which she and her mother lived, she wrote near Christmas in 1839, "Our carpenter arrived this evening and we held a consultation on the making up of my footstool."

As well as word pictures of frontier life in Upper Canada, Anne Langton made sketches of the interior of her brother John's log house as it appeared in the thirties. Despite the rude quality of furnishings, the sketches provide an impression of unmistakable woodsman's comfort in this bachelor's home.

Anna Jameson, who wrote of her travels in 1836–7, made no effort to hide her dislike of some aspects of life in Upper Canada, but she did appear to admire the native woods. While in St. Thomas she wrote: "There is here an excellent arrangement in Blythe House, the new home at Sturgeon Lake. The side chair on the right is of the Regency-period style that the English called a Trafalgar chair.

Public Archives of Canada

manufacture of cabinet ware and furniture; some articles of the black walnut, a tree abounding here, appeared to me more beautiful in color and grain than the finest mahogany; and the elegant veining of the maple-wood cannot be surpassed."

She admired too the foresight of an Irish clergyman and his family living at Erindale on the Credit River, not far west of Toronto. Mrs. Jameson reported that they had brought a full range of tools from the old country and were well trained to use them, and had built at Erindale a barn, forge, outbuildings, and "a carpenter's shop, a turning-lathe, in the use of which the old gentleman and one of his sons are very ingenious and effective . . . and a house comfortably furnished, much of the ornamental furniture being contrived, carved, turned, by the father and his sons. . . ."

The same Mrs. Jameson was one of several writer-travellers to visit Colonel Thomas Talbot at his fief on the Lake Erie shore. Her impression was one of stoic simplicity in the furnishings there:

S and T.   Anne Langton in the 1830s made several sketches of her bachelor brother's pioneer home above Sturgeon Lake. Two views of the main room in his log house indicate that he had then only the simplest kind of furniture and a

"Here no fauteuil, spring-cushioned, extended its comfortable arms—no sofa here. . . . Colonel Talbot held all such luxuries in sovereign contempt. In front of a capacious chimney stood a long wooden table, flanked with two wooden chairs, cut from the forest in the midst of which they now stood. . . ."

She added, however, that while there she was given a well furnished bedroom. The stoic standard may have prevailed in only one part of the house because Mrs. Jameson wrote in conclusion: "The interior of the house contains several comfortable lodging-rooms; and one really handsome one, the dining room. . . ."

Sir James Alexander, who travelled widely in Canada, was another who enjoyed the hospitality of the Talbot home. Recalling the visit, he wrote in 1849: "In the sitting-room there was a long

minimum even of that. The sketches show a few profession-
ally made late Windsor chairs, the kind that Mrs. Traill
called painted Canadian chairs, a simple rectangular table, a
crude home-made armchair, and bookshelves that may have
been made by a local carpenter.
Ontario Archives

table, a heavy press, shelves with books, and several
old portmanteaus." Less frequently used at the
present time, the word "press" was still then
commonly used to describe a cupboard, often one
which held linen or clothing.

More information about locally produced furniture comes from the 1844 work of James Bryce
Brown. After a residence of several years in the
western district, he published a book which includes this report:

> The following are specimens of prices of the
> description of furniture suited to the means of the
> working tradesman or small farmer:
> Common deal table, 8s. to 12s.; turned and
> painted chairs, 3s. to 4s.; French bed-stead of
> cherry wood, from 25s. to 30s.; feathers for bed-
> ding, 1s. 3d. to 1s. 6d. per lb.; chest of black
> walnut drawers, £2 15s.; . . . Furniture of the best
> description, made of mahogany, and also of the
> native woods, black walnut, maple, and cherry, are
> to be had of superior design and workmanship in
> almost every neighbourhood, and at reasonable
> prices.

The sad dearth of ready information available
to intending immigrants to Canada is implicit in
the generally consistent tone and the kind of basic
descriptions repeated so frequently by the authors
of settlers' guides. They employed many thousands
of words again and again attempting to correct
the old world's mis-impressions of the new. In a
revised edition of his work, Brown published in
1851 such information as this:

> Another prevalent mistake is, that inferior
> descriptions of tradesmen suit and find employment
> almost as well as the best in Canada—the colony,
> as individuals reason, being young, and therefore in
> a comparatively rude state, good workmanship is
> not in request. This may apply to small villages and

country settlements; but the case in regard to the towns is for the most part quite the reverse. In the principal towns of Canada, labour being usually well remunerated, the workmanship required is not inferior to that in the best towns in Britain. Inferior hands experience difficulty in getting employment, while superior tradesmen in most branches are highly prized.

Brown concluded by stating that good carpenters, joiners, and cabinet-makers were the most highly paid of tradesmen in Canada.

In 1905, J. Smyth Carter published a history of the eastern Ontario county of Dundas, and for his material he relied heavily on the tales of local old-timers. His description of earlier beds is particularly interesting:

> The bedsteads as first constructed were attached to the wall, a sort of stationary device. Following

these we find the high, moveable bedsteads, the posts towering towards the ceiling. . . . The bed proper being a good distance from the floor, sufficient space was secured underneath for the children's crib [trundle bed] to be stowed away during the day. Hanging about the base of the senior bed was a curtain. These beds were generally good, but owing to their height some ingenuity was required in order to get into them. The bunk came in as an article of utility, being useful as a seat by day and a bed by night. . . .

Carter's bunk is almost certainly the bunk-bed which is still to be found in eastern Ontario, particularly in areas with a Scottish heritage. The same tradition is familiar as the *banc-lit* in French Canada. A country piece of furniture, it serves as a settle or bench with back during the day, but its box-like base will open to serve as a bed when required.

U.   A water-colour view of the interior of Colonel Thomas Talbot's "castle" on Lake Erie shows it as it probably appeared in the 1830s. The upholstered armchair in the foreground is the most impressive piece of furniture in the room. The slat-back chairs are probably the kind that Mrs. Jameson described as "wooden chairs, cut from the forest in the midst of which they now stood". The stout cupboard with its four plain panelled doors and the H-stretcher table are familiar pieces, common then in many settlers' homes. The painter is identified as C. S. Brydges.

London Public Library Board

While we know little as yet of the furniture used to equip the various legislative buildings that have been used in Ontario, there were period reports and comments that give some impressions of how our forebears catered to the convenience and comfort of their lawmakers.

George Henry, who has already been quoted in these pages, visited York's House of Assembly in 1831, when its sessions were being held in the court house: "Each member has a desk, enclosing a secretaire for the deposit of his letters and papers."

While Anna Jameson said little about the actual furniture there, she had some acid comment to make of government quarters in York in 1836: "The hall of the legislative council . . . is certainly a spacious and lofty room, with a splendid throne and the usual superfluity of gilding and varnish; yet the interior decorations, (the admiration of the people here,) are in the vilest possible taste. . . ."

With the Act of Union which joined Lower and Upper Canada, the first building to serve as a Parliament for the United Canadas was a converted hospital in Kingston. According to a newspaper report in 1841, the Assembly was being furnished with eighty-four upholstered black walnut armchairs. They were covered in dark green moreen and each had a writing area attached to one arm.

In 1850, a Montreal *Gazette* report preserved details of the refurbishing of the old provincial Parliament Building when government headquarters were moved to Toronto. The newspaper correspondent was evidently impressed favourably by the chandeliers, the crimson carpets and draperies, and desks, described as having royal blue covered tops, and black walnut armchairs with crimson morocco cushions. Mrs. Jameson has left us no appraisal of this legislature, but whether in good taste or bad, it appears that the furniture was both sumptuous and colourful.

A remarkably informative collection of letters, shedding some light on the local furniture supplies of the late 1830s, is preserved in the Ontario Department of Public Records and Archives. Written by members of the Macaulay family, affluent and fairly prominent then in Upper Canada, the letters are much concerned with details of home management. Among the letters is an 1837 inventory of household furniture by John Macaulay, living on College Avenue in Toronto. He seemed surprised

V. An 1862 sketch of the sitting-room of Nith Grove, a modest farm home north of Hayesville in Waterloo County, makes it clear that Victorian clutter hadn't yet overwhelmed every rural interior. The unstudied style suggests a period of twenty to thirty years earlier. The box stove appears to be a model of about 1850, but the simple Canadian Windsor chairs, the large gate-leg table, and the bookcase of butternut or pine have a period flavour of about 1835.
Ontario Archives

at the total valuation, which was £ 2,000. Furniture contributing to that total included a dozen hair-bottomed mahogany chairs, a rosewood writing-desk with brass inlay, a mahogany piano, and, of particular interest, a mahogany sideboard with a marble top.

In 1830, as indicated earlier, York tradesmen had petitioned the colonial Assembly to protect them from American competition. The Macaulays, some years later, still did some of their household shopping across the lake in Rochester. They also inspected the Montreal markets in efforts to find household wares superior to those sold in York (renamed Toronto after 1834).

Specific references to the custom making of furniture in Toronto are incorporated in correspondence of 1837 to 1839 between John Macaulay and his mother, Ann Macaulay, who continued to live in Kingston. Toronto cabinet-makers referred to were the firms of Robson and Wilson and of Jacques and Hay. John was a most particular client and the records suggest he spent an appreciable amount of time inspecting the work of local craftsmen. A letter to his wife, then in Kingston, included a brief report of one such inspection: "I saw this evening a beautiful mahogany stand for music made by Wilson for Mr. Charles Richardson."

General practice up to about 1850 was for clients to order furniture directly from cabinet-makers and not, as later, from merchants. Most pieces were made to order. Chair-makers, however, were more likely to stockpile their products so that customers could purchase the ready-made article.

John Macaulay's letters certainly suggest that discriminating clients could at that time rely on the standards of fashion and quality more by shopping in Toronto than in Kingston. He ordered in Toronto a number of pieces of furniture for his mother and used the mail service to consult with her over their planning. One of John's letters makes clear the extent of client planning that a cabinet-maker was at times expected to incorporate in his work:

> I shall be able to make your writing-desk secretary very complete by adding to it a drawer which will contain a regular cash box with patent lock and key. I am not yet determined whether to put into it an ebony inkstand and have regular places made in the desk itself for bottles, etc. If I knew the exact size of your old ebony inkstand and you should like it, I will have a place made for it to stand in. I could get a sideboard made of plain solid walnut for about £12, if you would prefer it to the beautiful one at £18, of course it cannot be so handsome.

After the senior Mrs. Macaulay had written to approve plans, John replied with a report of immediate action in the Toronto workshops:

> I have purchased the side-board for you and shall send it down by one of the steam boats. It is well made of good wood, neat in figure and beautifully varnished. . . . I have agreed with Jakes and Hay for a neat little secretary for you, which will be moveable on casters, and contain all your writing apparatus. . . . I haven't yet given Wilson any order for the tables. . . . He can make a table to turn up like a card table, but the objection to this is, in my mind, that when open it may be too low, and when shut, a little too high, and on one side the joint will shew. The table might be a Pembroke one. . . . Then again, it may be made with two narrow leaves to turn down as you may please.

The sideboard reached Kingston in a few days and Mrs. Macaulay wrote immediately to John: "I am quite pleased with the sideboard. It does not take up too much room, and is a beautiful piece of wood, the old one stood the stove very well, and it was veneered, so I hope this will, if the wood has been well seasoned."

The cracking or lifting of veneer was obviously a matter of serious concern in houses heated by stoves, but John wrote with confidence of the sideboard's durability in his next letter:

> I have great hopes of it bearing stove heat well, for the best New York glue, which is better than English glue, has been used in the veneering. I have agreed with Wilson for a table of black walnut. It is to be a Pembroke table, with two narrow leaves, and will cost about three pounds, and be made of the best wood. It will be ready in the course of three weeks, when I will send it down with the secretary which Jacques and Hay are making.

At this point, although the secretary was not yet complete, John was already much pleased with it. He wrote with enthusiasm, "It is so convenient, and if it does not astonish the Kingstonians, then I shall wonder."

The secretary was damaged during its steamboat transfer to Kingston and a disappointed Mrs. Macaulay wrote that "little ornaments at top" had been broken off and lost. Back in Toronto, however, John ordered replacements and suitable veneering from the makers, and the damage was evidently repaired by a cabinet-maker in Kingston.

Scanty records have enabled historians to identify by name only a few furniture-makers working prior to 1812. With the growth after the war of population and of manufactures and services, the list of names becomes longer. After 1830, advertisements in the growing number of newspapers indicate that there were by then many makers producing a great amount of furniture in a considerable variety of styles.

W. Very few pieces of Ontario-made furniture are in any way labelled or branded by their producers. One of the few exceptions is this printed paper label affixed to the underside of a Boston rocker seat. It credits the chair to "Col. E. Buell Cabinet & Chair Factory. All work warranted. Brockville, C.W." The chair itself is probably a product of the 1840s.
Mr. & Mrs. F. M. Blayney, Waterloo

II.   An arrowback Windsor chair, one of a set of six which
was made, according to family tradition, in the eastern
Ontario village of Merrickville. Most comparable country-
style chairs were given a dark finish with stencilled decoration.
The freely handled decorative painting over a yellow base on
this chair is a fresh and unusual treatment. It was made
about 1840.

Canadian Industries Ltd., Montreal

In Brockville in 1831, the "New cabinet factory" of Thomas Church and Co. appealed to clients with reference to "their experience in the best shops in the principal cities of the United States".

The 1836 advertisement of William Dexter in Bytown offered potential customers "pedestal and framed side-board tables, Dining, loo, and card tables, ladies work tables, pembroke and dressing tables, secretaries, book-cases, wardrobes, chests of drawers, grecian and trafalgar chairs, sofas and bedsteads."

In the same advertisement he appealed for cherry and butternut boards and birch scantling. Dexter believed that success depended on moving with fashion's direction and in 1837 he advertised that "he has just returned from the United States with the latest New York and London fashions."

Another Bytown cabinetware firm, that of Kennedy and Blyth, advertised in 1838 that they "receive their mahogany direct from New York."

The word factory appeared in use by the 1820s. Poucett's chair factory at Niagara used an advertisement in 1828 for chairs with "Plain and Ornamental painting, gilding and glazing". Chair warehouse is a term also familiar in the 1820s and it may have been used by retail merchants as well as wholesaling chair-makers.

In York in 1815 there were craftsmen who listed themselves both as cabinet-makers and as joiners. In smaller communities the all-purpose professional survived throughout the nineteenth century, but in larger centres such as York a growing market encouraged as a rule much greater specialization.

In the early years transactions between producers and clients seldom involved actual money. Cash was in extremely short supply and everyone was accustomed to dealing in kind. With the growth of population and prosperity, the practice became less general in the larger centres. In Niagara, however, in 1830, cabinet-maker Joseph Merriam advertised that "country produce as well as lumber" would be accepted in payment for furniture. The barter system remained familiar in country towns for many years. The account book of Abram Southard in Picton reveals that in 1860 he was taking payment for furniture in all sorts of lumber, cheese, dried berries, butter and eggs, maple sugar, hickory nuts, and turnips. In one simple transaction he balanced a child's high chair against sixty-three pounds of buckwheat flour.

Furniture with marble tops was mentioned in earlier inventories, but possibly the first reference to its manufacture in Ontario came in 1847. In a Chatham newspaper the firm of G. Underhill & Co. advertised monuments and tombs and also centre tables and other furniture made of white marble imported from Vermont.

The trend to furniture in sets or suites, particularly for bedrooms, is to be noted in advertisements of the early fifties. A Hamilton firm described its bedroom furniture as "chamber sets in the most elegant styles with or without marble tops". The same advertisement reveals the growth of the practice of producing furniture before receiving actual orders. The phrase soon to be familiar in many cabinet firms' announcements was, "on hand or made to order".

Despite specialization in the crafts, there remained some firms which handled in considerable volume a fascinating variety of merchandise and services. One of the more ambitious claims was published in 1852 in Hamilton by the firm of Storror and Jarvis:

> Fashionable and durable articles of household furniture manufactured under their own superintendance. . . . Ladies needlework mounted on fire screens or ottoman boxes in a neat and elegant style. Funerals conducted on the most modern and economical principles. Auctioneering, appraising and paper hanging attended to. Goods packed, removed, exchanged, bought or sold on commission. Old furniture repaired, re-stuffed, and polished. Steam boats fitted up in a magnificent and at the same time economical manner. . . .

Funeral management was a natural adjunct to the furniture business since the making of coffins was obviously work for cabinet-makers. To this day, many furniture dealers in the smaller communities of Ontario still serve as funeral directors.

The appeal of fashionable American furniture for the wealthier city people has already been mentioned. Enterprising American business people, however, did not overlook the possibility of rewarding sales in smaller border communities and many advertised their wares regularly in Canadian newspapers. Typical was an Ogdensburg dealer who used a Cornwall newspaper in 1845 to advertise pianofortes from Boston and "new style" sofas, which probably meant they were made in the heavy fashion then popularized by the Baltimore architect John Hall. Offered at prices from $25 to $50 were upholstered mahogany rocking-chairs with seats and backs covered in haircloth.

Some ambitious cabinet-makers, as well as a growing number of merchants who sold but did not manufacture furniture, ordered furniture for resale from suppliers in the United States. In 1860, Picton's Abram Southard received furniture to the value of nearly $500 from Degraaf and Taylor in New York.

Southard, whose sales were limited to the Picton area, bought furniture from other Canadian firms as well. In 1859, for example, he received from Lewis Roenick in Belleville Boston rockers, scroll-bottom rockers, bent-back chairs, sewing chairs, and common high chairs. For Boston rockers

X.   In the village of Newburgh in Leeds County, James Hazelton by the 1870s operated a well-established furniture factory and also had an undertaking department with a horse-drawn hearse "which cost $400".
Leavitt: "History of Leeds and Grenville"

Southard paid $1.50 each; his selling price was usually $3.

The Southard account book provides a wealth of detail concerning the operation of a furniture-making firm in a small but important Ontario town. Although the period recorded is late, the materials, methods, and styles employed were probably very little different to those of twenty to thirty years earlier in this and in many other similar communities.

The small-town cabinet shop is revealed as a place where the local customer could expect a wide variety of products and services. Southard's records reveal that one could then order a walnut or mahogany sofa for thirty dollars or have one's duck decoys painted for seventy-five cents. Southard made bird-cages, walnut bureaus, mahogany ottomans, sets of dining-tables, oval frames, scroll bedsteads, and literally anything else one might have wanted in the furniture class.

He was familiar evidently with the trade-in manner of doing business because he is shown to have allowed one client five dollars for a high-post bed. His workmen put new flag (rush) seats in

chairs, and there were frequent entries in the records of upholstering and varnishing, or repairing and painting chairs.

Like cabinet-makers in larger centres, Southard relied on having work done by an independent turner. James Platt, who appears to have had a lathe and shop of his own, supplied him with sets of legs for tables and washstands as well as bedposts and spindles for cradles and beds. It's revealing in terms of developing specialization to learn from the records that Platt balanced the account in part by ordering from Southard two Boston rockers and a mahogany sofa.

Further specialization is indicated by account entries for carving work completed by outside craftsmen. They provided Southard with ornamental backs for sofas, corners for picture frames, table feet, and carved chair-backs. Payment for one chair back was thirty-eight cents.

Local agricultural fairs led even before the middle of the century to an annual provincial exhibition. By the time of the fair of 1852, exhibit classes had been broadened to include crafts and manufactures as well as farm stock and produce. The catalogue for the Provincial Exhibition held in Toronto in 1858 went into some detail in describing the furniture entries:

> Drawing room sofa, centre table, polished arm

Y. In the Huron County village of Varna in the 1870s, cabinet-maker George Diehl was still, as might well be expected in a provincial community, producing furniture in a variety of styles even then old-fashioned. The array to be seen in this old photograph includes a chest of drawers of late Empire tradition, a turned-post bedstead of a design popular in 1830, a late Windsor high chair, and a rococo-revival armchair.

> chair, pier table and other articles in black walnut are shown by the assignees of T. Fuller, Oshawa. . . . An elegantly designed lady's work table made by G. Fischer, Morristown, attracted considerable attention. The top of this table is composed of 1,220 pieces of inlaid wood. A lady's writing table by the same maker excited general notice. . . . A beautifully carved and highly polished birds-eye maple wardrobe manufactured by Jacques & Hay, Toronto, elicited the admiration of every beholder. There is also a handsome bedstead, dressing table, bedroom chairs, and washstand of the same material. This firm also exhibits a large quantity of splendid black walnut furniture, and a beautifully carved and polished oak side-board, which show that we have workmen in Canada competent to make the very best use of the beautiful woods which Nature has given us.

Professional and trade directories were scarcely known at all in Upper Canada until 1830, but by the 1840s they had appeared in most important communities. The information supplied by some is not entirely reliable but in general their publishers

MANUFACTORY AT OSHAWA, (East of Toronto, C.W.) ON THE **GRAND TRUNK** Railroad.

THOMAS FULLER & Co.,

MANUFACTURERS

OF

FURNITURE,

OF EVERY DESCRIPTION,

WHOLESALE AND RETAIL.

64 YONGE STREET, TORONTO.

MATRASSES, FEATHER BEDS AND PILLOWS ALWAYS ON HAND.

Toronto, October, 1857.

Z. The few illustrations to appear with Ontario cabinet-makers' advertisements of the earlier years of the nineteenth century were stock cuts from American typographic supply houses. By the middle of the century, in time for the exuberant lines of the rococo-revival style, the more ambi-tious furniture-makers sometimes illustrated their advertise-ments with a comparatively rich display of up-to-date wood engravings. This 1857 advertisement by the busy and prosperous Toronto firm of Thomas Fuller & Co. is typical.

have provided a most valuable store of information for later investigators.

One of the better regional directories makes it clear that by the 1840s almost every community worthy of the name had a cabinet-maker of its own. In 1846, the city of Toronto, with a popu-lation then of about 20,000, had twenty-five cabinet-makers, one chair-maker, five turners, five upholsterers, and three French-polishers. Kingston, which had a population of just over 6,000, listed ten cabinet-makers and two chair-makers. Even a village such as Lanark with only 250 citizens had one cabinet-maker, while towns with a population range from 1,000 to 2,000 had from one to five cabinet-makers each. Peterborough, a town of 2,000, claimed to have four chair factories in ad-dition to four cabinet-makers.

By 1851 the town of Hamilton could list among its business enterprises seven cabinet-makers, two upholsterers, two men who were both cabinet- and chair-makers, one who was an undertaker as well as a cabinet-maker, one chair and bedstead factory, and one cabinet and chair steam factory and upholstery warehouse.

Furniture-making had become a very busy trade. The colony was prosperous; its population con-tinued to grow and continued apparently to buy a great deal of home-produced wares from the cabinet- and chair-makers of the province. By 1857, when the population was probably a little over 1,000,000, there were in the province 800 firms or individuals listed as cabinet-makers, chair-makers, or specialists contributing to the furniture-making business.

The Illustrations

THE PICTURES which follow and which comprise the larger and more important part of this publication illustrate pieces of furniture, most of which I believe were made in old Ontario, all of which, I am convinced, were used to furnish nineteenth-century homes in the province.

There are very few pieces bearing any marks which identify their makers, an evidence of modesty that might be recommended to present-day manufacturers, whose labels may appear more lasting than their products. There are likewise few pieces of old furniture with flawless pedigree, few whose traditions of origin or ownership within one family can bear serious scrutiny.

It will be understood that some few pieces of the furniture illustrated will have originated outside Ontario. The historical evidence indicates that furniture of diverse quality did enter old Ontario from other nations and from neighbouring colonies, and some of my captions will suggest that certain pieces fall within that class.

There will remain some other pieces, particularly of common styles, which may have been made elsewhere. There certainly are examples of slat-back and Windsor chairs, for example, not likely to be distinguishable from those made in Lower Canada or the Atlantic colonies of the United States.

The sharing of styles and patterns in craft by neighbours has made the interchange of some products difficult to trace. If some examples of foreign make are commonly accepted today as properly Ontarian, one should recognize too that in recent years antiquarian merchants have eased the passage of much furniture made here into a United States market, where it has completely lost its identity.

Except for a very few pieces, all the furniture illustrated is at this moment to be found in collections within Ontario. The selection has been made in an effort to illustrate both the variety of style and the range in quality; the kind of furniture that was genuinely rare in its own period and that which was common and has become relatively rare in our day.

The relative size in which the different illustrations are reproduced is itself a key to the importance assigned to the furniture illustrated. The arrangement of the photographs too must in any picture catalogue reflect something of the prejudices of the author.

To this amateur of household furniture, it makes the greatest good sense to deal first with chairs, because that category is the most important of furniture groupings. The chair is the most personal of all furniture and is successfully designed only when its ornamental value does not outweigh its classic function of supporting a human frame in a position which preserves both comfort and dignity.

The ancient symbolic importance of chairs remains with us today in the throne of state or church, in the bench of justice, and in other special forms, none perhaps more important than the chairmanship of the corporate board. The chairs of very important personages remain quite special and set aside for their individual use.

There was a time when only a chieftain was entitled to use a chair; the people sat upon the ground. But the common folk have long since gained equal seating rights and their chairs are special because they exhibit a greater variety and subtlety in style than other classes of furniture.

It is logical that multiple seating units such as sofas and settles and settees should follow, because they are, of course, simply enlarged chairs. I have dealt next with beds because I believe we can regard them as modified chairs; particularly in the forms in which they appeared in early Ontario, beds are framed in a manner similar to many chairs. And like chairs, they are a very personal kind of furniture.

Case furniture comes next. This is a very large category whose basic example is the box or chest made of six boards, four to make sides and ends, one the bottom and one the top or lid, usually hinged.

The simple chest was the piece of old-country furniture most commonly brought here by settlers. For many newcomers it was the only furniture brought; for some time after it may have been the only piece of household furniture, and, in the shanty period at least, it served also as bench and table.

Most of mankind's impersonal furniture, the furniture intended to hold or store things rather than humans, has evolved from the chest. The chest of drawers was probably the earliest development from the box form. Deep boxes appeared with a drawer in the lower part; more drawers were added until the chest was filled and the top was no longer hinged but fastened down.

With or without drawers, the chest has been modified in many different ways to produce desks, sideboards, cupboards, bookcases, and other species and sub-species. The most familiar of the modifications are dealt with here more or less in some rational sequence.

Such subdividing allows for a degree of order in arranging catalogue pictures, but one is bound to be frustrated if one persists in trying to push every piece of furniture extant into a neatly labelled pigeon-hole. There are too many examples in which functions overlap.

The basic table, for instance, is a platform only, a plane raised from ground or floor level, a board as it was once called, on which to place certain things. But as soon as such a basic piece is modified by adding a drawer it becomes also a piece of case furniture, its relationship to the basic box clearly evident.

There are lesser categories which in the purest sense relate neither to the personal chair nor to the impersonal case or table. The mirror or looking-glass is one. The hall tree is another, and the rack for hanging spoons. But many of these are to be found with drawers or shelves incorporated, and one is enabled thereby to push them in one way or another into one of those handy pigeon-holes.

In the simplest terms there is only personal and impersonal furniture. Chairs and benches, beds and cradles make up the personal or people furniture. Chests and tables and their modifications make up, for the most part, the impersonal furniture, the furniture for putting things in or on.

The dates appended to the caption accompanying each illustration have been chosen by the author on a basis rather more empirical than properly scientific. They are intended to suggest the time span in which each piece is likely to have been made in Ontario. Similar designs may have been familiar at earlier dates in other parts of the western world and some may have been made at earlier dates even here in Ontario.

But the evidence generally does suggest that many styles were adopted here rather later than in other parts of the world. Likewise, such styles sometimes remained in fashion here after they had lost favour elsewhere. Whatever the truth, precision of dating is of lesser importance than the standards of design and workmanship in any craft.

Chairs

1. A provincial adaptation from high style in an older society, this purely eighteenth-century chair is a quite fine piece of furniture in the context of Upper Canada. Essentially English in tradition, it follows the simpler tradition of Chippendale patterns, which were already going out of style by the time the Loyalists first settled here. The wood is birch. The seat-covering fabric is modern. The chair was found in the Kingston area. Chairs very similar in design are known to have originated in Quebec and in Nova Scotia.

1780–1800

Mr. & Mrs. John Harbinson, Agincourt

2.   The elegance of Georgian England is echoed in this Ontario version of an eighteenth-century chair, inspired essentially by designs published in Hepplewhite's name. Made entirely of curled maple, it is the product of a competent, not an inspired, craftsman. It was made probably by a Loyalist who had some professional training before the move to Upper Canada.

1790–1810

Royal Ontario Museum, Toronto

3.   Very few wing chairs were made in Ontario because the style was out of favour before there was any considerable furniture production here, but an Ontario craftsman in Lanark County is believed to have made this good example about the late date of 1830. The style is that usually called after Hepplewhite and popular about 1790. The exposed parts of the frame are birch, and the front legs are slightly tapered. The upholstery is modern.

Mr. & Mrs. M. F. Feheley, Toronto

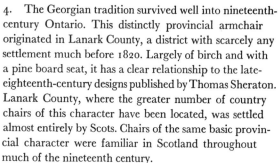

4. The Georgian tradition survived well into nineteenth-century Ontario. This distinctly provincial armchair originated in Lanark County, a district with scarcely any settlement much before 1820. Largely of birch and with a pine board seat, it has a clear relationship to the late-eighteenth-century designs published by Thomas Sheraton. Lanark County, where the greater number of country chairs of this character have been located, was settled almost entirely by Scots. Chairs of the same basic provincial character were familiar in Scotland throughout much of the nineteenth century.

1820–40

The Grange, Art Gallery of Ontario, Toronto

5. This armchair of country Sheraton character has unusually romantic, scroll-shaped back rails. The top rail particularly suggests the Empire style as interpreted here. The seat of this Lanark County chair is pine; the other parts are birch. The original finish was probably a brown stain.

1820–40

Mr. & Mrs. J. E. Flanigan, Brockville

6. A Georgian-style armchair from Carleton County owes its design generally to the Sheraton tradition, although the especially successful arms suggest a debt to the older Chippendale school. The main wood is birch, very popular with chair-makers for its strength, durability, and satisfactory working qualities, and its suitability for accepting a stain making it well suited to simulating walnut or mahogany. The board seat, as in most chairs of this type, is pine.

1820–40

National Museum of Man, Ottawa

7. The once frequent occurrence of this pattern in country Sheraton side chairs suggests it was made in considerable numbers by a capable chair-maker in Lanark County. Satisfying proportions and reeding detail on back stiles and rails make it a very pleasing provincial chair. Like others of its class, it has a flat board seat of pine with all other parts in birch. A brown stain is the original finish.

1820–40

National Historic Sites Service, Ottawa

8. The basic form of the joiner's Georgian-period chair survives in this example from Glengarry County, but some flavour of Regency style is added by the shaping of the back stiles and rails. This chair is the "carver" in a set of dining-chairs which remains today in the possession of a descendant of the original owner. The wood is birch; the original finish was a black stain or paint.

1820–40

Mr. & Mrs. Blake McKendry, Elginburg

9. Country Sheraton chairs originating in central and western Ontario were more often made of cherry, the flat board seat included. Another "carver" from a dining-set, this rather stout chair seems even more countrified than others of the type. The arms, however, have real Georgian distinction.

1820–40

Mr. & Mrs. John Harbinson, Agincourt

10. This armchair is one that exhibits in all its component parts its debt to Sheraton's pattern books. Its Ontario maker, however, may never have heard Sheraton's name; inspiration possibly was supplied by a finer mahogany chair once seen. It would be out of place in a formal drawing-room but it no doubt lent traditional dignity to a humbler home in Upper Canada. Stiles and spindles, as in many chairs of this type, are beaded. The woods are birch and pine; the original finish was brown stain or paint.

1820–40

Mrs. H. C. Walker, Toronto

12. A Lanark County chair quite similar to the side chair in Plate 7 probably came from the same workshop. In fact, it is possible that most chairs of country Sheraton style and having a Lanark County association may have been the work of one maker or firm. The practice of setting the front stretcher or rung a little distance behind the legs is an eighteenth-century tradition. The board seat is pine, the rest birch.

1820–40

Mr. & Mrs. Walter Beevor, Stirling

11. All chairs in this class are joinery work; stiles or posts and rails or rungs are fastened with mortise-and-tenon joints, each secured by a hardwood pin. The square back is basic to most Sheraton chair designs. The most frequently used wood in Ontario chairs of this class is birch. This Lanark County chair has vertical spindles refined by beading.

1820–40

Mr. & Mrs. Blake McKendry, Elginburg

13. The oddly distinctive arms, ending in an outward and downward curve, owe little to formal style books. The crude union of arm posts with seat rails suggests the arms may have been an afterthought. The maker of this Lanark County chair used ash in place of the more familiar birch. The seat is whitewood and the arm posts maple.

1820–40

14. A stubby armchair made for a child is under twenty-two inches high, but the provincial Sheraton character is the same as in other Lanark County chairs of adult scale. Front posts taper towards both the floor and the arm-rests above. The beading of the back spindles or balusters is a gesture towards refinement. The woods are the usual birch and pine.

1820–40

Author's collection

15.   An eastern Ontario child's chair seems to have been inspired more by the later Regency and Empire lines, but its basic construction is the same as other country Sheraton chairs. Made of birch and retaining much of its original brown paint, it is only nineteen inches in height.

1830–50

Upper Canada Village, Morrisburg

16.   The strange rendering of the arms of this chair **was** probably derived from a sophisticated prototype similar to some in Hepplewhite's *Guide*. This is another Lanark County chair of birch and pine, whose original finish was probably a brown stain. Back stiles and rails are beaded. Rear legs have been worn or cut down.

1820–40

Mr. & Mrs. Blake McKendry, Elginburg

17.   The arm design of this chair, culminating in a very short turned post, is a heavy country version of an English high style which appeared first about 1790. This one is a Lanark County chair of birch and ash. Like others illustrated here, the provincial Georgian seats are of uncompromising flat boards; the formal chairs which inspired them normally had upholstered slip seats.

1820–40

National Historic Sites Service, Ottawa

18.   This provincial version of a basic Georgian-period chair is crude but retains some distinction in its proportions. Unlike most chairs of the class which have been found in Lanark County, this one is largely of cherry. The top rail is curled maple.

1820–40

Author's collection

20. Two chairs from Renfrew County and of ruggedly distinguished peasant character are similar to others of the class but the shaped back splats suggest an inspiration derived from older Chippendale forms. The woods are birch with ash splats and pine seats. Some early brown stain survives.

1820–40

National Historic Sites Service, Ottawa

19. A chair from Victoria County has strange arms that suggest the character of wainscot chairs of sixteenth-century England. More likely, the odd outline is simply the work of a rural craftsman with a distorted concept of Georgian traditions that really went out of style fifty years before. Rear posts are of birch, the rest bird's-eye maple. The seat is a modern replacement and there is some possibility that the original was upholstered.

1830–50

Mr. Eugene Rae, Malton

21. For simple country chairs, these have quite distinguished centre rails of Regency character. A set of six appears to have been augmented by two made for children at a later date. The adult chairs have a medium brown stain with black accent lining and a dark purple finish on rectangular back-rail panels. The children's chairs have an even painted and grained finish to simulate mahogany. They were found in a nineteenth-century home in Prescott.

1820–40

National Historic Sites Service, Ottawa

22. Two from a set of Regency-flavoured dining-chairs found in Dundas County and made in the familiar birch and pine combination. The carver has arms derived originally from a classical Greek model. Traces of black and red paint remaining suggest they may have had an original finish to simulate mahogany. The period term was "mahoganized".

1820–40

National Museum of Man, Ottawa

23.   Although this armchair acquired in Lanark County was made largely in the pattern of other chairs of country Sheraton character, it is difficult to see past the unique front leg and post combination. The bow-legged look is the result of turning a familiar leg ninety degrees; it would look much more familiar if it curved forward rather than to the side. The original painted and decorated finish is of a character more familiar on fancy chairs and Windsors of the same period. The basic paint is black with yellow and green decoration. The main wood is ash but the seat is pine.

1830–50

Author's collection

24.   Bizarre is the proper word to describe this chair which was found in western Ontario. Although constructed in the same basic way as chairs of country Sheraton style, it may be more satisfactory to class it with pure folk art. The low-relief carving of a basket on the top rail is a simple version of a conventional nineteenth-century design, but the use of oak-leaf designs in such odd positions is unusual. The finials, four at the top and two pointing towards the floor below seat level, suggest those of ladderback chairs.

Nineteenth century

Uncle Tom's Cabin and Museum, Dresden

25. A fine banister-back armchair, this one was found in Dundas County. Fine turning of the arm posts and back members makes it a particularly graceful although uncompromisingly upright chair. Birch and hickory are the woods used; a red-brown stain appears probably to have been the original finish. The rush seat is woven in a pattern seen frequently in eastern Ontario.

1800–30

Mr. & Mrs. Blake McKendry, Elginburg

26. A much simplified banister-back chair from Oxford County is made of birch and hickory. The original finish, now removed, was black paint. The seat is modern, woven in a pattern not used in the period. The worn legs have been lengthened recently to approximate original height.

1820–40

Mrs. Marjorie Larmon, Burgessville

27. This banister-back chair of some individual distinction is made in a manner that suggests it was not designed as a rocker. Stout side stretchers, for example, would not be needed to provide stability in a chair with rockers. The woods are birch and ash with a crest rail of bird's-eye maple. The depth of the seat rails suggests it was intended probably to have a flat board seat. The present woven seat is modern. The maker, according to family tradition, was George Sutherland, who was born in Scotland in 1792 and settled in Glengarry County here before 1815. He was a great-great-grandparent of the present owner.

1820–30

Miss Margaret Cameron, Toronto

28. A very simple banister-back chair from Grenville County is made of maple with a brown finish. The older splint or bark seat has been covered with late fabric. The turning profile of the front stretchers or rungs is repeated in the back rails. Finials of the rear posts may originally have extended to points.

1800–30

Mr. & Mrs. Blake McKendry, Elginburg

29. The arm supports of this banister-back rocking chair are fastened to side seat rails but they extend to the rung or stretcher below, a characteristic noted in some chairs of early-eighteenth-century French Canada and New England. The ball feet are also eighteenth century in style. The flattened arrow shapes of the banisters may derive from Sheraton tradition. Short rockers are typical of early designs used when older chairs were adapted in the very early nineteenth century. The decorative paint is old but not original, possibly as late as 1850.

1800–30

Norfolk Historical Society, Simcoe

30. This banister-back chair is of a style popular in the United States in the first half of the eighteenth century; it very likely originated there. The rockers were added, their shape suggesting a date about 1840; the proximity of the lower side stretchers to the rockers indicates it could not have been designed as a rocking chair. The woods are ash and birch. Traces of colour indicate that its original finish was brown stain or paint.

Mrs. H. C. Walker, Toronto

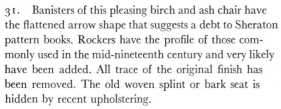

31. Banisters of this pleasing birch and ash chair have the flattened arrow shape that suggests a debt to Sheraton pattern books. Rockers have the profile of those commonly used in the mid-nineteenth century and very likely have been added. All trace of the original finish has been removed. The old woven splint or bark seat is hidden by recent upholstering.

1820–40

Mrs. H. C. Walker, Toronto

32. A banister-back rocker from Lanark County has the contoured arrow-shaped spindles commonly seen in Windsor rocking chairs of about 1830. Turning is simple but effective, although, as is frequently the case, the rear legs are plain. The wood is largely birch, the seat of woven elm bark. The original finish is covered by many coats of later paint. What appears to be a centre back rail is a later addition to guard against breaking banisters.

1825–40

Mr. & Mrs. J. E. Flanigan, Brockville

33. This slat-back chair has eighteenth-century characteristics and it may have reached Ontario from the United States. One older tradition is the bold character of turning, particularly in the front legs and front and side stretchers; another is the extension of the arm posts through the seat to the stretchers below. The profile of the arms and the vase-shaped foot terminals were familiar well before the beginning of Upper Canada. Rockers extend about the same distance behind as in front of the chair, like those of a cradle, the piece of furniture which no doubt first inspired rocking chairs. Chamfering of the rockers is a further noteworthy refinement. The wood is birch and the original finish was a brown stain. Rush is done in the most familiar traditional pattern but almost certainly is not original.

1760–1800

Mr. & Mrs. M. F. Feheley, Toronto

34. An eastern Ontario slat-back chair depends largely on its noteworthy turning of arm posts and mitre-shaped finials for a superior rating. Mushroom arm-post terminals are seen on American chairs as early as 1700. The rockers are of mid-nineteenth-century character and are not original to the chair. Traces of black stain or paint finish survive. Woods are birch, hickory, and ash. The seat is woven of inner elm bark.

1800–30

Mr. & Mrs. George Mason, Kingston

35.   Slim, tapering arm supports do much to give this simple slat-back chair a pleasingly light character. Found in Toronto, it is made of curled maple and has traces of nothing other than a clear varnish finish. The short rockers may well be original, as well as the splint seat.

36.   Splint seat of the same chair is woven in one of several attractive basket-weave patterns customarily used. Splint used in Ontario was probably most often of ash and hickory. The inner bark of elm and basswood was used in the same way. Both splint and bark were cut for use in the spring and were woven while soft and pliable. At other seasons, dry splint required soaking and softening in water before use.

1800–40

Mr. Eugene Rae, Malton

37. Concentrated local occurrence of chairs of this pattern suggests they were made in the Niagara Peninsula. With very simple banister back of some Sheraton-style influence, the chair is made of maple and hickory with a splint seat. Blue appears to have been a frequent paint colour chosen for these chairs. Arrow-shaped spindles are almost identical to those used in Sheraton-influenced Windsor chairs of the arrowback type.

1820–40

Jordan Historical Museum of the Twenty, Jordan

38. Except for its vase-shaped front feet and the subtle tapering of its banisters, this chair depends entirely on fine proportion for its distinct appeal. Exposed square ends to the front seat rail are derived from the eighteenth century and with some few exceptions they appear only with rush seats. Black paint finish is decorated with stylized gold leaves, tassels, and star bursts, suggestive of some English chair decoration of about 1800.

1810–30

Upper Canada Village, Morrisburg

39. Sheraton-style banister-back chair, found in Brant County, is made of birch and ash, and almost certainly was painted and decorated when new. The original rush seat has been covered with carpet strip of about 1850. The banister and front stretcher designs can be seen in Sheraton's publications. The feet have been cut down.

1820–30

Mr. Barclay Holmes, Vineland

40. A side chair of Sheraton style closely related to the preceding example, this provincial piece retains much of its basic black paint and some trace of yellow accent rings on posts and front legs. The panel in the top rail probably had an additional painted design.

1820–30

Black Creek Pioneer Village, Toronto

41. This chair should possibly be classed with the "fancy" chairs illustrated later in these pages but it is also distinctly related to the four preceding examples. The putty-coloured paint may be the original finish. The seat frame is that of the standard "fancy" chair design intended for rushing; the use of ash splint instead is most unusual. It was found in Prince Edward County.

1825–40

Mr. & Mrs. Walter Beevor, Stirling

42. This slat-back side chair combines romantic bow-shaped back rails of eighteenth-century tradition with the turned and then flattened rear posts characteristic of simple Windsor chairs of about 1830. The front legs are turned in the manner of "fancy" chairs of the same date. The seat frame is of the style usually intended for rush; the surviving woven elm-bark seat may not be the original. Woods are birch and hickory. The original paint finish was green. The chair was found in Lennox and Addington.

1820–40

Mr. & Mrs. Thomas L. Riedel, Bath

43. A painstaking maker required extra time to produce this chair with its considerable attention to decorative detail. Trumpet-shaped finials echo an eighteenth-century heritage but this chair evidently originated in nineteenth-century eastern Ontario. A second chair with back rails and arm-rests of this unusual pattern is known to have come from Prince Edward County. The woven seat is modern. Largely birch, it was originally finished in dark brown.

1800–40

Mrs. H. C. Walker, Toronto

44. It is neither easy nor entirely necessary to fit all chairs into neat descriptive pigeon-holes. This simple ladderback is modified by the influence of Sheraton-style Windsors in the raking and flattening of the back posts. The style of paint decoration is familiar both on Windsors and on "fancy" chairs in much of the first half of the nineteenth century. The base coat is black paint and the stencilled decoration is silver and gold bronzing. The rush seat appears to be its original.

1830–50

Mr. & Mrs. Blake McKendry, Elginburg

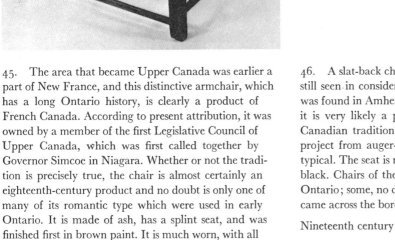

45. The area that became Upper Canada was earlier a part of New France, and this distinctive armchair, which has a long Ontario history, is clearly a product of French Canada. According to present attribution, it was owned by a member of the first Legislative Council of Upper Canada, which was first called together by Governor Simcoe in Niagara. Whether or not the tradition is precisely true, the chair is almost certainly an eighteenth-century product and no doubt is only one of many of its romantic type which were used in early Ontario. It is made of ash, has a splint seat, and was finished first in brown paint. It is much worn, with all the legs somewhat reduced, rear stretchers missing, and the third back rail broken.

1760–1800

Niagara Historical Society, Niagara-on-the-Lake

46. A slat-back chair in the simplest tradition of those still seen in considerable numbers in Quebec, this one was found in Amherstburg in the Detroit River area, and it is very likely a product of the surviving French-Canadian tradition there. Stretchers and rails which project from auger-drilled holes in squared posts are typical. The seat is rush. The hardwood frame is painted black. Chairs of the same style are familiar in eastern Ontario; some, no doubt, were made here; many others came across the border from Quebec.

Nineteenth century

Mr. & Mrs. Richard Brook, Simcoe

47. This slat-back chair with some Sheraton-style modification in the back is probably of Quebec origin and of a type that was marketed in eastern Ontario. The woven splint seat has straw stuffing, which makes it effectively a cushioned chair. Black is the original colour.

1820–40

Upper Canada Village, Morrisburg

48. A rocking chair of light character done in a bamboo style of turning suggests a style of the early nineteenth century. The design of what are undoubtedly its original rockers is much later, and a similar side chair illustrated by Carl W. Drepperd (*Handbook of Antique Chairs*, New York, 1948) is credited to a New York manufacturer in 1889. The finish is black paint with a decorative gold treatment of a "chinoiserie" character.

Black Creek Pioneer Village, Toronto

50. A Leeds County high chair is similar in style to others said by American antiquarians to be of early-eighteenth-century origin. This, however, is more likely to be a hundred years younger, illustrating the frequent survival of older styles in a provincial society. The exaggerated splay of the legs would reduce the possibility of the chair's tipping. The splint seat and the red paint finish of the birch components are probably both original.

1800–30

National Museum of Man, Ottawa

51. Somewhat less impressive than the preceding example, this high chair has good turning style in the arm support posts but the good finials have been omitted. Its original footrest was probably a victim of hard wear by succeeding generations of children. Splayed legs have been retained for stability's sake. Traces of paint below the present brown indicate an earlier finish of blue.

1820–40

Jordan Historical Museum of the Twenty, Jordan

49. A slat-back chair of possibly unique character is this Wentworth County example which almost didn't have arms. The pieces serving as arms are identical to the side stretchers below the seat. Shaving of the front face of the rear posts is a characteristic shared with many nineteenth-century Windsor chairs. The rockers, thin blades sometimes called "rug cutters", appear to be original. The paint finish is bright red with accent lining in black.

1830–50

Mr. & Mrs. Ronald Pequegnat, Guelph

52.   This fine comb-back Windsor has long Ontario association but it is of pure New England style and quite possibly was made in the United States in the late eighteenth century. The name S. MUCKE, presumably that of the maker, is twice stamped on the underside of the seat. The oval pine seat is fitted with handsomely turned hardwood legs and posts; the spindle back provides comfortable and reliable support for a human back; the shaped crest rail is a restrained piece of fine craft, terminating in the voluted manner of a classical Ionic column. Windsors were almost always made of common local woods and finished with paint. This one has a recently restored finish of dark green.

1760–1800

Upper Canada Village, Morrisburg

54. The arch-back or continuous-arm Windsor is a type that American authorities associate with New England. The arms and the back frame are fashioned from one continuous piece of tough pliable wood, like the hickory arch of this chair found in eastern Ontario. The turning profile of the ash legs, stretchers, and arm posts is less refined than some but satisfactorily bold. The whitewood seat is comfortably saddle-shaped. The original finish was red.

1780–1800

Dr. & Mrs. Peter Bell, Sharbot Lake

53. A standard member of the Windsor family is the hoop-back or bow-back chair, this one having been found in Grenville County although it is quite indistinguishable from those of the same pattern originating in the United States. The horizontal semi-circular rail forms arms as well as back frame and it supports the bowed member in which the principal back spindles terminate. The somewhat saddle-shaped seat of this example is of whitewood, the other members of birch and hickory. Windsors of this period were most often painted in solid colours, occasionally stained to simulate mahogany.

1780–1800

Author's collection

56. A simpler version of the traditional continuous-arm Windsor in Plate 54 is this light and airy example found in Ontario County. Countrified in contrast to the earlier chair, this one has legs turned in a manner suggesting the craftsman may have had only elementary ability at the lathe. The oval seat is pine; the other parts are largely hickory, a wood that can be steamed and bent into extreme curves without breaking.

1800–20

Mr. & Mrs. Reginald Owen, Whitby

55. This tall comb-back chair is in the same tradition as the Windsor in Plate 52, but the first-class turning work has been eliminated, as well as the fine finishing detail of the crest rail. Its very high back and excellent proportions make it still a handsome Windsor. It was found in the Kingston area and is almost certainly a product of Upper Canada. The seat is pine, the rest maple and hickory. The worn legs have been recently rebuilt to their original height.

1790–1810

Mr. & Mrs. Thomas L. Riedel, Bath

57. This bow-back Windsor side chair is an excellent representative of an eighteenth-century style once quite common here. This particular chair quite likely was made in the United States; there can be no doubt that many Windsors came into Upper Canada in the earlier years. Turning work is characteristic of better eighteenth-century work. Further refinement is accomplished by beading of the bowed back piece and by the saddle shaping of the pine seat.

1760–1800

National Museum of Man, Ottawa

58. This is one of a number of similar chairs believed to have originated in Kingston in the early years of the nineteenth century. Classed as a bow-back Windsor, it departs from the traditional American patterns, particularly in the distinctively different profile of the turned legs. The slab seat is heavier and less well shaped than earlier examples.

1790–1820

Mr. & Mrs. Azel Guest, Whitby

59. Crudely made Windsor chairs have survived in sufficient numbers to suggest that they were quite familiar in nineteenth-century Ontario. Chairs like this one, which was formerly owned by the Markham district Reesor family (York County), recall the character of medieval chairs from which the "modern" Windsor was developed. The restored black paint finish covers a whitewood seat and yoke piece and hickory legs and spindles. Box-style stretchers or rungs are used instead of the earlier H-form.

1820–60

Mr. & Mrs. John Harbinson, Agincourt

60. This crude Windsor armchair of elm and ash with only three legs possibly resembles the Gothic-period chairs which were strong enough to support a knight wearing armour. Legs and spindles have been shaped without the use of a lathe, probably with a draw knife. Despite the crude qualities of the chair, its elm seat has been shaped somewhat in the saddle tradition. What paint remains is black. The chair was found in the St. Lawrence River area of eastern Ontario.

1800–50

Upper Canada Village, Morrisburg

61.   Another chair that originated in the St. Lawrence Valley is even more crude. Legs and spindles have been roughly formed, probably with a draw knife, but with no attempt to make a smoothly finished product. Auger-drilled holes for box stretchers run completely through the legs. Components are of birch and ash. The old paint finish is red but it is not certain that such crude chairs when new were dignified with a paint finish at all.

1830–60

Upper Canada Village, Morrisburg

62.   A low-back Windsor in a home-made tradition required genuine skill to accomplish the graceful arrange-ment of shapely back-arm rail and the nicely raked spindles. Nails used to stabilize legs and spindles are hand-forged and therefore early. The chair, which now has several coats of paint, was located just east of London in western Ontario.

1800–30

Mr. & Mrs. John Harbinson, Agincourt

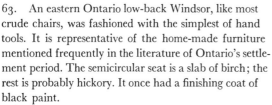

63. An eastern Ontario low-back Windsor, like most crude chairs, was fashioned with the simplest of hand tools. It is representative of the home-made furniture mentioned frequently in the literature of Ontario's settlement period. The semicircular seat is a slab of birch; the rest is probably hickory. It once had a finishing coat of black paint.

1830–50

Dr. & Mrs. Charles Danby, Kingston

64. A frontier low-back Windsor of some charm originated in Renfrew County. In place of the familiar round spindles in the back, this chair has three flat pine board splats. The slab seat is also pine, the yoke-like crest rail is soft maple, and the legs have been shaped with a knife from ash. With the chair that follows, this one resembles a country-made weaver's bench or stool to which a back has been added.

1820–50

Mr. & Mrs. Murray Copeland, Ottawa

65. Another low-back Windsor in the home-made tradition is this Prince Edward County chair with a slightly scooped pine seat and hand-whittled other parts of elm and ash. Three of the back spindles are heavier than the others and they fit auger holes drilled completely through the elm yoke rail.

1820–60

Mr. William Brebner, Lanark

66. Simplest of Windsor concepts is this child's chair, whose principal component is a virtual block of elm. That seat, with very slight surface shaping, is four inches thick. The legs are only two inches in length. The back spindles are fitted with a crest rail which is scarcely more than a bowed splint. Drilled holes in that rail indicate the chair earlier had some kind of device, probably a simple wooden rail, to restrain the occupant.

1800–50

Black Creek Pioneer Village, Toronto

67. Principal wood in this Windsor side chair is beech, common enough but little used for furniture-making in Upper Canada. The bowed back piece is hickory. The turning pattern of the legs is unusual and the character of the entire chair suggests an English rather than an American inspiration. It was found in the Kingston area.

1820–40

Mr. & Mrs. Thomas L. Riedel, Bath

68. While not a refined product to be compared with the best Windsors, this is distinctly not a home-made chair. It is the work of a provincial chair-maker and is that type of Windsor made and used as a garden chair in England in the eighteenth and nineteenth centuries. One rear leg is a poor replacement. Elm is the principal wood of this chair found in the St. Lawrence Valley.

1800–30

Upper Canada Village, Morrisburg

69.   A comb-back Windsor from a provincial workshop equipped with a lathe retains much of an eighteenth-century character above the seat level, but the seat and the leg structure, with box stretchers, are no earlier than 1820 in style. The seat is pine, the rest birch and hickory. It was found in Ontario County.

1820–30

Mr. & Mrs. Thomas L. Riedel, Bath

70.   This Windsor side chair shows distinct influence of Sheraton style in its squarely shaped back and in the modification of the turned central stretcher component into a flattened elliptical feature. The legs and back components are done in a manner sometimes described as bamboo turning. The brown paint finish is restored.

1800–20

Upper Canada Village, Morrisburg

71. A side chair which possibly originated in the Hamilton area, this Windsor shows Sheraton-style modifications in its generally squared back structure, the raked back posts with flattened faces, and the distinctive front stretcher with its flattened sausage-shaped feature. The chair was undoubtedly painted when new. The scored lines in the seat and the rings on posts and legs would have been emphasized with a contrasting paint. Box stretcher arrangement replaced the H-stretcher generally about 1800.

1810–20

Dundurn Castle, Hamilton

72. As well as the squarely shaped back, the medallion fitted between upper back rails is a distinctly Sheraton-style feature in this otherwise chaste Windsor armchair. The seat is pine. The hardwood components are turned in bamboo style; scored lines mark the high points of the turned pattern.

1810–25

Upper Canada Village, Morrisburg

73. It was Sheraton-style influence that was responsible for the square back of nineteenth-century Windsors. Another Sheraton detail in this side chair from Elgin County is the flattened arrow-like feature in the top rail. Unlike most simple Windsors of its period, it was not decorated in contrasting colours. The red paint surviving was its only finish.

1830–40

Mr. & Mrs. John Harbinson, Agincourt

74. The influence of the Sheraton fancy chair is evident in the shaping of the crest rail and the flattened faces of the turned back posts as well as in the decorative stencil design that still shows on the crest rail. The ground coat is black; the stencilled flowers are in silver bronze and yellow. Windsors of this pattern are familiar both in New York State and in New England, but it has occurred frequently in Ontario. This example, found in Toronto, is a scaled-down model only thirty-one inches high, probably made as a child's chair.

1820–30

Author's collection

75. A rod-back Windsor with comb piece above the back rail has legs raked at angles suggesting it was designed as a rocker. Many side chairs and armchairs, of course, were turned into rockers in the very early nineteenth century. The front and rear stretchers of this chair are unusually low. Seat is pine and the rest birch and hickory. Traces of paint suggest its original base coat was a mustard colour. It was acquired in Kingston.

1825–40

Mr. & Mrs. Thomas L. Riedel, Bath

76. A bow-back Windsor of later years, this one from Waterloo County has a largely restored black paint finish. Side chairs of this style were very common throughout the province, although armchairs are now seldom seen. The whitewood seat is always shaped from two pieces of lumber joined with a single glued butt. The hoop piece and the arms are of hickory.

1860–80

Mr. & Mrs. John Harbinson, Agincourt

78. The profile and raking of the back posts or stiles of this plank-seat chair make it something of a Directoire-style Windsor. The vase-shaped splat is derived from the Queen Anne style, which was old before the Loyalists came to Ontario, but it appears here in the manner used in formal Directoire- and Empire-style chairs. The two half-round scroll cuts in the underside of the crest rail are seen in many chairs influenced by American Empire. The paint finish is black over brown, with a well-worn stylized scroll-and-leaf stencil in gold, and seat striping and leg ringing in yellow. It was found in Frontenac County.

1825–40

Mr. & Mrs. J. E. Flanigan, Brockville

77. Because it has a slab seat into which legs and posts are fastened, this chair meets the basic definition of a Windsor or stick chair. In spirit it also might be called a Sheraton fancy chair, a class of chairs that belong primarily to that broad category labelled American Empire. The basic paint finish is the frequently used impressionistic rosewood graining, an effect achieved by using black paint over red. The superior stencilled decoration of melons, flowers, and foliage is done in gold. This is a rather out-of-the-ordinary chairmaker's product imported probably while still new from the United States. The name of the maker, James W. Robb of Wheeling, West Virginia, appears stencilled in gilt on the flattened front stretcher.

1825–35

Upper Canada Village, Morrisburg

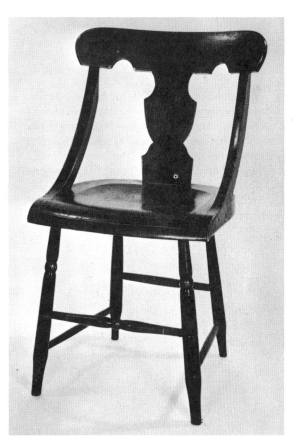

79. The rod-back chair, which combined a Sheraton-influenced Windsor structure with the decorative finish of a Sheraton fancy chair, was popular for more than fifty years. Seats were sometimes of pine but usually of whitewood; the turned components were birch, ash, maple, and hickory, usually in mixture. Most were treated with stencilled decoration. This one is more simply decorated by free-hand line work in red and green over a dirty cream base.

1825–45

Black Creek Pioneer Village, Toronto

80. The arrowback chair is the most familiar of Sheraton-influenced Windsors to have been made in Ontario. It differs from the rod-back only in having flattened arrow-shaped rather than tapered round-back spindles. It was common and popular at the same time as the Sheraton fancy chair, a framed chair usually with a rush, splint, or cane seat, and is probably the variety most often intended when period craftsmen advertised they were "Windsor and fancy chair makers". This eastern Ontario example has an unusual free-hand decorative treatment in blue and black over the basic grey.

1825–45

National Museum of Man, Ottawa

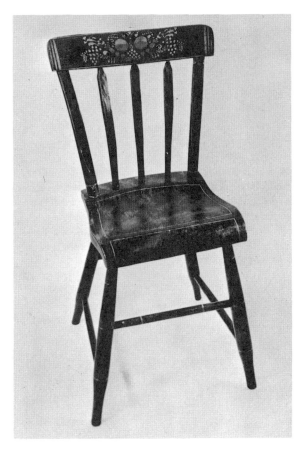

81. An arrowback Windsor verging on the crude, this eastern Ontario chair has the simplest turning pattern and roughly shaped arrow spindles, but, unlike most decorated chairs of that period, it has survived with its particularly colourful original finish intact. The seat has been given an impressionistic black and red graining. The stencil design is in gold. Striping or lining is yellow and the bands on the stiles, arrows, and seat are blue-green.

1830–50

Mr. & Mrs. Douglas Hough, Williamsburg

82. This chair with a back splat of some individuality is yet similar in structure to rod-back and arrowback Windsors. The splat and crest rail show Empire-style influence. The grained paint finish simulates curled maple. The accent lines are in black. The underside of the seat is branded "S. HASKIN", a chair-maker in the Leeds County village of Lyn.

1830–50

Upper Canada Village, Morrisburg

83. The branded mark of S. Haskin on underside of the preceding chair (Plate 82).

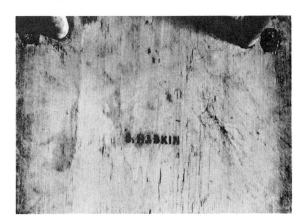

84. An Empire-influenced late Windsor from eastern Ontario, this chair has a faded but original finish. Unlike most chairs of the type, particularly those from a little earlier period, it has a simple black base finish rather than the familiar black over red combination; this no doubt was an economy move; certainly less care was given to decorating chairs as the years advanced. The chair is unusual in having a hardwood seat rather than one of whitewood. A chair made in identical pattern but with more stencilled decoration is in the collection of the National Museum of Man, Ottawa; it carries the name of its maker, N. Patterson, of the village of Lyndhurst in Leeds County.

1840–60

Author's collection

85. A late Windsor chair which suggests something of the balloon-back chairs that came with the rococo revival of the mid-nineteenth century. Similar simple kitchen chairs are known in Pennsylvania. The seat is pine, the rest hardwood. The base paint is green; the stencilled design with birds and a fountain in the centre splat is gold and silver. Other accent lines are yellow.

1850–70

Mr. & Mrs. Mogens Philip, Markham

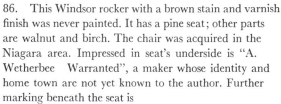

86. This Windsor rocker with a brown stain and varnish finish was never painted. It has a pine seat; other parts are walnut and birch. The chair was acquired in the Niagara area. Impressed in seat's underside is "A. Wetherbee   Warranted", a maker whose identity and home town are not yet known to the author. Further marking beneath the seat is

R. M. C.
Can.
A. F ——
Rochester

The initials are believed to be those of Ralph Morden Crysler, probably the one-time owner of the chair, who lived in Niagara before going to Rochester in 1841. He returned to Niagara in 1848. Whether he acquired the chair in Upper Canada or New York State is not yet known.

1820–40

Private collection

87. A pleasing Windsor rocker has the familiar black over red paint finish, decorated with a free-hand vine pattern and striping in yellow. Particularly among rocking chairs of this class, the back spindles were frequently bent to conform with the human back, making them, with their scooped seats, among the most comfortable of all chairs. This one was acquired in the Ottawa area.

1825–45

Mr. & Mrs. Blake McKendry, Elginburg

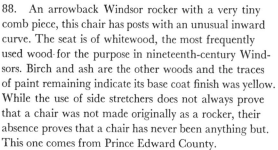

88. An arrowback Windsor rocker with a very tiny comb piece, this chair has posts with an unusual inward curve. The seat is of whitewood, the most frequently used wood for the purpose in nineteenth-century Windsors. Birch and ash are the other woods and the traces of paint remaining indicate its base coat finish was yellow. While the use of side stretchers does not always prove that a chair was not made originally as a rocker, their absence proves that a chair has never been anything but. This one comes from Prince Edward County.

1820–40

Mr. & Mrs. Walter Beevor, Stirling

89. Another arrowback Windsor made as a rocking chair has an especially graceful crest rail and a raked design that makes the entire product a satisfying composition of curving lines. It originated in eastern Ontario.

1825–45

Dr. & Mrs. Peter Bell, Sharbot Lake

90. An outstanding provincial rocking chair from eastern Ontario was made with an unusual three back rails added to a basic Windsor structure of Sheraton-style influence. Note also that it has no side stretchers. The painted finish with a basic black coat is remarkably well preserved, but close examination reveals that it is not the original. An earlier well-worn stencilled pattern can be traced below the present paint, indicating that professional finishers sometimes re-decorated chairs like new. The later accent decoration is in yellow and green.

1825–45

Upper Canada Village, Morrisburg

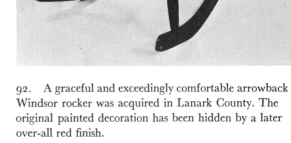

91.   Windsor side chairs of this period have stencilled designs that were frequently repeated. Rocking chairs before 1850 are more likely to exhibit decorative paint work of individual character. This chair from Wellington or Waterloo County has a black over brown ground coat and quite unusual decorative designs added in orange, green, and white. The crest rail is satisfyingly broad and the arrow-shaped spindles are unusually wide.

1825–45

Mr. & Mrs. Horace Dahmer, Guelph

92.   A graceful and exceedingly comfortable arrowback Windsor rocker was acquired in Lanark County. The original painted decoration has been hidden by a later over-all red finish.

1825–45

Mr. & Mrs. Blake McKendry, Elginburg

94. The old-style rockers of this unique Sheraton-style Windsor appear much like those of a baby's cradle, suggesting the source of the inspiration of the rocking chair idea. The back spindles are an odd mixture—four bamboo-turned and two arrow-shaped. Arm supports too are arrow-shaped and the arms themselves are flat. Unusual paint finish has a ground coat of middle green with a decorative pattern of foliage and flowers in dark green, red, yellow, and white. It was found in Waterloo County.

1820–40

Mrs. Marjorie Larmon, Burgessville

93. An arrowback chair has side stretchers so close to ground level that one is justified in suspecting the birch rockers were not original. There is every likelihood, however, that clients may have been able to order such a chair with or without rockers from the maker. The comb piece is unusually high. The chair has the common whitewood seat, with other parts of native hardwoods. The worn black paint with no further decoration added appears to be the original finish of this Glengarry County piece.

1825–45

Mr. & Mrs. Blake McKendry, Elginburg

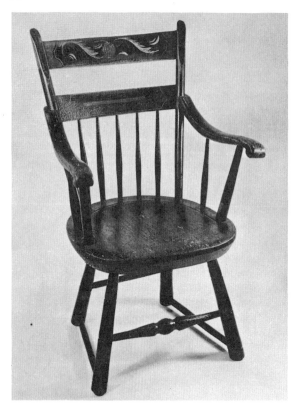

95. Acquired in Oxford County, this armchair of stout Windsor character has a handsome and well-preserved paint finish. The ground is black over red. The vivid panel in the crest rail is green, yellow, and red. The legs have been cut down several inches.

1825–45

Mr. & Mrs. Horace Dahmer, Guelph

96. Detail of preceding chair (Plate 95).

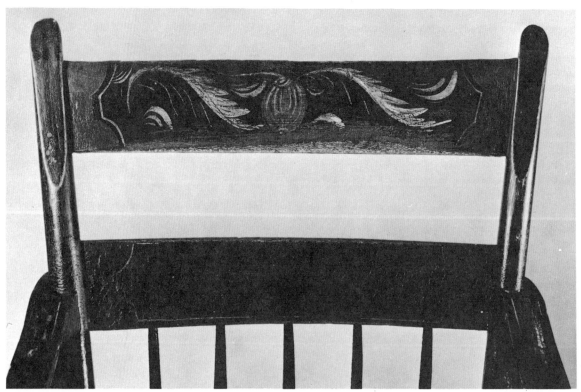

97. An armchair with well-shaped broad arrow spindles has, oddly, only one post and no spindles supporting each arm. Found in the Kingston area, it has a basic black finish with a grained effect over most areas. The surviving additional decoration, largely on the arrow spindles, is in yellow and red paint.

1830–50

Mr. & Mrs. John Harbinson, Agincourt

98. This Windsor-style armchair with Sheraton influence has flat arms, an unusual characteristic little seen outside the Wellington County area. The seat has a minimum of traditional Windsor scooping. The back, although raked, has virtually no comforting curve. The chair is probably later than most illustrated in this section. The paint finish is a modern restoration job approximating the original.

1830–50

Mr. & Mrs. Horace Dahmer, Guelph

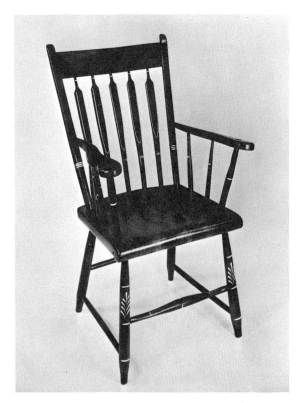

99. A particularly tall example, forty-six inches from crest rail to floor, this very comfortable armchair has a well preserved stencilled finish with a garland of grapes and cherries and a floral spray across the two back rails. Colours are green, red, yellow, and pink. As newspaper advertisements of the period make clear, paints in almost any colour desired were available from general merchants in Upper Canada even before 1820.

1825–45

Upper Canada Village, Morrisburg

100. An arrowback Windsor from the Markham area of York County, this chair has rockers sawn out in a pattern with that little extra flair that makes one chair stand out from others. The seat is whitewood, the other parts of several hardwoods.

1825–45

Mr. & Mrs. John Harbinson, Agincourt

101. An arrowback Windsor found in Brockville is of an unusual design with arms and crest rail adapted after those of formal classic-revival chairs. The arrow spindles are particularly graceful and effectively curved to provide the utmost in comfort for a relaxed human body. Originally it could well have had a stencilled decorative finish.

1830–45

Mr. & Mrs. J. E. Flanigan, Brockville

102. An unusual Windsor found in Lanark County is not one of the most beautiful country chairs but it does show the influence of fashionable town design. The back posts are set at an extreme angle, suggesting the line of Directoire design as made popular in the United States. The top rail has the scrolled half-round cuts familiar in many Empire-style chairs. The original decorated finish is hidden by later coats of paint.

1830–50

Mr. & Mrs. C. Ray Smith, Elora

103. Striving for distinction, the maker of this Sheraton-style Windsor gave it a crest rail much like that of formal dining-chairs, even to finishing it with a veneer of figured mahogany. The rest of the chair is made of the familiar native woods, painted black and accented with white and gold lines. Graceful back support is achieved with tapered spindles and with both spindles and posts curved to accommodate the human back with comfort. The flared seat with rolled front and rising back is made of three pieces of softwood and is the kind of seat familiar in the Boston rocker.

1830–45

Hiram Walker Historical Museum, Windsor

104. An odd interpretation of a Boston rocker, this Windsor of mixed antecedents has a seat with much exaggerated front roll. The back structure is rather too light to balance the heavy seat but the chair is clearly the product of an attempt to achieve genuine distinction. The seat has an impressionistic graining, plus red and yellow bands, and a panel enclosing green and yellow leaves and flowers. Seats of this type, with front roll and rising back piece, are scarcely ever used on chairs other than rockers. This one comes from Oxford County.

1830–50

Mrs. Marjorie Larmon, Burgessville

106.   Detail of the crest rail of the chair in Plate 105.

105.   The most florid of chairs, this example found in the Dunnville area has a spectacularly shaped seat which, together with its elaborate decorative treatment, makes it possibly unique in the Boston rocker class. The base-paint finish is the familiar impressionistic rosewood graining achieved with black over red. The greater part of the decoration is in gold. The detailed bird at the fore edge of the seat is in yellow and red bronze. The romantic scene on the crest rail, a military officer and a young woman, each mounted, meeting on a rustic bridge, is done in silver with some gold accents.

1830–45

Private collection

107.   A charming variant in the Boston rocker class is this chair found in Waterloo County. The shaping of the back posts and the crest rail, as well as the use of a vase-shaped splat instead of the familiar spindles, emphasizes the influence of Empire style on country chairs of this period. The perching birds on the splat are in yellow and red. Branches of strawberries on the crest rail are red and green. Lining on seat, posts, and rail is done in gold and yellow.

1830–50

Mr. & Mrs. R. L. Donaldson, Galt

108.   Windsor armchairs were frequently adapted for use as commode chairs; an owner had simply to cut a round hole in the stout plank seat. Many were also made specifically as commode chairs, often in the style of Boston rockers but with rockers wisely omitted. A box structure was usually added to support and hide a chamber pot. This specimen from eastern Ontario has a black and brown grained finish with gold stencil decoration of stylized birds flanking a fountain. Accent lines and rings are yellow.

1840–60

National Historic Sites Service, Ottawa

109. Another commode chair in the Windsor family has arms of a type used on later Boston rockers, continuous bent strips probably of hickory. The over-all paint is black. The handsome stencilled design, more elaborate than is normally expected on late chairs, is done in silver and gold. Additional lines and rings are in yellow. The chair was acquired in south-western Ontario.

1850–70

Dr. & Mrs. W. L. C. McGill, Brantford

110.   Detail of the crest rail of the chair in Plate 109.

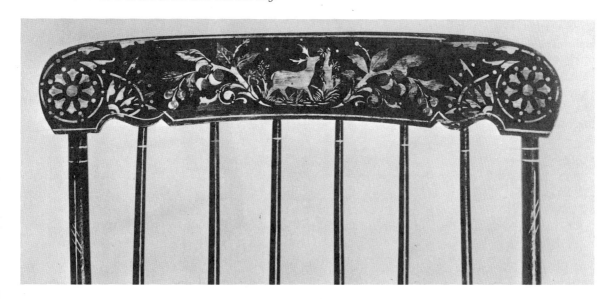

111. The low-back Windsor of the mid-nineteenth century is frequently called a bar-room chair by collectors. In the United States it is often called a firehouse Windsor. Like much antiquarian terminology, these are recent labels. Such chairs are related to but are massive in comparison to the graceful American low-back Windsors of the mid-eighteenth century. Turning profiles and decorative painting used are often similar to those of Sheraton fancy chairs. This good example from western Ontario has a pine seat. The yoke-shaped back and arm rail is built up from three or four thick sections of whitewood. The grained paint finish is old, but not likely to be the original.

1840–60

Mr. & Mrs. L. J. Ingolfsrud, Toronto

112. A low-back Windsor found in Lanark County has individual details that set it apart from the usual factory-made model. The back rail has a sharply defined camel hump. Curl return at the ends of the arms and at the fore edge of the seat is a worthy detail and the style of turning in the legs is possibly unique. It is unusual too to find rear legs turned to the same decorative pattern as the front. The original finish was probably brown.

1840–60

Mr. & Mrs. Blake McKendry, Elginburg

113.   A child-size version of the late low-back Windsor is this eastern Ontario chair only eighteen inches high. The well preserved original finish is bright red paint with decorative accents in black.

1840–60

Upper Canada Village, Morrisburg

114.   In mid-eighteenth-century chairs of the type, the special writing arm was almost invariably an integral part of the chair design. In the occasional mid-nineteenth-century low-back Windsor so equipped, the special arm, even though original to the chair, usually appears an afterthought in terms of design. This example, believed to have originated in eastern Ontario, has front legs derived from the Sheraton fancy chair and a seat related to that of the Boston rocker. Original paint finish has a ground of black over red with a mahoganized panel in the centre section of the back rail and another covering most of the seat. Trim around panels is green and white. Additional lines and rings are yellow.

1850–60

Mr. & Mrs. J. E. Flanigan, Brockville

115. Deterioration in design is evident in this low-back Windsor typical of later chairs of the class. The seat has very little surface shaping and the turned components have no more character than lengths of dowel. The back rail has less wood, less shaping, and less character than earlier examples. The chair is important, however, because it is among the few with a maker's label. The underside of the seat bears the label of W. H. Woodall of Hagerman's Corners in Markham Township, not far from Toronto. The original decoration is black over red paint with yellow lining and a simple stencil design in gold.

1850–70

Dr. & Mrs. J. Stephens, Kitchener

116. Label on the underside of the seat of the chair in Plate 115.

117. A hybrid chair introduces the heavy yoke-like back rail of the late low-back Windsor to what is in most respects a Boston rocker. The resulting product is interesting but not entirely satisfying aesthetically. It was found on Amherst Island. Much of the original black paint survives, but very little of the yellow lining and other decorative work. Absence of side stretchers guarantees that the chair was made originally as a rocker.

1850–60

Mr. & Mrs. J. E. Flanigan, Brockville

118. A unique low-back Windsor of the mid-nineteenth century, this heavy chair very likely served some special function. Overly deep and wide, it also has two iron inserts at the centre rear of the back rail. While these may have served as a mount for some extension, such as the head rest of a barber's chair, they may also have been intended only as reinforcements for that pieced yoke. While the seat is of whitewood, all other parts are of walnut, and the only finish used was varnish. It was found in Oxford County.

1840–60

Mr. & Mrs. Henry Dobson, Plattsville

119. A child's chair, or even a toy chair, this charmer is just under fourteen inches in height. Acquired in Leeds County, it may relate (like Plate 85) to similar chairs of Pennsylvania origin. It derives largely from Windsor and Sheraton fancy-chair traditions, but it may be that its balloon-style back was inspired by rococo-revival chairs of the mid-nineteenth century. The black base-paint finish is accented by gold lines and rings; the fine decoration of the back features two red roses and a foliage garland in gold.

1850–60

Author's collection

120. A fascinating late adaptation of Windsor structure has produced a pedestal-base chair with a central steel screw shaft for height adjustment and a spring and swivel facility for extra comfort and convenience. This is an office chair found in Waterloo County and made largely of whitewood and hickory. Its black paint finish is worn but the restrained yellow painted accent lines are still to be seen on seat and base.

1860–80

Miss Patricia Lockwood, Ottawa

121. The platform or spring rocker was a late-nine-teenth-century development that was frequently uphol-stered to some degree. This example, which preserves the general character of a Boston rocker, is out of the ordinary. The platform rocker did away with excessive wear to carpets; in fact regular rockers were often called rug cutters. Another advantage was stability; it didn't creep while in use. The rockers rock on a special base or platform with "silencing" fabric strips glued to their undersides. Several coil springs fasten the seat of the chair to the stable platform below.

1870–90

Mr. William Brebner, Lanark

122. Very much in the style of the classical Greek *klismos*, this side chair is representative of many pro-duced in Britain and North America during the early years of the nineteenth century. The bold carving of the crest rail is in a pattern very familiar among English chairs of the period, but the motifs are also pure Greek. This example is made of birch, stained to simulate mahogany, but since North American birch is known to have been used by British furniture-makers, one cannot be quite certain that this chair originated in Ontario. The padded slip seat was in general use with dining and parlour chairs of the period. The single-curve sabre leg comes direct from ancient Greek models.

1815–30

Author's collection

123. Another side chair of Greek Revival style is this walnut example. Although the pattern suggests a date about 1820, its scale is strange because the components were cut from lumber distinctly thinner than that normally used. The stencilled label on the frame which reads "D. Dubé Ottawa" identifies the chair as the work of Damase Dubé, either father or son, working in the capital in the 1880s. Evidently the earlier style retained sufficient appeal to justify a revival within the late-Victorian era.

1880–90

Mr. & Mrs. Blake McKendry, Elginburg

124. This walnut armchair with slip seat is frequently called a carver and is intended for the host who "carves the joint" at the dining-table. The basic inspiration of this chair is also the Greek *klismos*. Prototypes of these scroll-cut arms can be seen in Sheraton's drawings. Ash and pine are the secondary woods.

1820–30

Upper Canada Village, Morrisburg

125.   A slip-seat side chair of walnut retains the single-curve sabre leg of the *klismos* but its back structure is distinctly that of the Empire style as interpreted by American furniture-makers. It was found in the Niagara area.

1825–40

McFarland House, Niagara Parks Commission, Queenston

126.   This mahogany side chair is another of American Empire character. The original slip seat has been remodelled latterly in an unsuitable bulky manner. The lyre, an instrument used by the ancient Greeks, was an ornamental device much used on furniture of the classical revival. The leg with double curve is a modification of the single-curve sabre leg. As in many chairs of the period, figured mahogany veneer is used to further embellish the top rail, the splat, and the exposed faces of the front and side seat rails.

1830–45

Niagara Historical Society, Niagara-on-the-Lake

127. This chair of American Empire style is distinctive chiefly for its flared back posts or stiles which, unlike those of most chairs of the period, are not continuous with the rear legs. They curve forward and are joined to the side seat rails. Shaping of the crest rail and the back splat is typical of Empire style as used here. The chair is made of mahogany with the familiar figured mahogany veneer on crest, splat, and front seat rail.

1830–45

Mrs. Janet Ehnes, Bailieboro

129. An Empire-style carver exemplifies what might best be called provincial elegance of about 1830. Mahogany, the "correct" wood at that period, is used throughout, with figured veneer on crest rail and splat. The slip seat is covered with worn black haircloth, a durable upholstery material popular throughout the nineteenth century. This chair was found in Grenville County.

1830–45

Author's collection

128. "Greek" chairs of simplified line, with two un-decorated back rails and with front legs of sabre or ogee curve, were produced in considerable numbers by provincial furniture-makers in Ontario. This one is of local black walnut and has an unusually deep seat.

1830–50

Mr. & Mrs. W. N. Minhinnick, South Bay

130. Empire-style side chairs in black walnut were made by the Chatham firm of R. Smith & Co. The scroll cuts in the crest rails are less pronounced than in most of the period and the back splats are of very simple outline. Accenting walnut veneer is used on back rails and splats.

1830–50

Hiram Walker Historical Museum, Windsor

131.   This is the kind of chair that is frequently and safely called Regency. More specifically, it is a simple rendering of the classical-revival chair concept but with a nineteenth-century version of a Sheraton-style leg. The wood is curled maple. The slip seat is covered in the perennially popular black haircloth.

1825–40

Royal Ontario Museum, Toronto

132.   This walnut side chair comes from the Hamilton district and is probably representative of the kind of chair that contemporary writers advised intending settlers was available from furniture-makers in Upper Canada. The crest rail pattern is a countrified one, more familiar on chairs of rush- and cane-seat types. The centre-rail pattern has a Regency character. Both are enhanced with figured walnut veneer. The chair originally had a slip seat; its present needlework covering is of late-nineteenth-century style.

1830–50

Mr. & Mrs. Russell Harper, Alexandria

133. Two chairs from a set of eight once used in the board room of the old Canada Company offices in Toronto are in a neo-classical style familiar in Ontario in the second quarter of the nineteenth century. All the chairs are of black walnut with oak the secondary wood. The tapered octagonal feature of the turned legs is also frequently seen in tables of the period.

1830–45

Mrs. J. R. Robinson, Waupoos

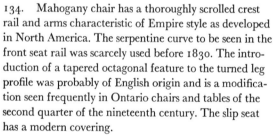

134.   Mahogany chair has a thoroughly scrolled crest rail and arms characteristic of Empire style as developed in North America. The serpentine curve to be seen in the front seat rail was scarcely used before 1830. The introduction of a tapered octagonal feature to the turned leg profile was probably of English origin and is a modification seen frequently in Ontario chairs and tables of the second quarter of the nineteenth century. The slip seat has a modern covering.

1830–50

Black Creek Pioneer Village, Toronto

135.   This Empire-style side chair of walnut has an elaborately cut splat and a crest rail with characteristic scroll cuts along the lower edge and modest carving above which seems to foreshadow that of rococo-revival-style chairs. The heart-shaped opening in the rail is a motif that was much used in such transitional chairs. In Ontario country towns, this model of late-Empire chair was still being made as late as 1860. The slip seat has a modern covering.

1840–60

Mrs. Janet Ehnes, Bailieboro

III.   The key piece in this parlour furnished in the classical-revival taste of about 1830 is the "Grecian" sofa with its distinctive scrolled end. The bookcase with restrained classic ornament is of the type often illustrated in furniture guides published in the period for the newly important middle class. The baize-covered pedestal table preserves an older Chippendale style, but the stencilled and gilt-trimmed "fancy" chairs are of a superior American design in the fashion of the day.

Upper Canada Village, Morrisburg

137. A framed chair of provincial Sheraton character has turned front legs of an unusual pattern. The original black paint is accented with stylized flowers in gold in a manner suggesting an imitation of the metal inlay work popular in some high-style chairs of the late eighteenth century. Cane seats, woven of a flexible rattan, were probably first used in China or India. The material and technique were introduced to England in the seventeenth century.

1815–25

Upper Canada Village, Morrisburg

136. This upholstered armchair is essentially of late-Empire style but with front legs which suggest the rococo- or antique-revival period which followed. It has the kind of combination of characteristics that makes it impossible to fit a great many pieces of furniture into neat pigeon-holes with period style labels. The mahogany frame is upholstered and covered with red plush suitable for the period. Castors were used only on larger and heavier chairs as a rule.

1840–60

Dundurn Castle, Hamilton

138. The Sheraton fancy chair, most familiar when it occurs with a rush or cane seat and a gaily stencilled decorative design, comes in a variety of forms. It might generally be described as a common chair of some Sheraton-style influence within an Empire-period framework. This handsome Ontario example has an especially attractive curved seat frame and a delicately scroll-sawn centre rail. The severely plain line of the crest rail raises some suspicion that it might be a replacement of a more ornate original. Except for side stretchers of ash, the chair is of curled maple throughout.

1820–40

Mrs. H. C. Walker, Toronto

139. A Sheraton fancy chair of curled maple acquired in the Cobourg area has a back very much like that of the English Trafalgar chair, a great Regency-period favourite. The outward curve of turned front legs first appeared about 1800 and was revived in later caned chairs after 1850.

1820–40

Mrs. Lenah Field-Fisher, Cobourg

140.   This Ontario chair of Greek-revival line is made of curled maple. The woven seat has been entirely enclosed by solid seat rails to reduce edge wear, achieving very much the structure of a chair with a slip seat.

1820–40

Mrs. H. C. Walker, Toronto

141.   Great imagination was exercised frequently in the making of Sheraton fancy chairs of curled maple. The scrolled centre rail of this pleasing example is a successful delicate rendering of an English Regency pattern, in its turn based on a Greek motif. The leg turnings, bowed front stretcher, and curved seat profile are similar to those of the earlier fancy chairs popularized in the United States.

1820–40

Mrs. H. C. Walker, Toronto

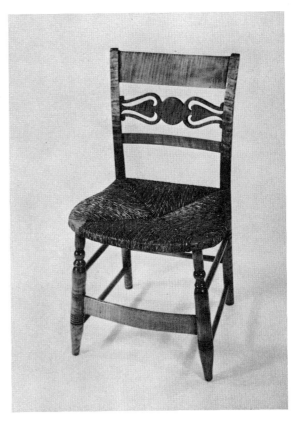

142. This neo-classical chair retains the simple sabre leg of the Greek *klismos* but the back splat and crest rail have been modified in the Americanized Empire manner. The side seat rails are shaped to merge gently with the curve of the back stiles and they terminate at the front in a return curve which suggests the inspiration for the rolled seat edge of the later Boston rocker. Both curled and bird's-eye maple are used in this chair.

1820–40

Upper Canada Village, Morrisburg

143. Located in the Niagara area, this neo-classical chair is characteristic of provincial Empire work in old Ontario. The wood is curled maple and the maker's name, S. Ely, is impressed on the underside of one seat rail.

1820–40

Royal Ontario Museum, Toronto

144. The shaping of the back splat appears to be a modification of the lyre motif often used to ornament neo-classical chairs. The handsome back rail is scrolled rather more discreetly than the average Empire-period work and is further embellished with matched burl maple veneer. Figured maple in its various forms was prized by old-time furniture-makers but they normally gave it a finish darker than that popularized among today's collectors.

1825–45

Mr. Paul Godfrey, Port Hope

146. This unique curled maple chair is one from a set which came from a home in Dundas County. The design of the chair back is particularly unusual although it might be compared to those of certain country chairs of France and Belgium. The cabriole legs at the front may foreshadow those of the mid-nineteenth-century rococo revival, but the use of cabriole legs at the rear is almost unknown. The serpentine curve of the front seat rail appeared in the style books at least as early as 1830 and was in general use in Ontario before 1850. The only safe classification for the chair is nineteenth-century hybrid.

1840–50

Upper Canada Village, Morrisburg

145. Neat pigeon-hole classification of chairs is not continuously possible; too many examples are hybrids. This chair has the shaped back splat and crest rail of a fairly formal Empire-style side chair, the type usually of mahogany and with an upholstered slip seat. In most other features it is a Sheraton fancy chair, which is also really an Empire-period variety, but one of common or countrified character. The scroll-sawn vase or urn-shaped splat is one of many pattern variations. The wood is largely curled maple and the chair was found in eastern Ontario.

1825–50

Mr. & Mrs. J. E. Flanigan, Brockville

147.   A flavour of the 1830s is particularly evident in the centre dip in the serpentine crest rail. The same curve is to be seen in the crests of many upholstered "easy" chairs of the kind popular just before the antique or rococo revival of the mid century. The entire chair, found in eastern Ontario, is of black walnut.

1830–50

Dr. & Mrs. Ferdinand Eckhardt, Winnipeg

148.   Typical of countless thousands of low-cost cane-seated chairs of the mid-nineteenth century is this example with its well-preserved painted and grained finish. The more painstaking graining of the two back rails, in the tradition of figured mahogany veneering, is edged in dark brown. Chairs of this general pattern were made in Ontario but they were also imported from American factories. Unless a chair bears a maker's mark, there is no reliable test to distinguish one from the other. This example was found in Dundas County.

1845–70

Mr. & Mrs. Douglas Hough, Williamsburg

149. A factory-made chair of walnut is one of the cane-seated models which were the specialty of a Bowmanville firm in the third quarter of the century. The impressed stamp on the rear of the top rail reads "G. P. Walter & Co. Bowmanville C.W.". Cheaper chairs were made of birch. Steam power and mass production methods were used so that each chair passed through the hands of six workmen before completion.

1860–80

Author's collection

150. This crudely painted, cane-seated, Empire-style side chair was found in Grenville County. The finish combines a painted black ground, a grained top rail, and gold lining and rings.

1830–50

Author's collection

151. The continuing Empire tradition is clear in this country-style side chair of walnut with its graceful if simple splat and its slightly different crest rail. The serpentine curve of the front seat rail is seen most frequently in caned chairs of the mid-nineteenth century. This is one of a set of chairs which came from the Picton area.

1840–60

National Museum of Man, Ottawa

152.   This outstanding example of the Sheraton fancy-chair class, quite possibly of American origin, was found in Toronto. The shaping of the centre back rail and the arms, together with the handsome stencilled decoration in gold, silver, and red, are particular features contributing to its superior quality. The ground-paint finish is black. Major American manufacturers of fancy chairs, including Lambert Hitchcock whose name is sometimes mistakenly used to describe all such chairs, advertised their readiness to export; many of their products no doubt entered old Ontario.

1815–35

Mr. & Mrs. Howard Pain, Toronto

153.   A Sheraton fancy chair of Prince Edward County background has a base paint of yellow ochre. Bands or stripes are in rust and the stencilled decoration on the back rails is a combination of green leaves and purple grapes.

1825–45

Miss Anne Farwell, Cherry Valley

154.   One of the finest Sheraton fancy chair designs known in Canada is illustrated by this example from a set of six found in the Belleville area. The finely scrolled top rail is evidently a tribute to the monarchial tradition. The body colour is dark green. The decoration, including the crown and the splendid linked centre rail, is largely in gold. The plumes are done in brown. As a design feature, the three-feather motif from the Prince of Wales' crest was used to embellish furniture in the eighteenth century. It is naïve to suggest that every instance of its use in Canada must have some association with the then heir apparent's visit here in 1860.

1820–40

Upper Canada Village, Morrisburg

155. This is a good average example of the Sheraton
fancy chair that is frequently and mistakenly called a
Hitchcock chair. Lambert Hitchcock was one American
manufacturer who produced a great many chairs of this
type but there were many others. Hitchcock's name has
been memorialized because he sometimes labelled his
products. Most manufacturers did not. Some of those
mass-production manufacturers marketed their wares
throughout the United States, in the Caribbean Islands,
in Mexico, and in Canada. Unless a maker's label appears, it is very difficult to distinguish imported from
locally produced models. Some recent study of stencil
designs suggests the incidence in old Ontario of some
decorative patterns not known in the United States. On
the other hand, it is quite likely that American-made
stencils were sold here and used to decorate locally made
chairs. The chair illustrated has the distinctive turned
characteristics, the specially shaped top rail, and the
stencil-decorated centre rail familiar in the average chairs
of this category. The base paint is black over a red
ground, a technique that no doubt began as a means of
producing a pseudo-rosewood finish. The stencil work is
entirely in gold, in bronze powder applied over a still
sticky varnish, to be more precise. The line work is yellow
and the border line around the stencilled work is green.
Accent rings on the legs and posts are yellow and green.

1820–40

Black Creek Pioneer Village, Toronto

156. Stencilled chair decoration typical of mid-century work retains charm but shows that less complex designs were used and less care taken in their application. There was an evidently hurried effort to give the black paint on each rail a grained effect. The quality of the gold and silver stencil application also suggests that a workman had no time to spare. Painstaking hand-craft was evidently losing out in a period when the machine was firmly establishing the pace of production.

1840–60

Mr. & Mrs. John Matthews, Stoney Lake

157. A fancy chair with quite impressive stencilled decoration was found in the Kingston area. Graining of the black base paint shows through the decoration on the crest rail. An opulent basket of fruit and sprays of flowers are stencilled designs done in silver and gold. Accent lines are in yellow.

1830–45

Mr. & Mrs. Esmond Butler, Ottawa

158. This popular chair model which has survived in considerable numbers evidently was made in many mid-century factories. In an illustrated American advertisement of 1853 it was called a "Grecian cane-back rocker" It was made sometimes of walnut, more often of maple or birch with a brown stain finish. This example, found in eastern Ontario, is unusual with its over-all black finish and stencilled floral decoration in the tradition of the fancy chairs. Chairs of this general model are known to have been made by G. B. Walter & Co. in Bowmanville.

1850–70

Dr. & Mrs. Ferdinand Eckhardt, Winnipeg

159. Scaled-down "Grecian cane-back rocker" is a faithful rendering of the pattern in child's size. This example, found in Prince Edward County, is in walnut. Picton and other ports in this county carried on a busy trade with American communities on Lake Ontario and it is at least as likely that such a chair originated in the Oswego Chair Factory as in a Canadian shop.

1850–70

Mr. & Mrs. W. N. Minhinnick, South Bay

160. This is a type made by the many thousands in steam-powered factories and advertised as bedroom chairs. Such chairs are lighter in design than most dining and parlour chairs and they are invariably caned. The turned and then slightly bent front legs are characteristic. This bedroom chair is made of maple and was found in the Bath district.

1850–80

Dr. & Mrs. H. C. Burleigh, Bath

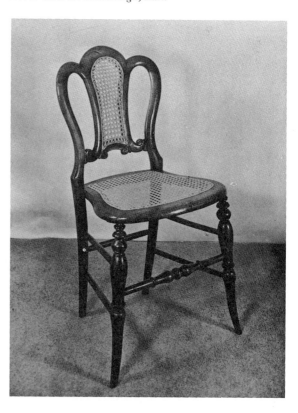

161. Another bedroom chair, this one was found in Kingston. It is of brown-stained hardwood, possibly beech. It preserves in modified form design features of earlier chairs — a style of turning to suggest bamboo, use of the classical lyre motif, and a centre back rail arrangement that harks back to a Sheraton style.

1850–80

Dr. & Mrs. H. C. Burleigh, Bath

162. The extremely popular style of the mid-nineteenth century was the rococo revival, variously labelled antique revival, French antique, and Louis XV revival, but today most frequently and inadequately called simply Victorian. The most readily recognized piece of the period is the balloon-back chair, which first appeared in the 1840s and was well known everywhere after 1850. The work of the revival period was much heavier than that of eighteenth-century rococo. The chair illustrated is a good representative example and one that very likely was made in Ontario. Of black walnut, it features better than average carving work among provincial chairs. The cabriole legs of a city-made chair would normally also have been embellished with some carved detail. This is one from a set that once belonged to James McCuaig, a Member of Parliament for Prince Edward County in the mid-Victorian years. The tapestry-type seat covering is modern.

1850–70

Mr. & Mrs. Howard Pain, Toronto

IV.   The parlour of a house in Frontenac County built about 1820. The character of the mantelpiece woodwork is similar to that of much of the basic cabinet furniture made in the area. A provincial Sheraton chair and a painted slat-back rocking chair flank the fireplace. In the small slip room behind the parlour there is a high-post Ontario bed.

Mr. and Mrs. Blake McKendry, Elginburg

V.   A tall chest of drawers from the Niagara Peninsula is an excellent example of nineteenth-century painted and grained finishing. The wood is pine throughout, but a clever painter has produced a case that looks like mahogany and drawers that, from a little distance, are indistinguishable from real curled maple. The drawers also have "crotch mahogany" bordering. The white ceramic pulls are original, suggesting that the piece dates from about 1850 to 1860.

Mr. and Mrs. Lynn McMurray, Toronto

163.   This is the common man's balloon-back chair, an
Ontario-made walnut chair with a minimum of demanding decorative work. The structure of the chair itself, the
style of leg, and the slip seat are unchanged from the
basic chair as it appeared during the various phases of
the long neo-classical period. Only the back is changed.
The needlework covering is of a style popular towards
the end of the century. Most chairs of this class were
covered originally with tough, practical haircloth. This
one was acquired in Durham County.

1850–90

Mr. & Mrs. L. J. Ingolfsrud, Toronto

164. A backwoods response to the balloon-back style is this crude chair of chestnut and maple from Huron County. The back splat suggests something of a formal style development of about 1860. The number and scale of the stretchers suggests that the maker was much concerned with stability.

1860–1900

Stratford Festival Foundation

165. A common countrified variant of the balloon-back comes with prudent braces linking back to seat rails. While increasing security the braces unfortunately destroy the appeal of the wasp-waist back. The invention of the coil spring in England in 1829 made possible the luxurious comfort of deep padded upholstering, used to the fullest extent in Victorian rococo chairs and sofas. This well-padded chair of carved walnut comes from Northumberland County.

1850–80

Mrs. Lenah Field-Fisher, Cobourg

166. This armchair with oval upholstered back is a nineteenth-century version of another French Louis XV period piece. Fitted pads on carved arms are characteristic. A front seat rail with a central decorative feature is common to many "Victorian" chairs. Castors were as a rule fitted to the front legs of such heavier chairs but seldom to the rear. The importation by antique dealers of many chairs of this period and style makes the distinguishing of local from foreign products usually difficult. This example from western Ontario has a carved frame entirely of native black cherry.

1850–80

Mr. Eugene Rae, Malton

167. Elegance was desirable but comfort was a matter of greater concern in much nineteenth-century furniture design. In the case of this chair, comfort was supremely triumphant. Associated with the Elizabethan revival that produced such a quantity of "spool" beds, a chair of this style was described in 1850 by Andrew Downing as "an easy chair, or lounge, better adapted for the siesta, than to promote the grace or dignity of the figure". No springs were used in this chair and the cushions are stuffed with excelsior. The upholstery fabric, of a pattern popular about 1860, may possibly be the original. The back cushion is loose. The frame of the chair, found in Haldimand County, is of black walnut.

1850–80

168. This walnut hall chair from Northumberland County is of a design illustrated in style guides as early as the 1840s but one popular till the end of the century. Intended more for decoration than utility, hall chairs almost invariably had uncompromising flat board seats. A pseudo-coat of arms evidently was often considered a good decorative feature; it very seldom had any other significance. Details were frequently of a Gothic-revival character.

1850–80

Mrs. Lenah Field-Fisher, Cobourg

169. Another black walnut hall chair, pretty much an exercise in neo-Gothic fretwork, displays the style of turning, best seen in the post finials, which originated in the 1840s but which was in more general use in the sixties and seventies. Like the preceding example, this chair has a family pseudo-crest incorporated into the decorative work of the back. It was found in Toronto.

1860–80

Mr. & Mrs. M. F. Feheley, Toronto

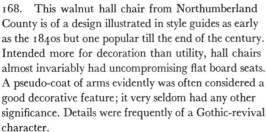

171. It looks like a wing chair — it is a wing chair. Precisely, it is a commode chair of wing-back character, made entirely of thin pine boards and still bearing its original dull red paint finish. A well-fitted plain board seat cover hides the chair's basic function. It comes from an eastern Ontario farm home.

1830–50

Mr. & Mrs. Michael McKenna, Ottawa

170. A home-made high chair that just doesn't fit into any category, this rather crude product from western Ontario suggests a familiar design for country dough-boxes or bread-kneading troughs. The wood is all pine; the paint finish is black. Some hand-made nails and some cut nails were used.

1830–50

Mr. & Mrs. John Harbinson, Agincourt

172. What must be one of the earliest neo-Gothic chairs in Ontario is this formal piece made entirely of black walnut. It was used by the presiding justice in the second court-house built in the town of Niagara in 1817. It is unlikely to be quite as old as the court-house itself. The chair, or bench as it might properly or ceremonially be called, continued to serve justice in the new court-house built in 1847 and when that building became the town hall after 1862 it became the chair in which the mayor presided over sessions of the council.

1820–30

Niagara Historical Society, Niagara-on-the-Lake

Family picture albums preserve a great deal of information not only about one's forebears and bygone fashions in personal clothing, but also of tastes and fashions in furniture. Seldom did a photographic artist pose his subject for a studio portrait without incorporating a piece of furniture, most frequently a chair. This group of *cartes de visite* from Ontario studios in the 1860s exhibits a considerable variety of styles in prop chairs, from a mid-century kitchen Windsor and a late-Empire armchair, to a rococo-revival armchair and side chairs, and Elizabethan-revival hall chairs.

Sofas
and Settees

173.   A waggon seat is a chair made double size. The slat-back type was probably very familiar in old Ontario and is referred to in the reminiscent late-nineteenth-century writings of Canniff Haight. It was used to provide a degree of comfort when an ordinary farm-waggon was pressed into service as a passenger vehicle. This example, made of maple and ash and having a woven bark seat, originated in south-western Ontario.

1830–50

Norfolk Historical Society, Simcoe

174.   A somewhat crude but distinctively Windsor-style waggon seat has a whitewood seat with other components largely of ash. The same model has been noted often enough in eastern Ontario to suggest that it was produced in quantity in some chair-maker's shop along the upper St. Lawrence. Now stripped of earlier finishes, this waggon seat evidently was originally painted and stencil decorated.

1840–60

Mr. & Mrs. Blake McKendry, Elginburg

175. A refined low-back Windsor settee, perhaps more frequently called a sittee when Upper Canada was young, is in the style of American pieces made in the late eighteenth century. The one feature not common to American Windsor products of that period is the centre back splat, which provides an interesting break in the long rank of slim, tapered spindles. The quality of turning work in the legs and stretchers is bold and satisfying and distinctively North American in character. The original finish was a sand-coloured paint; its seat is pine, the other parts birch and hickory. It was found in an old home in the town of Prescott.

1780–1800

Upper Canada Village, Morrisburg

176.   A country settee in a style of thirty to fifty years
later than the preceding example is this Sheraton-influenced arrowback Windsor which was found in eastern
Ontario. Like other settees it is really an enlarged chair,
although in this case perhaps a little heavier and bulkier
than the scaling-up justifies. The original painted finish
with stencilled decorations has long since disappeared and
the piece is presently finished in dark green. Broad front
and rear stretchers are common in Windsor settees of the
period.

1825–45

Upper Canada Village, Morrisburg

177. A Windsor-style settee which has a seat characteristic of Boston rockers and legs familiar on many Sheraton fancy chairs was found near Hawkesbury in Prescott County. Although none of its original finish survives, this is another piece which was no doubt once painted and decorated with colourful stencilled designs.

1830–45

Dr. & Mrs. Ralph Price, Port Perry

178. When rockers were added, the Windsor settee became a settee-cradle. This example, found in Middlesex County, has two holes bored into the seat's fore edge into which a kind of removable fence or gate was fitted to make the piece a secure cradle for baby. Its full length is just five feet and at the right end there remained space for mother to sit and rock. Like many removable accessories, the fence for this dual-purpose piece has been lost. It has a whitewood seat with the usual hardwood components and retains its original black paint finish with modest stencilled floral decorations.

1840–60

Mr. & Mrs. John Harbinson, Agincourt

180. Only three feet wide, this settee-cradle has no room for mother when converted to cradle use. The gate is secured in shallow mortise holes in the seat and by retaining pegs through the arm-rest ends. Some suggestion of the original stencilled decoration shows through the later coat of black paint. The convertible arrowback Windsor piece was found in Ottawa.

1825–40

Mr. & Mrs. Blake McKendry, Elginburg

179. A settee-cradle from Ontario County is complete with original removable guard. A second pair of holes, now plugged, at the left fore edge of the seat suggests that a second and shorter guard was originally provided to guarantee full security if mother was not available as sitter and rocker motive power. The well-preserved original paint finish is black with stencilled decoration largely of yellow with some red in the worn guard panel.

1835–50

Mr. & Mrs. Azel Guest, Whitby

182. In a completely Sheraton tradition, this is one of the most impressive sofas to have been found in Ontario in recent years. Acquired in Kingston, it is perhaps somewhat provincial in its execution but it certainly would have represented high style and elegance in the early days of Upper Canada. Stripped of all fabric covering and padding, the frame is revealed with a springy support of interwoven ash splints, taking the place of the familiar webbing. The entire back and seat frame was intended to be upholstered; the only wood to be exposed would be the eight legs and the free-standing and unusually shaped arm-rest supports. These members are of maple; the front and rear seat rails are of oak and the frame of the back of pine. A bound roll of rush, to serve as especially durable padding, is fastened along the front seat rail.

1800–20

Dr. & Mrs. William S. A. Dale, London

181. Tête-à-tête is a nineteenth-century term for a settee so designed that two persons can sit face to face. As the name itself suggests, it was conceived as a fashionable and sophisticated piece of furniture, but this late low-back Windsor version is a very unusual adaptation. It was found in Waterloo County. Although little trace of the original finish survives, it was almost certainly painted black and decorated with stencilled designs.

1850–60

Mr. & Mrs. Stanley Ashbury, Preston

183. Of a simpler Sheraton style, this sofa came from the home of the Reverend Mr. Robert Blakey, the first Anglican priest in the Prescott district of Grenville County. The legs, two at the front and three at the rear, are of brown-stained birch; all were once fitted with castors. The hidden frame is probably of pine. The seat has a firm board base rather than webbing support. The present upholstery and covering is modern.

1800–20

Mr. & Mrs. Blake McKendry, Elginburg

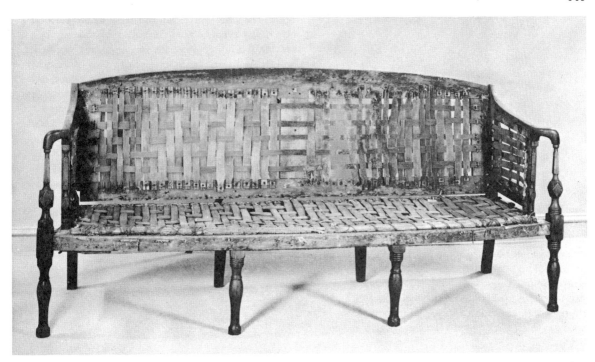

184. Although this sofa is primarily a simple provincial product, the few curving lines do owe some debt to formal design schools. The outline of the crest might be credited to a late Sheraton tradition, while the discreetly curved ends suggest the Grecian character of Directoire or early-Empire period. Seat and back were meant to have upholstery padding and covering. The crest rail, arm-rests, legs, and front seat rail, all intended to be exposed, are of black walnut. The sofa was found in Niagara.

1820–30

Mr. & Mrs. John Harbinson, Agincourt

185. The delicate Grecian couch of the neo-classical period was eventually interpreted in this manner by provincial artisans. Unusually long at eighty-eight inches, it differs from fancy parlour versions chiefly in the treatment of the legs. As well as being easier to produce, the stout turned legs of this and many other country couches and sofas no doubt satisfied both makers and clients as being more reliably strong and secure than the delicate sabre-shaped legs of the text-book models. Grecian sofas and couches are distinguished in having only a partial back, indicating that they were designed primarily for reclining rather than for sitting. This provincial example comes from Waterloo or a neighbouring county. Exposed wood at back and end is walnut, as are the legs. The seat rails are birch with a walnut stain. The present upholstery and covering are modern.

1825–40

Miss Jennifer McKendry, Kingston

186. An extremely crude country couch is this Glengarry County piece which probably was inspired by a couch similar to the preceding example. It is a homemade product of pine and butternut, originally having a red-brown paint finish.

1830–60

Mr. & Mrs. Russell Harper, Alexandria

187. This is high style in what should be called American Empire — the Empire period in France never knew a sofa like it. It was very likely ordered from a New York State maker by some proud and affluent Upper Canadian. Sofas of the period are quite noticeably heavier than those of Sheraton and Directoire designs. The legs, which appear as animal paws each reaching out from a complex of fruit and foliage, the whole carved in mahogany, are characteristic. This particular style of arm-rest is described by some furniture students as a cornucopia design, and the bolster pillows or squabs which fit against the arm-rests are also characteristic of Empire sofas. The carved crest of this type is familiar only on sofas of the earlier years of American Empire popularity; it still suggests a derivation from the capital of a Grecian-style column. Figured mahogany veneer was much used on flat and gently curving planes of such sofas. The black haircloth covering was a fabric very popular during the nineteenth century.

1810–30

Upper Canada Village, Morrisburg

188. This impressive sofa in American Empire style was located in Ontario County, although it may have originated in a fashionable city shop in either Upper Canada or New York State or possibly Montreal. In Upper Canada, turned and sometimes reeded legs were frequently used in place of the carved leg of the type seen on the preceding example. The curve of the arm-rest is closer to the Grecian inspiration of the earlier Directoire style and the squabs appear as a result super-fluous. Mahogany is the principal wood. Covering is the long-popular black haircloth.

1810–30

Mr. & Mrs. M. F. Feheley, Toronto

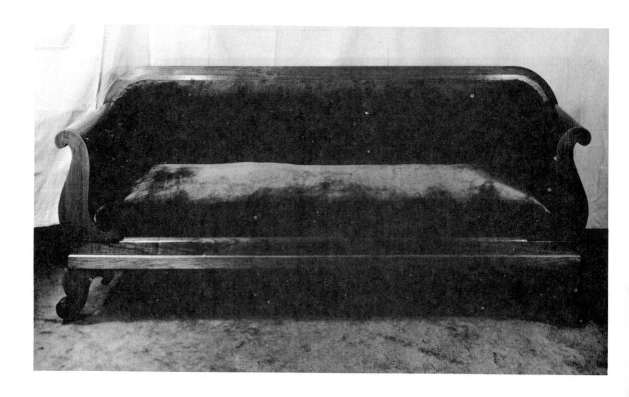

189. An Empire-style sofa found in Northumberland County has thoroughly carved arm ends and crest rail. The finials on the crest rail and more particularly those projecting at each end of the seat rail are unusual if not entirely attractive to all eyes. The legs would appear less chunky with their original castors. Some grace is also sacrificed, and this is common to many Empire sofas, because the curve of the arm-rest end does not rise directly from the horizontal line of the front seat rail. The wood, almost inevitable in such Empire pieces, is mahogany.

1825–40

Mrs. Lenah Field-Fisher, Cobourg

190. All the exposed wood of this provincial sofa is butternut; it was originally stained to simulate mahogany. The shaping of the arm-rest ends probably owes more to the Empire than to any other tradition; the profile suggests that bolster pillows or squabs were part of the original design. The legs are scroll cut in what is really a modified reversal of the arm-rest pattern. It was found in Northumberland County.

1825–40

Mr. C. Hardy Sifton, Cobourg

191. This country sofa with heroic curves comes from Elgin County. Although one may be tempted to relate its serpentine back to the camel-back Chippendale-style sofa, its over-all lines were more likely inspired by those of an Empire-period sleigh bed. If its back were removed, it would have much in common with the "Récamier" sofa, which falls into the Directoire category. Whatever its inspiration, it is a fascinating example of provincial adaptation. The frame and the legs are of pine and were probably originally painted black. Padding beneath the tattered covering is straw.

1840–60

Mr. Yosef Drenters, Rockwood

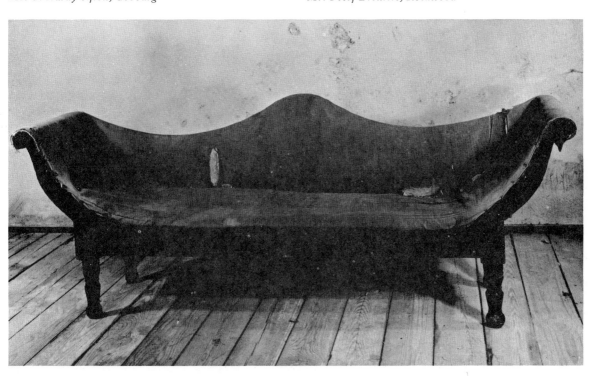

192.   Sofas after 1850 frequently were designed by
merging something of rococo-revival style with remnants
of Empire and even Directoire details; eclectic is the only
safe term to be used when describing them. The cameo
panelled back was extremely popular and a wealth of
ornamental carving was normal. This example, and
there were a great many like it produced in Ontario,
comes from Elgin County. All the exposed wood is
mahogany.

1850–70

National Museum of Man, Ottawa

193. This restrained rococo-revival sofa, the kind of piece most often intended by the catch-all term Victorian, came from the Picton furniture shop of Abram Southard. The exposed frame is black walnut. The fabric covering is modern and unlike anything used in period.

1850–65

Mr. & Mrs. C. Minaker, Milford

194. An Empire sofa of decidedly country character is this pine and maple piece found in Niagara. Red paint may well have been the original finish. A single long fitted cushion was probably intended for the seat but it is not at all certain that the arm-rest ends were upholstered when the sofa was new. The outline of the back is much similar to that of the very formal Empire sofa in Plate 187.

1830–45

Mr. & Mrs. Henry Dobson, Plattsville

195. This settee from eastern Ontario is structurally very similar to many low-post beds of the same period; even the seat rails come equipped with pegs, around which a rope "spring" was woven as support for the long seat cushion. The scrolled outline of the crest rail suggests something of Empire-period flavour. The original red paint finish survives.

1830–45

Author's collection

196. This settee from Essex County was designed like many beds of the period. Its basic form is the same; it has the bed-like arrangement to facilitate a woven rope "spring"; even the crest rail appears much like those of turned-post bed ends. The wood is curled maple. One long cushion or tick was no doubt intended to cover the seat. One or more cushions may or may not have been used at the back.

1830–45

Mrs. Marjorie Larmon, Burgessville

197. A settee found in the village of Bath is of a type particularly familiar in eastern Ontario. It appears to derive originally from the low-post bed form; in later years its turned members were designed in a way similar to those of the so-called spool bed. Such settees were especially popular for use in farm-house kitchens and on verandas. This example is made of pine and maple, and like most of its kind was intended to have a paint finish. Loose slats provide the seat support for a cushion filled with straw, raw wool, or sometimes feathers.

1830–50

Mr. & Mrs. Thomas L. Riedel, Bath

199. This is another settee which is really just a narrow low-post bed, to which a scroll-shaped back rest has been added as a kind of afterthought. The profile of that back board was inspired by some Empire piece. Turned members are birch; the rails, drilled for a woven rope "spring", are ash, and the back board is pine. The original finish was black paint.

1830–50

Mr. & Mrs. Walter Beevor, Stirling

198. This is a late country version of a Sheraton-style sofa in the same tradition as the refined piece in Plate 182. The turned, free-standing arm-rest ends make the most obvious common feature. Like the plain back board, the arm-rests, except for those turned posts, were intended to be padded and covered with fabric. The seat evidently was provided with a single long cushion. The rails and turned parts of this piece are birch, the rest pine. Exposed wood was finished with brown stain. It was found in Dundas County.

1830–60

Mr. & Mrs. William Johnstone, Dearborn, Michigan

200. Most of the later country settees are unnecessarily
heavy and with turned designs that are extremely
"spooly". This example from Grenville County retains
a light feeling, thanks partly to the very finely turned
back support spindles and partly to the "arcaded" treatment of the crest rail. The wood is largely ash and the
surviving original finish is a brown treatment of the kind
today described as varnish-stain.

1850–70

202. Another settle-bed, sometimes called bunk-bed and familiar in French Canada as *banc-lit*, this example is all pine with a mellow, well-preserved dark red paint finish. Its design is best described as traditional provincial, owing nothing to the rapidly changing schools of design of the nineteenth century. The hinges and hooks are products from some blacksmith's forge. Heavy moulding makes an effective crest above the handsome horizontal panels. The bunk-bed is evidently a Scottish as well as a French tradition and most Ontario examples have been found in areas where the first settlers came from Scotland. This piece comes from Lanark County.

1820–40

Mr. & Mrs. M. F. Feheley, Toronto

201. This seating unit of architectural character appears a traditional settle, but it is also a bed. The box-like seat is hinged at floor level; the retaining hook in the seat centre shows clearly where it opens to turn the settle into a large open box. A straw or feather tick can then turn the open box into an emergency bed. All pine, with handsome panels in the high back, this settle-bed from Simcoe County was originally finished in brown paint.

1810–30

Mrs. H. C. Walker, Toronto

203.   A settle-bed from Glengarry County has a back
which is scroll-sawn in an Empire-period pattern. The
entire piece is pine, finished with a base coat of red paint
with black brushed over it before the red was completely
dry. There is a narrow yellow line painted along the
scrolled back edge.

1825–40

Upper Canada Village, Morrisburg

204. Another Lanark County settle-bed betrays some
slight Empire influence in the profile of the back support
and in the discreet shaping which suggests the rolled arm
design of that period. This pine piece retains much of
its original red paint finish. The straw or feather ticks
used for emergency bedding were probably stored within
the closed box seat.

1825–40

Mr. & Mrs. Walter Beevor, Stirling

205. This settle does not serve as a bed but rather provides storage space in its seat-box area for fire wood. Two hinged lift hatches provide access to separate storage sections, the smaller one possibly for kindling, the larger for regular stove wood. The tradition of German Pennsylvania is apparent in the tulip and heart motifs, but wire nails used in its construction suggest the settle dates from the late nineteenth or even the early twentieth century. Its character is early, but the "modern" materials used indicate that provincial traditions in furniture-making sometimes survived to a very late date. This settle probably comes from Waterloo County.

1880–1900

Dr. & Mrs. Peter Bell, Sharbot Lake

Bedsteads

206. High-post bedsteads were common in Ontario's first fifty years. This example from Halton County has heavy maple posts, tapered above rail level but not below, a tradition that may possibly relate to earlier eighteenth-century styles. Chamfering of the heavy posts was the only attempt at refinement. The side rails and the head- and foot-boards are ash, and even the pine tester frame, joining the post tops, is the original. It is uncertain that the bed when new was given any finish coat; some traces of an earlier coat of shellac have survived. Slats fastened between the side rails support the bed, as early Ontarians would have called the mattress or ticks and other bedding material; bedstead was the specific term meaning the wooden frame which supported the bed.

1820–40

Mr. & Mrs. Ronald Pequegnat, Guelph

207. A "pencil post" bedstead has tapered octagonal posts of maple and low head- and foot-boards of pine. Posts taper from rail level both above and below. Square side and end rails, hidden by bedding, are drilled to enable a rope "spring" to be woven back and forth between them. Bed ends are fastened to sides by bolts which pass through posts to meet nuts mortised into the rails. The canopy frame is entirely a reproduction but is probably very similar to the original. This style with an arched canopy is called a field or tent bed and usually has shorter posts (these are fifty-one inches high) than bedsteads with testers. This example was found in Glengarry County.

1800–30

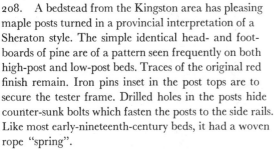

208. A bedstead from the Kingston area has pleasing maple posts turned in a provincial interpretation of a Sheraton style. The simple identical head- and foot-boards of pine are of a pattern seen frequently on both high-post and low-post beds. Traces of the original red finish remain. Iron pins inset in the post tops are to secure the tester frame. Drilled holes in the posts hide counter-sunk bolts which fasten the posts to the side rails. Like most early-nineteenth-century beds, it had a woven rope "spring".

1810–30

Mr. & Mrs. John Bowden, Ann Arbor, Michigan

209. The pervasive influence of the American Empire style is to be seen in the scrolled pattern of the pine footboard; the headboard, hidden by bedding, is iden-tical. The bird's-eye maple posts are turned in an unusual pattern, although the turning tradition would appear to derive from Sheraton styles. The posts are six and a half feet high and were intended, no doubt, to support a tester with bed curtains. This bedstead, according to family tradition made in South Monaghan Township, remains today in the family of the original owner.

1830–45

Mrs. Janet Ehnes, Bailieboro

210.   Beds were first made with high posts in order to support curtains which protected occupants from draughts. Since the drapery was often limited to the head area, the hidden posts were often given less decorative treatment than those at the foot. It follows that greater pains were frequently taken with the footboard than with the head. This Empire-style bedstead is a good example to illustrate both characteristics.

1815–30

Upper Canada Village, Morrisburg

211.   An Empire-period bedstead of local black walnut probably originated in the Niagara Peninsula. Its medium-height posts indicate it probably had an arched canopy, making it really a tent or field bedstead. The scrolled pattern of the headboard and the modified Sheraton-style post turning are familiar in many Empire beds. While eighteenth-century bedsteads generally had no footboards, it is an unusual oversight after 1820.

1820–40

McFarland House, Niagara Parks Commission, Queenston

212.   This high-post bed of restrained Empire character, most apparent in the shaping of the pine footboard, was acquired in eastern Ontario. The headboard and the maple head-posts have little ornamentation. While preserving something of the pattern of Sheraton style in turning and fluting, the foot-posts are considerably heavier and are representative of the general tradition in high-post beds as late as 1840.

1820–40

Upper Canada Village, Morrisburg

213. Roped beds with low turned posts, simple head- and foot-boards, and square side and end rails were very common in the second quarter of the nineteenth century. Scrolled head- and foot-boards and the turned profile of posts are frequently similar to those of high-post Empire-style beds, but for the most part they are provincially simple and not closely bound to the formal styles of period pattern books. The posts are usually maple, sometimes birch; the head- and foot-boards are almost always pine and the stout side and end rails are most often of ash. The finish most commonly is a red paint or stain, or, as some authorities prefer, a red filler.

1820–40

Upper Canada Village, Morrisburg

214. A doll's bed from the Niagara Peninsula betrays more Empire-style influence than many of the low-post beds it resembles. The rails are much more stout than required but the provision of pegs made it possible for some little girl to complete the toy bed with a properly authentic rope "spring". The piece is largely maple with a painted and grained finish of the non-objective school. The little bed is two feet long and its posts are twenty-two inches high.

1820–50

Dr. & Mrs. Ralph Price, Port Perry

215. Spirited provincial turning makes this low-post
bed of maple a charming country piece. Only the shaping
of the pine headboard really preserves any true suggestion of Empire styling. Substitution of a turned rail for a
footboard was a familiar feature of such beds. This one
was found in Prince Edward County.

1830–45

Miss Anne Farwell, Cherry Valley

216.   Very common in the second quarter of the nineteenth century, the low-post bed in Ontario occasionally
exhibits charming individual character. One with impressively strong character in its turning quality is this
example from Lanark County. Large acorn finials cap
each post and appear also as terminals to the Empire-
style rolled rails atop head- and foot-boards. The turned
parts are birch; one end-board is pine, the other butternut. The entire bedstead was originally painted red.

1830–45

Dr. & Mrs. Ralph Price, Port Perry

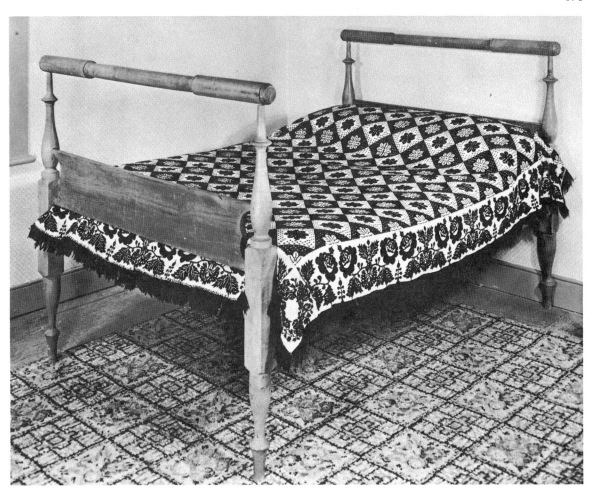

217. Simple turned-post bedstead of very light feeling is of a country style particularly familiar in western Ontario. This one was found in Waterloo County. Its most distinctive feature is the turned rail joining the post-tops at each end. This style of bed often has turned round side and end rails, threaded at each end so that the whole structure is held together by wooden screw joints. Turned parts are maple; the end-boards are pine. Some traces of a clear finish, probably shellac, survive.

1830–50

Mr. & Mrs. Horace Dahmer, Guelph

218.   A craftsman much addicted to ball turning was
responsible for this Waterloo County bed of knobby
Empire-period character, although he strayed from the
general tradition in making the head higher than the
foot. Side and end rails that hold the bed together are
circular and threaded at each end to screw into the posts.
Turned parts are of maple, the end-boards pine. The
original finish is a dark brown stain, accented on the
crest rails by gold stencilled decorations now so worn as
not to show in the photograph.

1830–60

Mr. & Mrs. Horace Dahmer, Guelph

219.   A mahogany Empire-style bedstead with identi-
cally matching ends is clearly of a formal style that
inspired the country version illustrated in the preceding
plate. This one was found in the Niagara Peninsula.
The romantically scrolled work, dressed up with figured
mahogany veneer, is framed by heavy posts and rails.
Fluted sections in the turned posts provide some relief
from a blocky geometric character whose most prominent
features are the unusual finials which are really cubes
with their corners planed off.

1830–50

Author's collection

220.   A child's bed of Regency character has low posts
which were shaped without a lathe and yet retain the
impression of turned work inspired by a Sheraton style.
The pedimented headboard encloses two pleasing fielded
panels. Lattice-like sides make it almost a crib. The wood
is largely ash and the brown stain finish is original. It
comes from Lanark County.

1820–40

Author's collection

221. A thoroughly basic bedstead for a child is this eastern Ontario product made largely of birch. Unlike those of larger beds, its side rails are mortised, pinned, and glued permanently into its posts. The square posts are chamfered above and below rail level. The brown paint coat is probably the original finish. Slats laid between side rails would support bedding.

1830–60

Miss Jennifer McKendry, Kingston

222. Perhaps this might be called a trundle or truckle bed, the very low kind intended to be stored below a full-size adult bed. With a full post height of sixteen inches, it would fit beneath some of the older and traditionally very high beds, but to satisfy the meaning of the word trundle or truckle, such a bed should have rollers or castors. Its wood is butternut and the finish is black paint. Mortise joints are close fitting and without glue; the tightly strung rope makes the entire frame rigid. It was found in Dundas County.

1820–50

Dr. & Mrs. Peter Bell, Sharbot Lake

223. A narrow low-post bed from Hastings County has turned posts of maple and turned end rails of black walnut. The rope rails also are of maple. Slight modification would make it a settee (see Plates 195 and 196).

1825–50

Mr. & Mrs. Thomas L. Riedel, Bath

224. The sleigh bed, or French bed as it was called in its period, is a North American version of the Napoleonic Empire-style bed. It was meant to be used with one side pushed against a wall and with a regal canopy hung from the ceiling and draped over each flaring end. The wood, as in this example acquired in Ottawa, was almost invariably mahogany. Simpler country versions were made of lesser woods and usually painted and decorated.

1825–50

Mr. & Mrs. W. N. Minhinnick, South Bay

225. Spool beds can be classified as the most popular
expression of a short-lived Elizabethan-revival style, but
it's more important to recognize that they represent the
massively successful application of steam-powered factory
methods to the large-scale production of cheap furniture.
The turning work is more frequently in the ball-and-
ring pattern than in a true spool shape. Better-quality
models were made in walnut and cherry; many cheaper
beds were made of lesser woods and stained or painted.
The style first appeared a few years before 1850 and
persisted in one form or another for about thirty years.
This example is of birch and whitewood with a dark red
paint finish and is representative of the general style in
the later years of its popularity.

1860–80

Cradles

226. Fashionable new styles in furniture seldom had much effect on traditional approaches to cradle-making. Charming provincial simplicity was the general rule, as illustrated in this cradle from the old French settlement on the Detroit River. Scratch-carved into its bottom board is the name "I. St. Louis", probably Isidore St. Louis, a member of a family long resident in Essex County. Like many cradles made in Quebec, it is framed with corner posts, into which sides and ends are mortised. The familiar tradition in cradles among English-speaking settlers was box-like construction without posts, corner joints being dove-tailed or rabbeted. While Quebec cradles were usually made of pine or butternut, this example is a combination of black walnut and cherry, both common in south-western Ontario.

1820–40

Hiram Walker Historical Museum, Windsor

227. A cradle of French-Canadian style, showing also some Empire influence in the decorative device at the head, is made entirely of black walnut. Found in Essex County, it is a good example illustrating the survival of their own traditional styles among descendants of the original French settlers of the Detroit River colony. Although sides and ends suggest panelled construction, each is a single board channel-moulded on the outside. French-Canadian cradles are commonly of framed construction with corner posts extended high enough to make manual rocking convenient.

1825–50

Hiram Walker Historical Museum, Windsor

228. Of traditional box-like construction, but with simple though effective efforts to make it romantically decorative, this all-cherry cradle comes from western Ontario. Its basic form, without corner posts, was general across most of Ontario. Hand-grips were frequently cut into cradle sides. Brass knobs, the same as used for pulls on small drawers, were sometimes applied as in this example so that a cord might be fastened across the cradle to secure the covering over the baby.

1800–50

Dr. & Mrs. Peter Bell, Sharbot Lake

229. Hooded cradles were no doubt developed for the
same reason as high-back settles and wing-back chairs —
to protect the occupant from draughts. Some decorative
effort was normally expended on the hood; in this case
it was given a handsome arch, trimmed with a simple
but extremely effective moulding. Found in eastern
Ontario, its wood is pine and its finish red paint.

1810–40

Upper Canada Village, Morrisburg

230. A hooded cradle found in Hastings County is made of pine and retains its original red paint finish. Rockers are of birch or maple and, as in most cradles, are decorated by a scroll-cut pattern at each end.

1820–40

Mr. & Mrs. Walter Beevor, Stirling

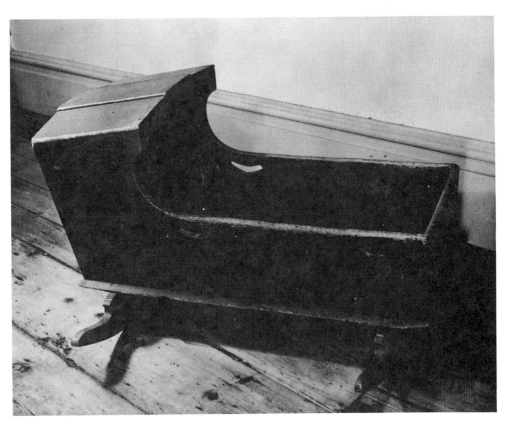

231. Whether crude or fine, the cradle's basic form
changes very little, but there can be many ways of treat-
ing a hood; this way is distinctly unusual. The rockers
are heavy and the corner joints rabbeted rather than
dove-tailed. The wood is pine but its paint finish is not
the original.

1830–50

Black Creek Pioneer Village, Toronto

232. Squared box construction is an earlier form than
cradles with flared sides and ends. Added finials, to make
rocking by hand more convenient, were also familiar on
cradles long before Ontario's earliest settlement. This
cradle, found in Durham County, could be an eighteenth-century product brought north by Loyalist settlers.
It could just as easily be an Ontario product illustrating
the provincial tradition of preserving old styles into a
period in which they have been largely forgotten. The
rocking handles are maple, the rest pine. The surviving
old finish is dark brown paint.

1800–30

Dr. & Mrs. Ralph Price, Port Perry

234. Most Ontario-made cradles are box-like in construction; Windsor cradles are uncommon, but here is a good example found in the Niagara Peninsula. Just like Windsor chairs, it was made by inserting a set of spindles into holes drilled into a single board. A dark brown stain makes identification of the wood uncertain, but it is probably largely of maple or birch.

1810–30

McFarland House, Niagara Parks Commission, Queenston

233. This very charming provincial cradle from Durham County has an outstanding and well-preserved painted and grained finish, one achieved with a dark brown paint used over a light brown ground. The interior is painted black. The rockers are of ash; the rest of the cradle is pine.

1830–50

Mrs. Janet Ehnes, Bailieboro

235. Suspended cradles may truly be earlier in form than those on rockers since they no doubt developed from a time when some early parent hung a baby in a basket from a tree bough. A more formal prototype can be found among Sheraton's drawings. This example from Lanark County can swing in its stout turned frame or on its own rockers when placed on the floor. The cradle proper is of butternut, the frame maple. Red paint appears to have been the original finish.

1820–40

Mr. & Mrs. J. E. Flanigan, Brockville

236. Another suspended cradle found in Lanark County has no rockers at all. The frame with its proportionately massive turned base was apparently designed with absolute security in mind; this one would be impossible to upset. The cradle-box is of pine and the frame of ash. The apparently original finish is red-brown paint.

1830–45

Mr. & Mrs. Blake McKendry, Elginburg

237. The eccentric character of this Windsor cradle can be explained by attributing it to a chair-maker. The arrowback head of the cradle is similar to the backs of many provincial chairs and the sides are clearly no more than extended chair arms. The maker faced a totally unfamiliar problem when required to enclose the foot of this hybrid cradle and his use of a chair back rail is not entirely satisfying. It was found in Durham County and the woods are birch and whitewood.

1840–60

Mr. & Mrs. Thomas Lawson, Port Hope

238. This cradle from western Ontario is not the simplest box form like most but is framed with sides and ends mortised into corner posts. The inspiration is clearly the Empire period's sleigh or French bed. The wood is entirely cherry.

1830–50

Chests

239. Without the slightest suggestion of sophistication, this pine chest is representative of many made not by cabinet-makers but by carpenters and joiners. It is a simple six-board chest whose end-boards have been scroll-cut to make legs. Butt joints at the corners are secured by nails. The lid lifts on butt hinges. The original finish is a base coat of yellow ochre with a "finger paint" design of dark brown.

1800–30

Upper Canada Village, Morrisburg

240. Excellent quality in joinery work is illustrated in this panelled pine chest found in Prince Edward County. The back, although it might seldom be seen, is identical to the front with four finely finished fielded panels. The stiles (vertical framing members) at each corner extend to the floor to reinforce the bracket feet; even so, the lower part of the bracketing has been broken away. No evidence of any protective or decorative finish survives.

1780–1820

Mr. & Mrs. Thomas L. Riedel, Bath

241. Blanket chest is the term most generally applied to antique boxes of suitable size no matter what their actual uses might have been, but this rather fine walnut example certainly must have been a featured piece of bedroom furniture, used to store woollens and linens. The bracket base is a provincial rendering of a Hepplewhite line. The principal inlay design in maple, a rectangle with scooped corners, is a motif of vaguely classical origin popular in the eighteenth and the earlier part of the nineteenth centuries. As a decorative design it was used by Ontario furniture-makers for both raised and recessed panels, for inlay work, and even in ornamental painting. This chest was acquired in Norfolk County but is similar in character to other pieces originating in the Niagara Peninsula.

1800–30

Mr. & Mrs. L. J. Ingolfsrud, Toronto

242. Dome-top chest of rugged character is of a traditional northern European design. German settlers brought many to Ontario; others no doubt were made here. Typical of German-influenced travelling chests are the iron binding of the corners and the wrought-iron strap hinges, key-hole escutcheon, and heavy carrying handles. The chest itself is of pine with a slapdash decorative finish of wavy black bands over a red ground paint.

1800–30

Black Creek Pioneer Village, Toronto

243. Decorated by an inspired and unfettered hand, this colourful chest probably provided a bright and cheerful accent in some stark pioneer home. Blanket boxes provide the greatest variety in painted decoration among Ontario furniture. On no other piece of furniture did old-time craftsmen or householders venture so boldly into ornamental colouring. This dove-tailed pine chest with its rudimentary bracket base is done in an exciting black and brown free-hand design over a yellow base.

1820–60

Black Creek Pioneer Village, Toronto

244. Small-size boxes of light stock, usually with gently arched tops, are still to be found but rarely with their original colourful finishes. This one, only twenty-three inches long and fourteen inches high, is an outstanding example of exuberant provincial painted decoration. Colours are red, green, yellow, and blue. The inspiration for such decorated boxes may come from the Pennsylvania-German tradition. The wood is sycamore, which is unusual in Ontario furniture but is native to the south-western part of the province.

1820–50

Mr. & Mrs. Howard Pain, Toronto

245. Structurally the same as the preceding example, this small pine box, twenty-seven inches long, is painted in a very different style. Over a yellow ground coat the swirling patterns with neat grained border trim are done in orange, green, and brown. It was found in the Niagara Peninsula.

1820–50

Dr. & Mrs. Peter Bell, Sharbot Lake

246. Small boxes which might be used to store many different household items were favoured objects for whimsical ornamentation. An example is this Ontario County box, eighteen inches long, completely covered by marquetry decoration; rather than an art object, it became an exercise to display the craftsman's ability. The basic box is pine. The dark background on sides and ends is cherry veneer; the light inlay pattern is in bird's-eye maple. The pattern on the lid is cherry inlaid on the pine.

1830–60

Mr. & Mrs. Azel Guest, Whitby

VI. An extremely fine black walnut blanket chest is a Lincoln County piece dating between 1800 and 1820. The bracket base is unquestionably superior to known comparable examples. The brass pulls on the three drawers are new but of the same style and quality as those first fitted to them.

Mr. & Mrs. John Harbinson, Agincourt

VII. A cherry chest of drawers in a Sheraton style was found in the Niagara Peninsula. The characteristically Sheraton combination of a bracket base with turned feet is very little seen in Ontario work. The inlay designs fall far short of sophisticated standards, yet set this chest quite apart from most comparable pieces of local origin. It was made probably between 1810 and 1830.

Dr. Alan Laws, Toronto

247. A specialized form among very small chests is the tea caddy, a box of decorative character in which precious tea was stored and secured by a lock. It was an eighteenth-century tradition and one more familiar in the homes of the affluent, but by the time this provincial caddy was made in Brant County, probably in the mid-nineteenth century, tea was less expensive and as likely to be stored on a kitchen shelf. This caddy was made, according to tradition, by a young man for his bride. The chief wood is bird's-eye maple and the trim butternut.

1850–60

Royal Ontario Museum, Toronto

248. This blanket chest from Leeds County has a bracketed base, which incorporates a central carved shell ornament, suggesting an earlier tradition than that expressed in most country boxes. The row of fine waving tulips with red and yellow flowers does more, however, to lift this piece out of the ordinary class. The background paint is dark green and the foliage light green. The lid lifts on blacksmith-made strap-iron hinges.

1810–30

Mr. & Mrs. John Harbinson, Agincourt

249. Ontario chests with turned feet are much less common than those with bracket feet or with no feet. Equally noteworthy in this dove-tailed pine box from Halton or Wellington County is the striking finish with a feathered brown design over a yellow base paint.

1820–40

Author's collection

250. While the label establishes not only an owner's name but also a date, this may well be an earlier chest given a fresh decorative finish during Confederation year. Apart from its very small bun-like feet, this Waterloo County box is of the standard dove-tailed pine construction familiar through much of the nineteenth century in all parts of settled Ontario. The surviving finish is yellow with red-brown graining accented by painted panels of imitation curled maple. Lettering and date are in black.

Mr. & Mrs. Horace Dahmer, Guelph

251. This is very much an average Ontario chest, made in the most simple style through much of the nineteenth century. The decoration, both inside and out, makes it an unusual example among the many basic chests which still survive. A butternut piece with a brown grained finish, it is further embellished with sprightly stylized flowers in red and yellow. Much faded but still visible on the back of the chest is the lettering: "Magery Kennedy's chist   Kenyon   Presented by Dr. Kennedy August 30 1854". Kenyon is a township in Glengarry County. The interior of the chest is trimmed with two kinds of mid-nineteenth-century wallpaper and a wood engraving clipped from a periodical of the 50s.

Mr. & Mrs. Russell Harper, Alexandria

252. While the evolutionary development from basic chest to chest of drawers was not actually accomplished in old Ontario, there are many evolutionary pieces to be found. The incorporation of one or two drawers into the base of a lift-top chest was the first step in the development of the chest of drawers. That first-step piece itself turned out to be quite useful and its kind continued to be made along with simple boxes and chests of drawers. This Waterloo County example, with the drawer case area effectively marked off by a line of moulding, survives with its original finish. The base paint is brown with a subdued accenting of black.

1830–50

Author's collection

254. The sloped and hinged top may suggest a bin for flour or grain storage but chests built in this fashion were also used for storage of bedding and out-of-season clothing. The use of walnut as the principal wood and the naïvely executed maple inlay work of Masonic devices makes it apparent that a clear finish was intended. Inlaid initials "S" and "C" flank the repaired area where there was once a keyhole. The drawer pulls are probably late replacements. The chest comes from Ontario County.

1820–40

Mr. & Mrs. M. F. Feheley, Toronto

253. Another Waterloo County chest into which drawers have been introduced has a scrolled bracket base whose basic pattern was much used in Ontario case pieces. It also has a cunning lock device to secure the two drawers: a long dowel slides down through a latching device behind the face of each drawer; only when the lid is lifted can the dowels be raised to release the drawers. For a canny builder, this meant that only one lock instead of three was required from a hardware supplier. The original painted and grained finish, suggestive of crotch-grain mahogany, is done in light brown and black or very dark brown.

1840–60

Miss Jennifer McKendry, Kingston

255. A blanket box of pine from Waterloo County survives with a virtually pristine painted and grained finish. Perhaps the decorator was thinking of mahogany when graining the main area of the box and certainly bird's-eye maple when doing the drawer faces. The character of work in the accent panels above suggests some hybrid wood. Provincial work of this kind appears to have remained popular in the "German" parts of Ontario later than in other sections.

1840–60

Royal Ontario Museum, Toronto

256. This high chest with lift top and with four drawers built into its lower case area was found in the Kingston district. It has a reasonably successful mahogany-style grained finish over its everyday pine. In evolutionary terms, it's easy to see that the addition of a few more drawers and the fastening down of its hinged top would complete its transformation into a chest of drawers. The split-baluster trim is an Empire-period device. The combination of a bracket base with turned feet is out of the ordinary in country furniture but it does appear to echo designs seen in Hepplewhite and Sheraton schools.

1825–40

Mr. & Mrs. John Harbinson, Agincourt

257.   The proper classification term for this piece is probably chest-on-chest. The upper section is a lift-top chest which fits into a recess in the lower section, which has a single large drawer. The upper section is of simple board construction with strips of moulding and turned pulls applied to suggest three drawers which do not exist. The lower section is of stile-and-rail construction enclosing moulded panel ends. It was acquired on Amherst Island. The surviving old finish is red paint. The wood is pine.

1810–40

Dr. & Mrs. Ralph Price, Port Perry

258.   This looks like a chest of drawers but the upper four drawers are not drawers at all. It is a lift-top chest with one long and two short drawers in the lower part. The suggestion of drawers above was accomplished by applying strips of moulding and wooden pulls that never pull. The wood is pine and the grained finish suggests an aspiration to mahogany. The decorative trim on the front stiles was done with oak leaves cut from leather and fastened with tiny nails. The chest was found in Lanark County.

1830–50

Mr. & Mrs. Blake McKendry, Elginburg

Chests
of drawers

259. Traces of Sheraton and Hepplewhite traditions are to be seen in chests of drawers more frequently than in any other category of Ontario furniture. This example is provincial in execution but it perpetuates a familiar Hepplewhite design incorporating the flaring "French" bracket-foot base. The sides and top are maple. A narrow band of inlay (stringing) draws a fine accent line along the top edge and another across the base. Drawers are veneered in mahogany with an edge trim of curled maple. The oval brass escutcheons may just possibly be old but the brass bale pulls are new, replacing originals that were probably the turned wooden variety. The chest was found in the Kingston area.

1800–20

Royal Ontario Museum, Toronto

260. A more countrified but still recognizable rendering perpetuates a Hepplewhite tradition in eastern Ontario. This butternut piece with walnut finish was found in Renfrew but it almost certainly originated farther south. Reeding of the edge of the top surface is a subtle and economical means of increasing refinement. The mushroom-shaped brasses are the original.

1800–30

Mr. & Mrs. Blake McKendry, Elginburg

261. This handsome Hepplewhite-style chest of drawers originated in the Niagara Peninsula. The top is curled maple and the ends cherry, their exposed front edges faced in curled maple. The pine drawers are veneered with curled maple, the veneering of the two uppermost drawers being contrived in a panel pattern. A narrow walnut moulding surrounds each drawer face. Wooden pulls are walnut. A nearly identical chest of drawers now in the Royal Ontario Museum collection also came from the Niagara area and certainly originated in the same workshop.

1800–20

Mrs. H. C. Walker, Toronto

262. Bow-front and serpentine-front chests of drawers are familiar but this example with an oddly arched centre section is quite out of the ordinary. The tradition otherwise is still generally of the Hepplewhite school. Top and sides are birch; drawers have a light figured mahogany veneer on pine. Tradition is that it belonged to the Barnhart family and that it remained in a home on Barnhart Island in the St. Lawrence River until that island became United States territory under the terms of the Ashburton Treaty.

1800–20

Miss Dorothy Short, Ottawa

264. Still graceful, the bracketed base of Hepplewhite high style has been reduced to its most simple satisfying form in this cherry chest of drawers from eastern Ontario. The brass pulls are new but, judging by old scars on the drawer faces, are probably very similar to the missing originals.

1810–30

Dr. & Mrs. Charles Danby, Kingston

263. Some feeling of Georgian-period formality remains but this curled maple chest of drawers with gently bowed front is more to be classified as good Ontario provincial design. Drawer faces have a butternut base veneered with curled maple and bordered with mahogany. The original pulls are of pressed glass in brass mounts.

1810–30

Mr. & Mrs. M. F. Feheley, Toronto

265. Another countrified chest of drawers retains a hint in its bracket base of the styles of the Hepplewhite and Sheraton era. The wood is all curled maple. The brass pulls although new are probably similar to the originals they replace. The chest was acquired on Amherst Island.

1800–30

Mr. & Mrs. Thomas L. Riedel, Bath

266.   The execution is perhaps more coarse than in some of the preceding examples but a striving for the fine air of fashion was of some importance to the provincial craftsman who produced this bracket-base chest of drawers. Although the wood is pine, it was painted and grained, the case a dark brown to suggest walnut or mahogany, and the drawers to imitate curled maple veneer with contrasting dark wood borders. It was found in Glengarry. The brasses are new but probably similar to its originals.

1810–30

Mr. & Mrs. Blake McKendry, Elginburg

267.   This chest of drawers of later form retains some earlier characteristics, notably a bracket base of curled maple whose pattern suggests some designs of the mid-eighteenth century. Drawer faces and top are of black walnut. The sides are pine and their exposed front edges together with the drawer dividers are veneered with curled maple. A central compartment with a hinged door is out of the ordinary but by no means unique. The decorative heart in the door panel and the eight-point star in the drawer face below are veneered features in mahogany and maple. Tradition is that it was made by George Sutherland who was born in Scotland in 1792, emigrated to Glengarry before 1815, and is a great-great-grandfather of the present owner.

1820–40

Miss Margaret Cameron, Toronto

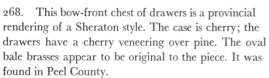

268. This bow-front chest of drawers is a provincial rendering of a Sheraton style. The case is cherry; the drawers have a cherry veneering over pine. The oval bale brasses appear to be original to the piece. It was found in Peel County.

1800–20

Mr. & Mrs. Robert Bull, Brampton

269. The chest of drawers with swing mirror attached was a Sheraton-style innovation and this countrified example has such long legs that it might even be classed as a provincial Sheraton dressing-table. It is a cherry and maple piece, acquired in Kingston.

1830–40

Gibson House, North York

270. Only half an inch short of six feet high, this chest of drawers from Waterloo County is a country-made Hepplewhite-style piece with some Pennsylvania flavour. The usual wood for a chest in this style is walnut but this one is pine throughout, painted and grained to simulate bird's-eye maple. The brass pulls and escutcheons appear to be the original.

1810–30

Royal Ontario Museum, Toronto

271. A tall chest of drawers, fifty-five inches high, is almost certainly an American piece made about the mid-eighteenth century and which may well have come to Ontario in Loyalist times. It falls among the Chippendale styles and the pattern of its bracket foot suggests it may have originated in New England. Brasses are all new but scars on the drawer faces indicate the originals were of this Chippendale-period butterfly type. The principal wood is black walnut, the secondary pine. It was found in Toronto.

1740–80

Mr. & Mrs. Azel Guest, Whitby

272. This black walnut chest from Lincoln County is just over fifty-four inches high. Its quarter columns are plain and its bracket feet seem perhaps a little lighter than the scale of the piece demands. Its mushroom-shaped brass pulls are almost certainly the original. They are smaller than one would expect, but the wide variety of pulls used on pieces of this particular school suggests that the makers generally used whatever was most readily available.

This and the seven chests of drawers that follow are in a particular class and of a style that show that old traditions die hard among provincial craftsmen. Here is preserved, with little trace of later inspiration, a North American Chippendale style that in the United States was out of favour before the end of the eighteenth century. Principal points of recognition are a moulded cornice, vertical quarter columns at the front corners, lip-moulded drawers, and, most obvious of all, ogee-curved bracket feet of a classical Chippendale line.

All the pieces here illustrated probably originated in Lincoln County. Some have been attributed to John Grobb and to one or more members of the Fry family, but further research will be required before specific attributions can be entirely accepted. Whatever their names, the makers evidently came from a Pennsylvania-German background. Some of the pieces may date as early as 1800, others as late as 1860.

1820–40

Mr. & Mrs. L. J. Ingolfsrud, Toronto

VIII.   This bird's-eye maple chest of drawers in a Chippendale-survival style has possibly the finest ogee bracket feet to
be seen on any Ontario furniture. Although it was found in
York County, its style suggests that, like other pieces of this
school, it was probably made in Lincoln County, possibly
between 1820 and 1840. The brass pulls are new.

Mr. and Mrs. John Harbinson, Agincourt

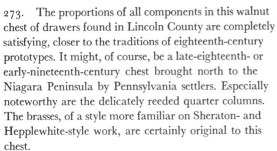

273.   The proportions of all components in this walnut chest of drawers found in Lincoln County are completely satisfying, closer to the traditions of eighteenth-century prototypes. It might, of course, be a late-eighteenth- or early-nineteenth-century chest brought north to the Niagara Peninsula by Pennsylvania settlers. Especially noteworthy are the delicately reeded quarter columns. The brasses, of a style more familiar on Sheraton- and Hepplewhite-style work, are certainly original to this chest.

1800–20

Mr. & Mrs. L. J. Ingolfsrud, Toronto

274.   Detail of the foregoing piece illustrates the handsome ogee curve of a Chippendale-style foot and the fine reeding of a quarter column.

275.   This Chippendale-style walnut chest of drawers impresses initially with its very mass but it also exhibits such refined details as reeded quarter columns and a very finely reeded frieze below the moulded cornice. The ogee bracket-foot profile is unusually deeply indented at one point. The mushroom-shaped brass pulls appear to be the original. The chest was found in Lincoln County and the present owner attributes it to Fry. It is sixty-eight inches high.

1810–25

Mr. & Mrs. John Harbinson, Agincourt

276. The quarter columns of this bird's-eye maple chest of drawers are less refined than others illustrated but the fine ogee feet may possibly make it the case piece with the most successful Chippendale-style bracket base in Ontario. The cornice is made of a section of half-round moulding. The top of the chest is pine. The brass pulls are new; scars suggest it once had pressed-glass knobs. It was found in York County, north of Toronto, but probably originated in Lincoln County.

1820–40

Mr. & Mrs. John Harbinson, Agincourt

277. A Chippendale-style chest of drawers featuring spirally shaped quarter columns is otherwise virtually identical to the preceding example. Even its measurements are almost precisely the same. It too was found just north of Toronto although its design suggests it may have originated in Lincoln County. The case is pine, as is the bracket base, and both are finished with a walnut stain. The drawer faces are of bird's-eye maple. The opalescent pressed-glass pulls may or may not be the original. Like most of the chests in this group, it has solid shelf-like dividers, sometimes called dust shelves, separating the drawers.

1820–40

Mr. & Mrs. H. Larsen, Sydenham

278. A curled maple high chest of drawers in Chippendale style may possibly be a later product than the preceding examples. Cornice treatment has been reduced to a simple cove moulding and a less demanding, thin flat moulding applied to the edges has been substituted for the traditional lip moulding of the drawer faces. The tradition of decorative brass escutcheons has also been sacrificed. The original pulls appear to have been American pressed-glass knobs. The chest was acquired in the Niagara Peninsula.

1830–50

Mr. & Mrs. F. M. Blayney, Waterloo

279. Chippendale character survived well into the nineteenth century as indicated by this Lincoln County piece, which also features an unusual but unmistakably late-Empire-style pediment. The white ceramic pulls, which may be the originals, are of the type produced by several United States potteries after 1850. Local black walnut is the principal wood; as in most chests of this group, pine is the secondary.

1840–60

Gordon & Audrey Griffith, Jordan

280. The last of the Chippendale survival pieces illustrated should possibly be called a bureau desk. It is a chest of drawers which also does service as a desk. Above the long drawers is a writing slide with two tiny glass pulls. A panel between the two pairs of short drawers slides up and back to reveal seven curled maple drawers of sizes suited to desk functions. The principal wood is cherry. The front corners are accented by unusual three-quarter pilasters which derive from the Empire style. The gallery, which combines a scrolled pediment with wings comprised of turned spindles, is unusual but it occurs on a number of pieces from this Niagara Peninsula school of furniture. The name Fry appears on the underside of one drawer but the first name has been obliterated. The original pulls are pressed glass.

1830–50

Mr. & Mrs. F. M. Blayney, Waterloo

281. An Ontario late-Sheraton-style chest of drawers displays the full-height corner pillars which belong to that design tradition. The top of the chest is shaped to cover the tops of the pillars and they appear more an integral part of the case than the heavier pillars and pilasters of later Empire-period pieces. The small scrolled pediment provides some hint of an incoming Empire style. The case is maple and the drawers are faced with bird's-eye and walnut veneering.

1810–30

Royal Ontario Museum, Toronto

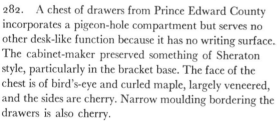

282. A chest of drawers from Prince Edward County incorporates a pigeon-hole compartment but serves no other desk-like function because it has no writing surface. The cabinet-maker preserved something of Sheraton style, particularly in the bracket base. The face of the chest is of bird's-eye and curled maple, largely veneered, and the sides are cherry. Narrow moulding bordering the drawers is also cherry.

1825–40

Dr. & Mrs. H. C. Burleigh, Bath

283. The bow-front drawer treatment familiar as a Hepplewhite and Sheraton tradition was to some little extent carried over to American Empire-style pieces. The overhanging top drawer is an instantly recognizable feature of the period. Flanking turned and carved pillars or pilasters were first seen in the Sheraton period but in the Empire treatment they became heavier, more prominent, and sometimes more intricate. This example, found in the Niagara district, has drawers veneered in curled maple over pine; the case and trim are cherry.

1820–40

Mr. & Mrs. W. Helwig, Niagara-on-the-Lake

285. If the foregoing example is a city version of early-nineteenth-century American Empire style, this chest of drawers is its small-town cousin. The use of S-shaped supports is a fashionable variant to turned and carved pillars and pilasters. The stylized acanthus-leaf carving which ornaments those supports and the pediment is a little out of the ordinary. The case is butternut and maple with a red-brown stain to suggest the more costly mahogany. The drawers are of solid bird's-eye maple. The brown flint-enamel pottery pulls of the 1850–70 period are not original.

1820–40

Dundurn Castle, Hamilton

284. This high-style American Empire chest of drawers may well have been purchased in New York State by some affluent and fashion-conscious early citizen of eastern Ontario. The wood is mahogany with figured mahogany veneer on drawers, the drawer dividers, and the pediment. The small top drawers overhang those below and seemingly are supported by the typically Empire carved pilasters, which in turn are mounted on stout and again typically Empire-style feet carved in the form of paws. The light-coloured wooden pulls are not the originals.

1810–30

Upper Canada Village, Morrisburg

286.   The real country cousin in this Empire group, and a piece of much ingenuous charm, is a chest of drawers with drawers painted with a brown mottling over a yellow base. The case is painted a solid brown. The rather heavy and ambitious turned work is actually made easier to accept by the contrasting effect of the whimsical style of painting. The incised carving which flanks the large upper drawer is a countrified response to the formal relief carving of the kind seen on the two preceding Empire pieces. The opalescent pressed-glass pulls are of a kind produced in American glass factories in the second quarter of the nineteenth century.

1825–40

Dr. & Mrs. C. Stuart Munro, Unionville

287.   The high chest of drawers in a simpler Empire tradition is walnut. The overhanging top drawer, which has a convex moulded face, is like those on many chests of the class in having no visible pulls; recessed finger grips in the lower edge are used to open it. Using some chest space for shelf-like compartments was also frequent; this one has two compartments, one in the centre, another behind the pair of bogus drawer fronts at left centre.

1820–40

Dundurn Castle, Hamilton

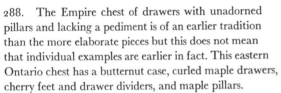

288. The Empire chest of drawers with unadorned pillars and lacking a pediment is of an earlier tradition than the more elaborate pieces but this does not mean that individual examples are earlier in fact. This eastern Ontario chest has a butternut case, curled maple drawers, cherry feet and drawer dividers, and maple pillars.

1820–40

Mr. & Mrs. Murray Copeland, Ottawa

290. A restrained Empire-style chest of drawers from Waterloo County is outstanding among country pieces for its striking painted and grained finish. The wood is pine throughout but finished to simulate a mahogany case with figured mahogany drawers and pediment. The pilasters are black with gold stencilled decoration in the tradition of the popular Sheraton fancy chairs.

1840–60

Mr. & Mrs. Henry Dobson, Plattsville

289.   Only the pediment with its "chimney-pot" ends betrays an Empire tradition in this otherwise extremely simple chest of drawers found in Waterloo County. The case is whitewood and the pediment bird's-eye maple. The drawers are veneered in bird's-eye and trimmed with a thin walnut moulding.

1830–50

Dr. & Mrs. W. L. C. McGill, Brantford

291.   A country chest of drawers with an impressive gallery was probably inspired by a Sheraton-style piece of furniture, but this gallery is bigger and more dramatically scrolled than anything in the style books. The simply designed case of pine with butternut drawers appears originally to have been given a simulated mahogany finish or, in the language of the period, mahoganized. It was found in Lanark County.

1825–50

Mr. & Mrs. Blake McKendry, Elginburg

292.   There are many country chests of drawers similar in style to this basic piece from eastern Ontario but few with such a fascinating painted finish. The usual aim of a grained treatment was to simulate some costly wood but in this case the painter appears to have designed an entirely new wood. The base coat is a terra cotta colour and the graining is done in black.

1840–60

Mr. & Mrs. Walter Beevor, Stirling

293. Details of florid Empire styling were often modified to produce pleasing romantic features in simpler country furniture. This chest of drawers from the Kingston district is thoroughly Empire in inspiration but a far cry from some of the elaborate examples here illustrated. The case is maple and butternut. The pediment is of curled maple and the drawers of bird's-eye.

1830–50

Mr. & Mrs. W. Helwig, Niagara-on-the-Lake

295. Massive scrolling and much use of ogee curves were the special features of furniture modelled on the patterns of John Hall's 1840 book, *The Cabinetmaker's Assistant*. Some call it a late-Empire style. This chest of drawers of curled maple, much of it veneered on pine, is more acceptable to present-day taste than most Hall prototypes. The concave treatment of the top section with its two small drawers is an unusual feature that greatly increases its appeal.

1840–60

Mr. Paul Godfrey, Port Hope

294. A Durham County cabinet-maker chose features from both early and late Empire traditions to produce this piece. The upper section with a serpentine-curved cherry drawer and lacking a pediment suggests the earlier; the front feet are of a style popular after 1840. The top and sides are of butternut and the drawers and facing of bird's-eye maple. The top drawer, top edging, and drawer mouldings are of cherry.

1840–60

Mrs. Janet Ehnes, Bailieboro

296. The Sheraton tradition of an attached swing mirror became more frequently used at mid-century and after. Contrasting styles suggest that this chest of drawers, which may be as early as 1830, could have been "brought up to date" by the addition of a looking-glass about 1860. The mirror frame and supports are of walnut, contrasting to the darker woods of the chest case, cherry sides and top, and crotch mahogany veneer on its front. The drawer faces are veneered in bird's-eye maple with mahogany inset escutcheons. The chest came from Prince Edward County.

Mr. & Mrs. Hugh McMillan, Rockwood

297. The revival of the chest of drawers with swing mirror attached is illustrated by this piece which has evidently been in an old Hamilton home since it was new. The chest itself with its serpentine front could perhaps be classified as a late-Sheraton-style expression, even to the half-round flanking pilasters which are of the same tradition seen in Plate 281. The mirror supports suggest a Gothic-revival inspiration and are in distinct contrast to the chest proper. The wood is mahogany and figured mahogany veneer. The use of castors on such furniture was infrequent before 1850 but became common afterward.

1850–70

Whitehern, Board of Parks, Hamilton

298.   This chest of drawers found in Waterloo County suggests something of dressing-table design and does have features in common with the country Sheraton piece in Plate 269. There is depth enough on the upper shelf to accept a separate looking-glass. The drawers with ogee curved faces are of late-Empire tradition and have finger grips at their lower edges. The principal wood is cherry; the legs are maple.

1840–60

Mr. & Mrs. Guy Andrus, Kitchener

299.   This chest of drawers acquired in Toronto is included less for the sake of its beauty than for its odd features and hybrid character. It has a late-Empire case with a bank of overhanging drawers in a combination that became very popular by 1845; the larger square drawers are still called bonnet drawers. The turned feet are of a basic design used frequently from 1820 on. The style of wooden pull, like a knob set in a saucer, is to be seen fairly frequently on some central Ontario furniture about mid-century. The carved walnut escutcheons were much used on country-style rococo-revival pieces but usually with hand pulls to match. The brackets are in a fretwork tradition used to ornament much furniture in the late years of the century. The laminating of bird's-eye maple and walnut strips in the case sides was surely done solely for novelty's sake.

1860–80

Dr. & Mrs. W. L. C. McGill, Brantford

Desks
and Secretaries

300. This slope-front desk in a Hepplewhite style is a Loyalist period piece; it was brought from Pennsylvania to Ontario in 1783 by an ancestor of the present owner. The case is largely of cherry with some interior fittings of curled and bird's-eye maple. The brasses throughout are original. As an early import, it is the kind of piece after which some old Ontario-made furniture may well have been modelled.

Forms of desks and secretaries differ considerably, but the most familiar of the genus is that which is clearly a modified chest of drawers, having in its upper part a writing section enclosed by a hinged and sloped front. A second form, almost indistinguishable from a chest of drawers when closed, has an entirely vertical front, but what appears to be the top drawer face is actually a hinged panel which drops to serve as a writing surface. Since conflicting terms are often used, let it be established that in this book the former variety is to be known as a slope-front desk, the latter as a bureau desk.

1760–80

Mr. & Mrs. Donald Dunham, Milliken

301. A pine slope-front desk found in Grey County is a countrified version in the same Hepplewhite tradition as the much finer preceding piece. Few country pieces with the flaring French foot have survived and it is likely that relatively few were made in Ontario. The brasses are new but scars on the drawers indicate that the originals were probably similar. Black paint was the original finish.

1800–20

Mr. & Mrs. Howard Pain, Toronto

302. A slope-front desk found in Ottawa is largely of birch with an over-all walnut finish. The French foot is not retained but the bracket base is otherwise the same as in the preceding example. As in most desks of this class, slides to support the hinged front in a writing position are fitted one on each side of the upper drawers.

1810–30

Mr. & Mrs. Walter Beevor, Stirling

303. A basic, perhaps the better word is crude, version of the slope-front desk is this maple piece found in Dundas County. Although it would have been easier, and to some eyes more attractive, to complete this desk with simple bracket feet, the maker apparently considered it more fashionably correct to install chunky turned feet in the front. The finish is a much worn red stain or paint.

1830–50

Upper Canada Village, Morrisburg

305. This piece of furniture looks like a desk but isn't. It is a late-nineteenth-century baking cabinet made largely of poplar. The slope front, supported on familiar desk-style slides, serves as a pastry or bread board. The largest drawer is a flour bin and it can be reached when the cabinet is in open working position through a hinged hatch in the upper compartment. The lower drawers have cast-iron pulls and the interior drawers small white pottery knobs. This piece was found in St. Catharines and others like it are said to have originated in Toronto.

1880–90

Mrs. Floyd Crabtree, St. Catharines

304. There are many old desks in Ontario with a gently sloped front which itself is intended as the writing surface. Hinges are fitted at the upper edge so that the panel must be raised to gain access to the interior where writing materials are stored. Most are simple counting-house-type desks — box desks on legs — but this is an unusual modified chest of drawers type in a restrained Empire style. Found in the Kingston area, it is pine and birch with a worn red finish that suggests more a stain than a paint. The spirally shaped legs and the unusual reeded work transform what could have been a severe design into one of considerable romantic character. The bale brasses appear to be the originals.

1820–40

Dr. & Mrs. Peter Bell, Sharbot Lake

306. Desks with sloped lift tops almost invariably require a user either to stand or to sit on a tall stool. Examples like this are frequently called schoolmaster desks, but the incidence of such desks even today suggests that there must have been many more desks than schoolmasters. The truth is that they were used in stores, in homes, on farms, and perhaps even in schools. They were made too as box desks, without legs, for use on tables and counter tops. The example illustrated is of a common design but of a not-so-common material, figured maple.

1830–60

Mr. & Mrs. Gladstone Thomson, Port Hope

307. A variant form is the desk with a sloped writing surface which is fixed in position. Perhaps it could as easily be classified a writing-table. Two drawers provide limited storage and the space between is to accommodate the writer's knees — this desk can be used while seated. The decorative gallery is of an unfamiliar fretwork pattern. The woods are birch and whitewood and the original finish was a brown stain. It was found in Lanark County.

1850–70

Ministry of Industry and Tourism, Ontario

308. Even less common is this folding box desk on frame in a provincial Sheraton style with a pediment of Empire flavour. Found in Ottawa, it is made entirely of cherry. The mushroom-shaped brass pulls have facings with rosette patterns.

309. When the compact box desk is opened, it offers a felt-covered, sloped writing surface, which itself is hinged at its centre to allow access above and below to the storage area of the box.

1820–40

National Historic Sites Service, Ottawa

310. A slope-front desk without a bank of drawers below is not common in Ontario furniture. This is a pleasing provincial version of a Sheraton style, made of butternut with birch legs and having a long drawer of curled maple. It was found in Grenville County. The familiar technique used to inhibit warping of the writing panels of almost all slope-front desks is readily seen in this illustration: a narrow section of the same wood is glue-jointed to each end of that panel with grain running at right angles to it.

1820–40

National Historic Sites Service, Ottawa

311.   The table desk is a form developed from the basic
writing table. Drawers useful to writing needs flank a
kneehole space in this provincial Sheraton-style piece
made of cherry. This form with its flat writing top occurs
much less frequently in Ontario than other desks; the
flat-top desk without legs but with full pedestal ends
containing drawers became familiar, particularly for
office use, after 1850.

1825–40

Mr. Paul Godfrey, Port Hope

312. This thoroughly countrified version of a table desk
was found in Lanark County. It is made of pine and
had originally a black paint finish. Chamfering of heavy
square legs is frequent in country pieces but the treatment at the foot is unusual; whether or not by design,
the maker has produced something that just suggests the
spade foot of formal Hepplewhite tradition.

1830–50

Mr. & Mrs. Blake McKendry, Elginburg

313. Some call this form a bureau desk — it looks like a chest of drawers when closed; and in North America the word "bureau" has been corrupted so that it is often used to mean chest of drawers. It may also be called a fall-front desk; the upper drawer front falls forward to become a writing surface and to reveal a compartment with pigeon-holes and small drawers. The entire compartment actually is a drawer and must be drawn out the distance shown in this illustration to serve adequately as a writing desk. The hinged writing surface is supported by arc-shaped metal pieces called quadrants. This example, found in Durham County, is of a late-Empire style. The case is cherry and the drawer fronts, the chest face, and the interior fittings are largely of curled and bird's-eye maple veneered on pine.

1835–50

Mrs. H. C. Walker, Toronto

314. Except that it lacks the requisite doors, this piece from eastern Ontario is very much a provincial rendering of the form of the delicate tambour desk popular in Britain and the United States about 1800. Tambour doors are flexible, consisting of thin strips of wood glued to a fabric backing, and in such a desk as this would slide in grooves into recesses at either end of the cabinet. It is a sophisticated concept and the provincial cabinetmaker who produced this birch piece possibly felt that the no-nonsense framed doors were more suitable. The writing-surface plan is the same as for most tambour desks; a hinged lid opens forward and is supported by a pair of slides like those familiar in slope-front desks. The writing surface and the panelled doors are of curled or wavy birch.

1810–30

Naval & Military Establishments, Penetanguishene

315. This secretary of ingenuous provincial workmanship is a modified version of a heavier Empire style; its formal-parlour prototype would have very stout turned pillars, possibly supporting the top drawer of the chest section. The unusual rendering of this example, although its shorter turned legs appear possibly to be an afterthought design, is actually less cumbersome than the high-fashion model. It came from a Lanark County home and is made of mahogany and crotch mahogany veneer, with pine and butternut as secondary woods. The slope front, of an almost imperceptible slope, has diminutive slides below, which present their broad rather than the usual edge surfaces for support. The glazed cabinet section above, as in most Ontario secretaries, is a separate unit, making it easier to move the entire piece of furniture.

1825–50

Mr. & Mrs. Murray Copeland, Ottawa

316. This Sheraton-style curled maple secretary or secretary-bookcase is from Welland County. What appears to be a very large drawer is really a hinged panel which falls forward to provide a writing surface. The Sheraton tradition combining turned feet or legs with a scrolled apron is not frequently seen in Ontario furniture. Fine detail finishing in this piece extends to the wooden pulls, each of which is decorated with an inlaid star pattern.

1810–30

Miss Marion MacRae, Toronto

317. Another curled maple secretary or secretary-bookcase has a large fall-front panel; when lowered, that panel rests on the fore edge of the table-like base and presents a felt-covered writing surface with a gentle slope. The glazed bookcase section preserves a more pure and satisfying Sheraton tradition while the base betrays a later character with its less delicate proportioning and heavy turned legs.

1830–40

Dundurn Castle, Hamilton

318. A secretary all of cherry comes from south-western Ontario. Its large fall front is panelled to match the pair of doors above; the writing surface inside is covered with black oilcloth. The uppermost section has adjustable shelves which are fitted snugly but not fastened to notched supports. Like the preceding example illustrated, this piece is made in two sections and as such could properly be called a secretary on frame.

1830–50

Mr. Gordon Postlewaite, Ottawa

319. An exceptionally fine secretary in curled maple is in the same continuing Chippendale tradition as that group of chests of drawers illustrated earlier and is attributed to the same Lincoln County cabinet-maker or makers. This piece exhibits the same distinctive features — quarter columns at the front corners, lip-moulded drawers, and fine ogee curved bracket feet. It too was acquired in Lincoln County and is made entirely in an eighteenth-century style. Most parts are of solid curled maple; only the small drawers and small door in the writing compartment are veneered in burl maple on pine. The brass pulls are all original. The writing surface is provided with folding metal supports but in actual fact it is supported when open by the edge of the chest base.

1820–40

Mr. & Mrs. M. F. Feheley, Toronto

320. The same secretary showing open writing compartment.

321. A desk which appears to have come from the same workshop as the secretary preceding was also found in the Niagara Peninsula. Only the horizontal moulding immediately above the fine bracket foot base differs somewhat in its profile. The pressed-glass pulls are of American manufacture and very likely are the originals.

1820–40

Mr. & Mrs. L. J. Ingolfsrud, Toronto

322. Still another desk in almost the same pattern is this cherry piece whose quarter columns and cove moulding at two levels are ebonized. Small drawers in the writing compartment have bird's-eye maple veneering. It is the only piece of this particular Chippendale-survival style with a tradition claiming origin definitely outside Lincoln County. A former long-time owner attributed it to a maker named Fuller, living in the village or township of Canboro in Haldimand County. Canboro, however, is not far from the Lincoln County communities to which comparable pieces are credited, and the possibility that this attribution is correct would suggest there may well have been a school, rather than just one or two furniture-makers, working in this survival style.

1820–40

Mr. & Mrs. John Harbinson, Agincourt

323. Still in the same Chippendale-survival style, this desk of cherry was acquired in the Lincoln County district where John Grobb worked. The interior fittings are finer than in most comparable pieces; small drawers are faced with curled maple. The brass ring-pulls and the small opalescent pressed-glass pulls are probably original. The large drawers above and below possibly were once fitted with similar but larger opalescent glass knobs. The white ceramic pulls are almost certainly later replacements. The slope-front writing panel is supported by a pair of brass quadrants. The distinctive gallery of spindles is to be seen also on some chests of drawers of this school.

1820–50

Gordon & Audrey Griffith, Jordan

324. This is a provincial secretary of bird's-eye and curled maple which is believed to have come from the Niagara Peninsula. The upper enclosed shelf section fits flush with the top of the slope-front desk unit. Its lines are so simple as to defy any close association with formal fashion standards. The contrasting turned and split-ring moulding which borders both panels and drawers is a type that was most frequently employed in the second quarter of the nineteenth century. The mushroom-shaped brasses are the original.

1830–50

National Gallery of Canada, Ottawa

325. A richly handsome secretary that was once the property of the Baby family in the Windsor district of Essex County is made of walnut and its front is veneered entirely in burl walnut. The entire design is reminiscent of eighteenth-century character but it has modifications that place it closer to the mid-nineteenth century. The ogee bracket foot is more chunky, less graceful than the earlier model that inspired it. The corners of the desk unit, the glazed shelf section, and even the moulded cornice have been smoothly rounded, a development that appeared not much before 1850. The bracketed border pattern in the glazed upper doors is a slightly earlier innovation. The pleated silk curtain tacked behind the glazing is new but replaces a similar curtain which may have been installed when the secretary was new; the treatment itself is a style introduced in Regency times.

1840–50

Hiram Walker Historical Museum, Windsor

326. A pine secretary found in Hastings County is in distinct contrast to the preceding example. This one is very much a country version, its slope-front desk section retaining a much earlier character than the bookcase unit above. Only the bracket-foot pattern is particularly out of the ordinary.

1830–50

Mr. & Mrs. Richard Hart, Picton

327. The choice of display items behind the glazed doors may confuse the definition but this romantic piece of furniture is really a secretary or secretary-bookcase. The drawer with its ogee-curved front is the hinged fall-front kind which opens to provide a writing surface. The adjustable shelves in the glazed section above were designed to hold books. The wood is walnut and figured walnut veneer. The eclectic mid-nineteenth-century style of this piece has distinct similarities to two other pieces illustrated in this book (Plates 376 and 412); all of them have been found in the Cobourg district.

1840–60

Mr. & Mrs. L. J. Ingolfsrud, Toronto

Cupboards

328. Open dressers are early in tradition if not always
in fact; historically, the cupboard with open shelves is
older than that enclosed by doors. Judged by style alone,
this could be a late-eighteenth-century piece, but it comes
from rural Lanark County where there was scarcely any
settlement earlier than 1820. This is kitchen furniture
and in the kitchen the changing winds of fashion were of
little concern. Such cupboards were made by carpenters
and joiners, frequently no doubt while the interior
woodwork of a house was being completed.

Decorative scalloping of end-boards, easy to accomplish as illustrated here, was possibly less frequent than
might be imagined. The projecting piece at each end at
floor level is called a shoe and is the visible end of an
inset cross-piece which makes it easier to move the large
cupboard without damage. The original red finish is very
much worn.

1820–30

Dr. & Mrs. Charles Danby, Kingston

329. A pine dresser with worn but original red finish
was found in the lakefront area of Ontario County.
Style, materials, and workmanship make a relatively early
origin possible; the shaping of the end-boards at counter
level, is certainly eighteenth-century in tradition.

1790–1820

Dr. & Mrs. Ralph Price, Port Perry

IX.   The open dish dresser was a popular piece of country furniture even as late as 1850. This one was found on a farm in Carleton County. An unusually interesting feature is the fretwork patterned frieze. The inevitable wood in such pieces is pine; the restored paint finish is also the most familiar among such country pieces of the first half of the nineteenth century.

Gibson House, North York

330. Popular tradition has it that pine furniture of the work-kitchen class was home-made. The truth is that most of it was made by persons who obviously had some training at least as carpenters or joiners. This large and handsome dresser was made by someone much skilled in joinery; note particularly the unusual and painstaking mortise-and-tenon work where the thick counter-ledge piece joins the vertical ends. The craftsman also devoted skilled attention to moulded panelling, to beading of edges, borders, and plate rails, and at the cornice to a fine kind of scalloping that verges on the sophisticated. The enclosed cabinet section, thirty-two inches from front to back, is unusually deep. Like so many old kitchen cupboards, its first coat of finish was red paint. It was found north of Toronto in York County.

1810–30

Mr. & Mrs. Howard Pain, Toronto

331. A smaller kitchen dresser of pine was acquired in Wellington County. Greater attention to detail, as in the doors which each have four panels instead of one, usually attests to an earlier origin. The particular profile of the moulding combination in the cornice, however, suggests a date closer to the middle of the nineteenth century. The late white ceramic pulls are not likely to be original.

1830–45

Private collection

333. The workmanship is of lower standard than in the other dressers illustrated but the maker made special efforts to ornament this pine cupboard. Exuberant fretwork makes it an appealing piece of provincial craft. Panel work in the doors adds further interest. Treatment of the cornice, almost a flat bevelled moulding, suggests a date towards 1850. It was made probably in Northumberland County.

1835–50

Mrs. Janet Ehnes, Bailieboro

332. Decorative attention to the small compartmented shelves adds considerably to the appeal and interest of a handsomely designed pine dish-dresser from Glengarry County. Note that plates are intended to lean forward on shelves when plate rails are provided. An open dresser with the same detail in shelf design, and acquired on the St. Lawrence front, is now in the National Museum of Man collection in Ottawa. The surviving upper shelving of another cupboard with this unusual treatment and which originated in Glengarry is in the collection at Upper Canada Village. It is almost certain that the three pieces came from the same workshop.

1800–30

Mr. & Mrs. Blake McKendry, Elginburg

335. Cupboards of architectural character and with decorative detail reminiscent of eighteenth-century Adam style have been found in significant number in the district along the Bay of Quinte, from Kingston to Belleville. This example came from a village north of Napanee. It is entirely of pine and shows traces of an original red paint finish.

1820–40

Dr. & Mrs. H. Allan Burnett, Wellington

334. A corner cupboard was sometimes built as an integral part of the finishing woodwork of a room, much as a mantel piece was built as a permanent immovable fixture. But most corner cupboards were movable, although size and weight tended to inhibit frequency of moving. They were often of architectural quality; the cornice and trim of this corner cupboard from Hastings County differs very little from the familiar trim used on principal entrance doorways in frame houses of the early nineteenth century. This piece is pine, retaining some traces of its original blue paint finish. Corner cupboards were sometimes painted as part of a room's woodwork trim. And most of the earlier examples appear to have been made in one piece.

1830–40

Mr. & Mrs. Walter Beevor, Stirling

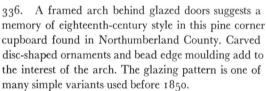

336. A framed arch behind glazed doors suggests a memory of eighteenth-century style in this pine corner cupboard found in Northumberland County. Carved disc-shaped ornaments and bead edge moulding add to the interest of the arch. The glazing pattern is one of many simple variants used before 1850.

1830–40

Dr. & Mrs. H. C. Burleigh, Bath

337. The inspiration for the glazing of this corner cupboard is Georgian English, as is the treatment of the frieze just below the cornice. Most unusual, possibly even unique, is the fall-front writing panel in the centre area. A single slide support is recessed in the centre of the rail below it. It is unusual, too, in a provincial piece to find brass hinges such as those used for the glazed doors and the fall front; the maker reverted to more familiar cast-iron hinges for the lower pair of doors. The wood is pine; the original finish was red-brown paint. The cupboard came from Halton County.

1820–40

Mr. & Mrs. Howard Pain, Toronto

338. Only a provincial craftsman, unrestrained by rigid codes of design use, could have used such a gleefully bold approach in interpreting the classical style as revived by the brothers Adam. With its combination of turned feet and a bracket skirt, there's something in the base too of the classical style generally credited to Sheraton. The compounded geometric design of the glazing pattern is a fascinating one even if not a smoothly finished concept. The cupboard, which originated in the Kingston area, may not be a best or a finest but it certainly ranks high among flamboyant late Georgian. The wood is pine but its original finish is not known.

1800–30

Royal Ontario Museum, Toronto

339. This illustration shows how many corner cupboards were fitted permanently into a room corner; in present-day terms, it was built in. Baseboard and chair rails are fitted flush against cupboard sides. The architectural character of this piece from the Kingston area is made almost overwhelming by the striking reeded pilasters.

1820–40

Upper Canada Village, Morrisburg

340. Narrow corner cupboards in this eighteenth-century pattern are common in Britain but little known in Ontario. This pine two-piece cupboard found in Lanark County is a provincial piece with the most familiar of all English Georgian glazing patterns. Although much worn, the original blue-green paint finish is quite evident. Oddly enough, although such narrow corner cupboards are relatively early, they are often made in two pieces. The upper section fits snugly behind a half-round moulding applied to the top of the lower section.

1800–1820

Dr. & Mrs. Peter Bell, Sharbot Lake

342. A corner cupboard with bowed front is very unusual in the Ontario experience. In this piece, found in
Glengarry County, the frame of the cupboard, the
panelled doors, and the three shelves inside all are bowed.
The ornamenting of the frieze, principally a piece of
appliqué fretwork, is not familiar in other Ontario furniture. The panels in each door are set forward from the
bevelled moulding to give them a sculptured quality. The
wood is pine, retaining much of its original red paint.

1800–30

Mr. & Mrs. M. F. Feheley, Toronto

341. A narrow corner cupboard of design very similar
to the preceding piece has an air suggesting it was among
the furnishings of a town rather than a country house.
The finishing detail work is finer. The wood is butternut
which evidently was originally finished with a walnut
stain. The somehow incomplete look of the bracket base
returns suggest that the cupboard was "built in" in its
original house in Brant County.

1810–30

Mr. & Mrs. R. L. Donaldson, Galt

343. For an Ontario country piece, this corner cupboard of butternut has a distinguished cornice; the two design components within it are to be found in formal English furniture of the Sheraton style. The pointed-arch motif is repeated in the lower pair of doors. The panel effect is unusual too; the arched panel design is routed out of a single board. Each of the three shelves in the upper section have a concaved and beaded forward edge. The cupboard comes from Lennox and Addington County.

1825–40

Mrs. H. C. Walker, Toronto

344. Reminiscence of the eighteenth century has faded; this cupboard from rural York County is almost entirely a forthright product of the nineteenth century. Detail treatment throughout has nineteenth-century flavour; the cornice moulding has a well-fed or well-packed rather than an elegant look; even the bracket feet bear little resemblance to Georgian prototypes. The long narrow panels in the returns and in the lower doors are all bevel with no central features — a nineteenth-century treatment more familiar when applied to the doors of houses. The woods are curled and bird's-eye maple.

1830–50

Royal Ontario Museum, Toronto

345. An odd provincial treatment of the classical revival has resulted in a heavy and extremely wide (sixty-six inches) cupboard with rudimentary pilasters, but these are surmounted by scarcely any cornice worthy of the name. Setting back the upper shelving so as to provide a convenient ledge became increasingly frequent towards mid-century. Like most country pieces, this corner cupboard from Leeds County is all pine. The original paint finish was yellow.

1830–50

Mr. & Mrs. Russell Harper, Alexandria

346. A large two-piece corner cupboard of butternut from western Ontario has the kind of modified Chippendale-survival ogee bracket feet often seen on furniture in those counties west of Lake Ontario. Its original finish was a brown stain. An out-of-the-ordinary detail is the lip-moulding of the doors.

1830–50

347.   This corner cupboard is a good example of the Pennsylvania tradition manifest in old Ontario. Foremost of the transplanted characteristics is the use of rounded arches to cap the glazed panels. The particular pattern of the bracket base is another; it is familiar on much furniture, including the common dry sinks, of western Ontario. The painted and grained finish is outstanding and one of the very best examples of this kind of work to survive in Ontario. The general style of the cupboard is eighteenth-century but most of the details are later. The cast-iron button latches, which appear original to the piece, are also of a kind not in general use before 1850. The grained finish is an impressive example of a popular art, one in which those settlers of Pennsylvania background excelled. The cupboard is all pine; its finish is intended to suggest mahogany with drawer and door panels in curled maple. It comes from western Ontario.

1840–60

Dr. & Mrs. Peter Bell, Sharbot Lake

348.   A Georgian-period tradition preserved by settlers from Pennsylvania was the building of corner cupboards with classically inspired Chippendale expression. But the results in nineteenth-century Ontario were hybrids. The cupboards here, frequently massive in size, came out in a distinctive provincial Chippendale-Empire style. The Chippendale contributions are the broken-arch pediment and the pleasing rounded arch formed by the glazed cabinet doors. The Empire tradition is most apparent in heavy pilasters or pillars, or both, and overhanging drawers with ogee curved fronts. This example, found in Wellington County, is all pine and it retains much of its original brown paint. Like most of its kind it was made in two pieces.

1840–60

Mr. Yosef Drenters, Rockwood

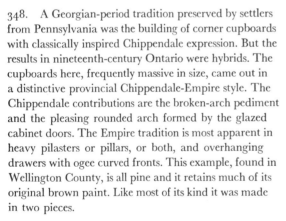

349. Cupboards of this hybrid character are usually massive; this example, seven feet high and four feet across the front, is a diminutive exception. Scarcely ever do cupboards of this type appear with a single glazed door. Its broken-arch pediment is a more than normally successful rendering of the traditional eighteenth-century design. The wood is pine and traces of old finish suggest it was originally mahoganized. Like others of its kind, it comes from western Ontario.

1840–60

Gordon & Audrey Griffith, Jordan

350. Like the design of this Waterloo County cupboard, its well preserved grained finish is of mid-nineteenth-century character. Books of the period illustrate painting and graining techniques of this quality. The cupboard is representative of its class in size — one hundred inches tall, sixty-two inches wide. Even though it is built in two sections, it is no small task to move it. Like most of its kind it has four turned feet at the front — one at each angle intersection — and a fifth at the rear corner. The graining is a brown-over-ochre treatment; contrasting darker brown is used in the bevelled fielding of the lower door panels. Special large and heavy hinges are used on the glazed doors of these cupboards; they project so that the pin on which the hinge swings is about two inches forward from the door face. This allows a door to swing open freely without interference from the bulky pilaster beside it. Oddly enough, the lower doors are almost invariably fitted with the usual butt hinges so that they can swing open only ninety degrees before being blocked by the flanking pillars.

1850–60

Mr. & Mrs. Donald Dunham, Milliken

351. Another unusually small cupboard of this distinctive Pennsylvania tradition is this piece found in Perth County; it is actually a little under seven feet tall. The rounded arch has been flattened and the flaring character of the distinctive pediment much subdued. What appears traditionally as a keystone feature surmounted by a finial has been transmuted here to an exuberantly carved sheaf of grain. It is unusual, too, in being built in one piece. The mustard-yellow paint finish is new but replaces what is believed to have been the original.

1840–60

Mr. Donald Pero, London

352. Small cupboards designed to be hung in a corner were not evidently common in Ontario; most that survive appear to have originated in western Ontario. This example in pine is of deceptively simple style; the regionally familiar treatment of the cornice moulding and the low-relief impression provided by those fielded panels must be credited to a workman with respect for good craft even in the making of a humble piece of furniture. The cast-iron button latch appears to be original. The original blue-green paint finish has been recently restored. The cupboard is fifty-seven inches high.

1840–60

Dr. & Mrs. Peter Bell, Sharbot Lake

353. Another small hanging corner cupboard, this one forty-seven inches high, displays the same kind of cornice moulding as the preceding example. This one is pine, has its original blue paint finish, and was found in Waterloo County.

1840–60

Dr. & Mrs. C. Stuart Munro, Unionville

354. A satisfying rendering of eighteenth-century classical-revival style makes this one of the finer pieces of furniture to survive from old Ontario. It is a well-disciplined piece of work in which the quality of design and craft is understated and ornament is subdued. This is a black walnut cupboard for storing household linens, in its period called a linen press. The bracket base is chastely Chippendale in derivation; so also the reeded quarter columns at the front corners of the base section. The upper section displays a simpler treatment of reeding on a flat corner edge. Decorative door panels and a reeded frieze add further interest. The bale brass pulls and escutcheons are old and probably original. It was found in the Niagara district.

1790–1820

Mr. & Mrs. John Harbinson, Agincourt

355. A linen press in walnut has characteristics that link it possibly to that tradition of Chippendale-survival work believed to have originated in Lincoln County. The old-style ogee bracket feet, quarter columns, and lip-moulded drawers are the primary common features. The cornice and the long, narrow fielded panels in the doors tie this piece firmly to the nineteenth century, probably its earlier years. The cupboard is in two pieces; the upper section has storage shelves. The mushroom-shaped brasses are original.

1820–40

Dundurn Castle, Hamilton

356. The very basic version of linen press has shelves hidden by two doors and drawer space below, just like the two preceding examples. It was found in Leeds County and its humble pine still retains some of the original blue paint finish. Turned "turnip" feet of this character were much used on case furniture in Ontario after 1820.

1830–50

Mr. & Mrs. Esmond Butler, Ottawa

357. A pine armoire of a design very familiar in Quebec was found on a farm in Russell County in the Ottawa Valley. It is, of course, a product of the French tradition in Canada and was made in the late-eighteenth or early-nineteenth century. No matter on which side of the Ottawa River it was actually made, it evidently was among the household furniture of an early citizen, probably French-speaking, of old Ontario. Traces of old finish indicate that, like so many other pieces of country furniture, it was once painted red.

Mr. & Mrs. Kenneth G. Roberts, Ottawa

358. In the search for distinctive label words, some would be tempted to call this a *kas*, an exotic word that in North America is primarily associated with massive wardrobes that the Dutch made and used in their Hudson River settlements. But this is a piece of Pennsylvania-German tradition, and the appropriate word in that vernacular is *schrank*. Whatever one chooses to call it, this western Ontario piece is one of the very finest in the province. This is refined provincial work in an eighteenth-century manner. Note particularly the excellent early-style ogee bracket feet and the hand-forged hinges, each with a flaring tail anchored to the cupboard frame. The wood is cherry. Old scars indicate that oval bale pulls of brass were the original drawer hardware. The elaborate escutcheon plates are perhaps less certain.

1790–1820

Mr. & Mrs. Henry Dobson, Plattsville

X.   A black walnut linen press, almost certainly originating in the Niagara Peninsula, features fine Chippendale-style ogee bracket feet, finely reeded quarter columns at the front corners, and a delicately moulded cornice. The drawers are edged in curled maple. The bale brasses are probably original. Although it is in an eighteenth-century style earlier popular in Pennsylvania, this Ontario piece probably dates from about 1820.

Mr. & Mrs. M. F. Feheley, Toronto

359. A wardrobe and a linen press may appear very similar but the wardrobe has a cabinet section in which clothing can be hung while the linen press provides shelved storage space. This pine wardrobe from Waterloo County has a grained finish, the larger area in a medium brown tone, the raised panels in darker brown, and the bevelled fielding in a yellow-brown. The quarter columns, just simple quarter-round moulding at the front corners, are painted green. Massive wardrobes like this normally were built in three sections — the base with drawers, the cupboard section with doors, and a separate cornice unit; the whole can be broken down readily to make occasional moving a little easier.

1830–50

Royal Ontario Museum, Toronto

360.   A wardrobe of similar inspiration but of distinctly nineteenth-century character is this butternut piece from Waterloo County. Older-style bracket feet survive and the cornice piece is moulded in a graceful ogee curve. The stars on each door are inlaid ornaments done in contrasting walnut and maple. The large wardrobe, over seven feet high and nearly seven wide, was built in three sections. The base with drawers is one unit, the cabinet or closet section with doors another. The section above the half-round moulding that caps the doors is the third unit. All fit snugly together but can be separated to make moving at least possible.

1825–50

Mr. & Mrs. Henry Dobson, Plattsville

361.   Much simpler in style, this basic country wardrobe
is yet in the continuing tradition of the two finer pieces
preceding. This one was built in two sections and it is
interesting to note that the moulding at the top of the
drawer unit is identical, though inverted, to the moulding
of the cornice above. It is made of pine and painted and
grained, the case pieces to simulate mahogany, the
drawers and the door panels bird's-eye maple. It originated in Halton or Wellington County.

1830–60

Dundurn Castle, Hamilton

362.   A wardrobe found in Welland County and made
largely of figured cherry is a basic piece of furniture but
one designed with an awareness of changing nineteenth-
century style. The long narrow panels, the split-ring
moulding, and the prominent cornice moulding with
rounded corners are mid-century characteristics. Inset
escutcheon pieces are ivory and, as in many cabinet
pieces, the key serves as door pull. The moulded cornice
is removable.

1840–60

Private collection

363. Excellent use of classical detail makes this a properly Greek and a thoroughly architectural cupboard. It was found in Lennox and Addington, just north of Napanee, and it resembles closely some of the finer doorways of early frame houses along the Lake Ontario shore. The eminently satisfying way in which the pilaster capitals are merged with the cupboard's cornice, the skilful blending of moulding profiles, and the varying of relief impressions indicate that here was a workman who thoroughly understood the revived traditions of classical Grecian style. The wooden pulls are later additions. The cupboard is pine and its original finish was blue.

1810–30

Professor & Mrs. A. R. C. Duncan, Kingston

364. This outstanding two-piece cupboard in black walnut is in that special tradition of Chippendale-survival pieces associated with Lincoln County. Although at this writing there is yet no supporting documentation, the furniture-maker often credited with this and similar pieces is John Grobb, who worked near present-day Vineland. Noteworthy features are excellent panelling, a creditable cornice, rudimentary quarter columns at front corners, and ogee curve bracket feet (presently requiring repair).

1820–40

Gordon & Audrey Griffith, Jordan

365. This pine two-piece kitchen cupboard is another
example to illustrate the strong craft influence brought
to Ontario by Pennsylvania settlers. Classical-revival
style is given individual expression; the treatment of the
pilasters, which make two right-angled turns before
reaching their capitals, is certainly a matter of severely
bending a style. The present pulls are late replacements.
1825–40

Mrs. H. C. Walker, Toronto

366. A pine and whitewood two-piece cupboard has that distinctive open counter found primarily in areas where immigrants from Pennslyvania settled. It is a kitchen piece, found in Waterloo County, with its original red paint finish in fine condition.

1830–60

Mr. & Mrs. Ronald Pequegnat, Guelph

367. A pine one-piece cupboard combines a cornice treatment more or less of Sheraton inspiration, a pair of pure Grecian pilasters, and a set of pointed-arch panels usually called Gothic; provincial craftsmen, unhampered by traditional rules, excelled at mixing styles and periods. It was found on Wolfe Island, in the St. Lawrence River near Kingston.

1830–50

Mr. & Mrs. Walter Beevor, Stirling

368. A "built-in" cupboard of architectural character originated in the Kingston district; although now installed in a different house, it probably appears now much as it did when newly completed. The neo-classic treatment was probably done by the craftsman who did the interior woodwork of the original house. The elliptical "sunburst" designs below the capitals remained popular long after the time of the brothers Adam, with whose names they are often associated.

369. Detail of the treatment of a capital of the same cupboard.

1820–40

Mr. & Mrs. M. F. Feheley, Toronto

370. The panel treatments as here combined make this country cupboard from Carleton County particularly noteworthy. It is also one of the few eastern Ontario cupboards to have a completely open counter-height shelf between enclosed upper and lower sections. Entirely of pine, it was originally painted a red-brown colour; the grained finish is later-nineteenth-century work in brown over yellow.

1840–60

Dr. James Hiscock, St. Mary's

371. Common in that district, black walnut was sometimes used even in making a basic kitchen cupboard in south-western Ontario. This walnut two-piece cupboard was found in Lincoln County, and, although pretty obviously a nineteenth-century product, it still retains the much earlier Chippendale-style ogee curved bracket feet.

1820–40

Mrs. Joanna Milder, Dundas

372. Cupboards with adjustable shelves were intended for books. In the case of this black walnut example there can be no doubt; on the underside of the removable cornice piece there is written in period script: "John Gortage Maker of this Book Kase Amherstburg April 6 1859". This modified, less-flaring treatment of the old ogee bracket-foot design is very familiar in nineteenth-century furniture of south-western Ontario.

Fort Malden, Amherstburg

373. Economy of line, economy of ornament, and economy of material together contribute to the thoroughly pleasing impression made by this bookcase of late-Georgian character. Found in Stormont County, it is a walnut two-piece product of a craftsman working entirely in a British rather than American tradition. Turned feet like these came into common use as alternate choice with a bracket base in the early years of the nineteenth century.

1810–30

Upper Canada Village, Morrisburg

374.   A two-piece cupboard of restrained Empire style is made of butternut and has a walnut stain finish. Plate rails, in this case narrow wooden strips nailed to the upper surface of each shelf, indicate that it was intended for storage and display of dishes. If the same model had shelves which could be adjusted according to clearance height required, one would assume it to be a bookcase.

1830–50

Todmorden Mills, East York

375. The heavy swelling brackets of the base section of this eastern Ontario cupboard were clearly inspired by that late-Empire style codified by John Hall in his 1840 book *The Cabinetmaker's Assistant*. The treatment of the pediment above, with its "chimney pot" ends, is also of Empire origin but of an earlier tradition. The wood is butternut stained, as it so frequently was, to suggest walnut.

1840–50

Upper Canada Village, Morrisburg

376.   An eclectic approach after 1850 found furniture-makers producing pieces impossible to classify neatly according to style. This bookcase of mahogany is representative; it has some vestige of Empire about it and yet it certainly isn't just an Empire piece. The pattern of the glazed panel doors was possibly exotic in the old Ontario of its period, but it is a design familiar in some eighteenth-century English furniture. It was found in Durham County, but it has some affinity of design and feeling with two other pieces of furniture associated with the nearby community of Cobourg (see Plates 327 and 412).

1850–60

Mr. C. Hardy Sifton, Cobourg

377.   A bookcase from Norfolk County and made according to local tradition by a cabinet firm in Simcoe is in a classical-revival style similar to designs published in the many editions of J. C. Loudon's *Encyclopaedia* from 1833 to 1867. It is a style more familiar in Ontario after 1850 than before. The maker used walnut and figured walnut veneer.

1850–70

Norfolk Historical Society, Simcoe

378.   This is essentially a plain country cupboard of a very common design, but the maker aspired to some degree of elegance and so he set the little cupboard apart by providing it with doors of lattice pattern glazing. The wood is walnut and the piece comes from Waterloo County.

1845–60

Mr. & Mrs. O. T. Fuller, Ottawa

379.   A red-painted pine cupboard from Renfrew County is of folk-craft tradition and really owes nothing to the style books. Crudely made if contrasted to elegant city work, it exhibits nevertheless thoroughly honest provincial charm.

1850–70

Dr. & Mrs. Ralph Price, Port Perry

381.　Even after 1850 the classical revival was still a source of inspiration to country furniture-makers. This large pine cupboard built in two pieces was found in the western part of Halton County. The white ceramic pulls and the spring latches appear to be original. The paint finish is dark brown.

1850–60

Mr. Yosef Drenters, Rockwood

380.　A pine two-piece country cupboard from Renfrew County is a simple product which relies for its appeal on the pattern of moulded panels. The cornice is built up with three tiers of the same moulding. The original paint finish was red.

1840–60

Mr. & Mrs. Blake McKendry, Elginburg

382. A quite astounding piece of provincial work is this splendidly conceived and heroically scaled piece of Ontario folk craft, an impressive example of the classical revival interpreted in country style. The wood is butternut. Its original finish was red paint and the present brown and yellow graining dates probably from about 1880. The fascinating pattern of the glazing work is possibly unique. The white ceramic pulls appear to be original. The woodwork of the house in Mono Mills, Peel County, from which it came, was apparently de-

signed by the same craftsman. Entrance doorway, partition doors, chair rails, wainscot, and fireplace mantel all were treated in the same boldly imaginative neo-classic way. Despite its size, eighty-seven inches high and seventy-three wide, the cupboard was made in one piece.

1840–70

Mr. Yosef Drenters, Rockwood

XI.   The Pennsylvania-style corner cupboard is a superbly deceptive piece with its excellent painted and grained finish of mahogany and figured maple applied to common white pine. It is a western Ontario cupboard of mid-nineteenth-century origin, yet preserving much of the traditional style of the late-eighteenth-century years. The splay-leg high chair in its original painted finish is an eastern Ontario product which similarly carried over an earlier tradition into the early nineteenth century.

Dr. & Mrs. Peter Bell, Sharbot Lake

383. The repeating Gothic-arch motif in the glazed doors of this Grenville County cupboard gives it a most unusual herringbone pattern. The wood is pine and the grained finish, more a rosewood than a mahogany simulation, is a restoration of the original. There is no finish or even cornice moulding on the left end since the cupboard was built to fit in a corner.

1835–50

Mr. & Mrs. Horst Ruhs, Carsonby

384. A two-piece cupboard from Waterloo County shows persistence of the classical tradition primarily in the application of half-round moulding strips which rise from three plinths just above the bracket base. The scalloped cornice and central appliqué strip simply prove that a country craftsman didn't have to take neo-classicism entirely seriously. The brown-over-yellow grained finish is about 1880 in style.

1830–50

Mr. & Mrs. M. F. Feheley, Toronto

385. A most handsome two-piece pine cupboard from Peel County displays excellent use of the classical-revival style, effectively humanized by the adaptation of a provincial tulip design to the neo-classic capitals. This is very fine country-style work, but like many provincial cupboards its lower section is quite noticeably plain; the major effort was applied to the upper section. Now stripped, the original finish was red.

386. Detail photograph shows fine rendering of provincialized classicism. Reeding in the frieze, spirally carved moulding, and the romantic, bead-moulded arch behind the glazing are effective features contributing to the cupboard's excellence.

1825-40

Mr. Eugene Rae, Malton

387. The chief interest of this two-piece pine cupboard from Waterloo County lies in the crude low-relief carving representing trees, birds, fish, coiled serpents, and a fan. The glazing of the doors derives from a Georgian English tradition. Although little finish survives, there is enough showing on the rail-piece below the glazed doors to show that it was once given a stylized graining.

1830–50

Royal Ontario Museum, Toronto

388. A large two-piece cupboard found in Lambton County combines an ambitious if ingenuous use of classical tradition in its upper section with a thoroughly utilitarian treatment of its base. This piece is a little over seven feet tall, a little more than six feet wide. The wood is pine and the original finish was red.

1840–60

Mr. & Mrs. Azel Guest, Whitby

389. Primarily a utilitarian kitchen piece, this small cupboard serves as a food safe. In a tradition evidently brought from Pennsylvania, the panels of pierced tin allow for ventilation and also provide scope for decoration. This example comes from the Niagara Peninsula and its wood is cherry.

1860–80

Mr. & Mrs. Horace Dahmer, Guelph

390. A very familiar kitchen cupboard, low enough actually to be regarded as a kitchen sideboard, is that with enclosed shelving below and two drawers above. Most of them appear in a rather simple Empire tradition, sometimes betrayed only by the familiar overhanging drawers. The formal dining-room sideboard of this basic design (see Plate 407) is much less common than the kitchen variety in Ontario. This example in pine, retaining its original red paint, is superior in design to most.

1830–50

Dundurn Castle, Hamilton

391. A second kitchen cupboard-sideboard is of an Empire style a little later than that of the preceding example. From Peterborough County, it is pine with a red stain finish. The lozenge-shaped escutcheons are maple.

1845–60

Mr. C. Hardy Sifton, Cobourg

392. The third example of this familiar class is a pine piece from Glengarry County. Pointed-arch panels, a somewhat different pediment, and a contrasting red and yellow paint finish make it a distinctly individual example among its many provincial fellows.

1850–60

Upper Canada Village, Morrisburg

Sideboards

393. This curled maple bow-front sideboard is an Ontario product in an unmistakable Hepplewhite style. The castors with square cups fitted to the legs may possibly be original to the piece but the bale brasses on the drawers, although quite suited to the style and period, are not. Scars show that the older pulls were circular wooden or brass knobs. The lozenge-shaped escutcheon inlay pieces are of walnut.

1800–20

Royal Ontario Museum, Toronto

394. A Hepplewhite-style sideboard of skilled design and craftsmanship is this fine piece whose full history is unknown but which has long been among the furnishings of the Governor General's official residence in Ottawa. The principal wood is curled maple; each drawer face has a veneered border of mahogany, cherry, and maple. The brass pulls appear to be the original. The decorative work in the four front legs and that in the arched area below the centre drawer is not inlay but a shallow routed pattern which has been accented with a dark stain.

1790–1810

Government House, Ottawa

395. A sideboard that was once the property of Sir John Beverley Robinson, Chief Justice of Upper Canada, gives the impression that it is a piece over which some cabinet-maker strove mightily to express fashion's full flowering without actually understanding the design of models from which he took his inspiration. This is Empire rendering, English Empire or Regency as it is frequently called. The Robinson sideboard owes more to the British than to the American manner of interpreting the French tradition. The pillars which terminate in carved paws would normally, in a North American interpretation, have been used only if the sideboard had pedestal ends, encasing drawers or cabinets. The effect, however, has been to produce a relatively light piece of furniture from a basic design that often results in something overwhelmingly heavy. The woods are cherry and curled and bird's-eye maple. The wooden pulls are not the original; restoring its Empire-style circular brass pulls would greatly improve it.

1825–40

The Grange, Art Gallery of Ontario, Toronto

396.   Another Empire-style sideboard of unique design
is this Prince Edward County piece made largely of
butternut and having a restored red paint finish. Front
legs in this form and as free-standing supports are most
unusual; they are more familiar when used as pilaster
pieces flanking enclosed cabinet pieces. The drawer faces
are of unusually thick wood and are cove-moulded in a
dramatic and unusual way. Whether or not one likes this
sideboard, it is an excellent example of the kind of work
done by some provincial cabinet-makers who incorporated individual expression into currently fashionable
style.

1830–45

Upper Canada Village, Morrisburg

397. From Durham County, this is a countrified version of a simple Sheraton-style sideboard. It has a butternut case with legs and drawers of curled maple. It appears originally to have had a pediment piece which ran along the entire back.

1830–50

Mr. & Mrs. Gladstone Thomson, Port Hope

398. This simple walnut sideboard acquired in Prince Edward County is a forthright, pleasing provincial expression more than an adaptation of some sophisticated but passing style. It is much enhanced by the raised, fielded panels of its two large doors and by the unusually patterned bracket base. The profile of the moulding of the top surface edge is one that was much used at mid-century. The drawer pulls are late replacements.

1840–60

Mrs. Alix Gronau, Hamilton

399. Towards the middle of the nineteenth century, Ontario cabinet-makers made many sideboards which are simple, solid, and remarkably free of excess ornament, and yet which usually retain some suggestion of Empire tradition. This small sideboard found in the Niagara district preserves the overhanging bank of drawers and a decorative pediment. The chief wood is black walnut; two forms of figured walnut are used on the drawers and the pediment.

1840–50

McFarland House, Niagara Parks Commission, Queenston

400.   This sideboard is representative of the better quality of design publicized in Loudon's *Encyclopaedia* after 1830 as "Grecian" furniture. In actual fact, the only thoroughly Greek motif to be seen is the carved ornament at each end of the pediment. This is a display piece that features a great deal of handsomely figured mahogany veneer; the secondary wood is pine. Because it has a rich and formal appearance, many present-day observers would assume it to have been imported, but there is no good reason why it may not just as likely have been made here. It stands today in the restored Toronto home of early citizen John Howard; tradition has it that it stood there during Howard's lifetime.

1835–50

Colborne Lodge, Toronto Historical Board

401. It could be classed a desk but it is more likely to have been planned as a small sideboard. It is largely of black walnut but the sides of each pedestal are butternut. The doors are each one single piece of walnut; a routed line has given each a pointed-arch panel effect. It comes from Grenville County.

1840–60

Mr. & Mrs. David Bartlett, Manotick

402. This is one of a pair of matching small sideboards in walnut, made evidently to fit two niches in the early-nineteenth-century Toronto home of D'Arcy Boulton, Jr., now restored as a period exhibition house. The sideboards illustrate the general style that Loudon in his London-published *Encyclopaedia* of 1830 promoted as Grecian. The handling of the walnut veneer banding is very similar to that in the wardrobe on page 9, Plate C, which also may have been made to Boulton's order.

403. A shelf above the top surface is surmounted by a scrolled pediment whose central feature is a carved representation of the Boulton family crest.

1825–40

The Grange, Art Gallery of Ontario, Toronto

404.   A small-size, though unusually tall, Empire-style
sideboard has a cherry case with carved cherry pillars
and feet. The two doors have panels of curled maple and
the long drawer is of bird's-eye. The other drawers and
the face trim are veneered in mahogany. The tall, narrow
drawers are fitted to hold wine or liquor bottles. The
brass-mounted glass pulls on these drawers are probably
original; the wooden pulls are replacements. Tradition
suggests a Kingston district origin.

1825–40

Sombra Museum, Sombra

405.   An Empire-style sideboard with an eastern Ontario background is made largely of walnut and figured
walnut veneer. The two drawers with wooden pulls in
the centre section are veneered in curled maple, stained
to blend with the rest of the piece. The pediment has a
dramatically panelled centre feature. The turned pillars
supporting the overhanging bank of drawers are comparatively light and unencumbered by the frequently
overdone carved ornament.

1825–35

Upper Canada Village, Morrisburg

XII. Furniture in the early-nineteenth-century French-Robertson house includes a butternut and figured maple chest of drawers that reflects contemporary neo-classic taste, a side table of late Sheraton style in curled maple with ebonized legs, and a Windsor side chair of a pattern once very familiar in eastern Ontario.

Upper Canada Village, Morrisburg

406. The cabinet-maker who produced this Empire-style sideboard was striving apparently for contrasting texture effect. The case is largely of cherry; the drawers are of curled maple veneer; the flanking turned pillars are of bird's-eye maple, as is the feature inlay strip above the bank of three drawers; the case ends are of butternut and the small Gothic-arch inlaid panel above each pillar is mahogany. The secondary wood is pine. The two deep drawers in the centre were intended for wine or liquor bottles. The pediment with broken arch would have been more successful with bolder treatment, greater flair. The sideboard was found in Lennox and Addington County.

1825–40

Dr. & Mrs. J. D. L. Howson, Peterborough

407. Mahogany was the fashionable wood for Empire sideboards, but local black walnut, being cheaper and more readily available, was often used in its place in Ontario. This compact example found in Northumberland County is the work of a cabinet-maker who made good use of figured walnut veneer on the varied planes of its face. The two drawers with convex facing can be opened with recessed finger grips. This kind of formal sideboard no doubt inspired the commonly seen Ontario cupboard or kitchen sideboard which duplicates its form in a simpler way and in lesser woods.

1825–40

Mr. C. Hardy Sifton, Cobourg

408. For an Empire-style sideboard, this is a piece remarkably lacking in ornament. If the pediment and the unusual scroll-shaped feet were removed it would be a severe piece. The wood is cherry, with pine secondary, and it was acquired in Waterloo County. One scroll foot is missing.

1835–50

Todmorden Mills, East York

409. An eclectic sideboard with a Norfolk County heritage is an unusual provincial piece with its row of bowed pilasters probably modified from the late-Empire style associated after 1840 with the Baltimore architect-author John Hall. The gallery formed of short spindles is quite out of the ordinary. The wood is black walnut with pine secondary.

1840–60

Norfolk Historical Society, Simcoe

410. This is an example of the John Hall late-Empire style in full bloom. The ogee curve is freely used on drawer fronts and in the flaring brackets that support the drawer section. The scroll form of foot is also very much a John Hall feature. The pointed-arch panel was used freely in cabinet doors of Empire work after 1830. The wood is butternut with a mahogany stain finish. It originated, by tradition, on the St. Lawrence front.

1840–50

Miss Dorothy Short, Ottawa

411. A heavy but fascinating provincial sideboard from Lanark County is probably a mid-century piece which borrows individual features from several different formal styles. The general character suggests the Empire but the pediment may have been borrowed from the rococo revival. The delightful pair of cocks, in appliqué, belongs exclusively to the inventive cabinet-maker. The wood is largely ash and the original finish was a brown stain. Wooden pulls applied to door panels are later additions; like many cabinet pieces, the doors were secured by locks and the keys served as pulls.

1850–70

Mr. & Mrs. Michael Palko, Spencerville

412. An eclectic sideboard displaying rich and effectively matched use of figured walnut veneer has the smoothly rounded corners and the top surface moulding that indicate a mid-nineteenth-century origin. There remains some feeling of the long-popular Empire style, but the bracket base is unusual in association with it. The distinctive shaping of the door panels is to be seen in two other pieces of furniture illustrated in this book (Plates 327 and 376). All three may have been made in Cobourg.

1850–60

Mrs. Lenah Field-Fisher, Cobourg

Clocks

413. This tall clock found in Ontario County has a sober pine case of a basic design little changed from a familiar British pattern of the very early eighteenth century. Hinges are of the rudimentary staple form and the door which provides access to the weights and pendulum appears never to have had a lock to secure it. Traces of old finish indicate it was once mahoganized.

Although clocks as time-keeping devices are essentially machines and therefore do not fall into the usual categories examined in this book, clock cases as such really do constitute a special class of furniture. Clock movements found in Ontario originated for the most part in the United States or Britain, but the cases, or at least the tall clock cases, to house them were many of them made here.

1780–1820

Mr. & Mrs. Azel Guest, Whitby

414. Designs of Chippendale tradition were the most favoured for tall clock cases, and the broken-arch pediment atop the hood is the most familiar and the most readily recognized feature. The reeded quarter columns at the front corners of the long, thin section called the waist are also characteristic of the Chippendale style, as are the particular kind of bracket feet here illustrated. This clock came from a home in Durham or Northumberland County. The case is all pine and it was probably finished originally with a simulated mahogany treatment.

1780–1820

Mr. & Mrs. Azel Guest, Whitby

415. Chippendale tradition is perpetuated in this clock case from Brant County, but the hood has been handled with less skill than the lower section. The delicate bracket base departs from the Chippendale line; it is rather a reflection of a Hepplewhite style. The chief wood is cherry and the accent pieces are curled maple.

1820–40

Royal Ontario Museum, Toronto

416. Contrasting patterns of cherry, bird's-eye maple, a little curled maple, and a single band of mahogany veneer just below the hood provide a richly varied texture for this provincial Chippendale-style clock found in Lanark County. The spiral quarter columns and the cherry-banded door are particularly effective. Considering the standards of workmanship in most parts of the case, it is strange that the short columns flanking the clock face are simply squared rather than decoratively turned in the familiar tradition.

1800–30

Mr. & Mrs. J. E. Flanigan, Brockville

417.   The tradition acquired with this tall-case clock claims that it was made for a Scottish settler in Grenville County in 1817. The case itself, made of butternut and finished with a dark brown stain, very likely is of local origin, but the face bears the name R. Whiting — and Riley Whiting's Winchester, Connecticut, shop turned out a great many clock movements between 1808 and 1835. His name is frequently seen on clocks found in Ontario. Like many provincial clock cases, the design and execution of its pediment is its weakest feature. The tradition of quarter columns on the waist section is replaced by a wide chamfer feature which is itself reeded.

1820–40

Miss Charlotte McDonough, Beamsville

418.   Perhaps the first impression is that this piece of furniture is a very successful exercise in veneering, displayed in rich colour and variety of texture. The second impression is that it is a tall-case clock and one that retains the basic feeling of the classically popular Chippendale design. But the bracket pattern at its base is Sheraton in derivation. The octagonal panel in the base, the moulding that borders it and also the pediment arch, and the odd use of scalloped trim at each side of the hood all are contributed by nineteenth-century taste. The veneer work is largely of bird's-eye maple and figured walnut; cherry is the principal wood in the hood. The clock works are German and the case was probably made in the Markham area of York County.

1830–50

Royal Ontario Museum, Toronto

419.   Formal tall-case clocks in mahogany frequently have brass finials mounted on the hood. For a simple, reminiscently Chippendale case of provincial pine, somewhat heavy, urn-shaped finials of local birch are substituted. Traces of red-brown finish survive. The clock was found in Lennox and Addington County.

1820–40

Mr. & Mrs. John Player, Waterton

420.   Very much a country clock case, this one has an ingenuous fretwork border to its hood. The wood is pine, painted and grained probably with mahogany in mind. Decoratively painted bands, now scarcely visible, are similar to those on the Woodruff clock which follows.

1830–50

Upper Canada Village, Morrisburg

421. A simply rendered country version of the classic Chippendale clock case is this pine example with mahogany-style grained finish. Subdued vertical bands with diagonal stripes can still be seen on the hood. Both clock face and the wooden case bear the lettering "R. W. Woodruff   Burford   U.C." The case no doubt was made in Mr. Woodruff's shop, but the wooden works, similar to those in the familiar Twiss and Whiting clocks, probably came from Connecticut; provincial clock dealers frequently lettered their own names on the faces of clocks for which they made cases.

1830–40

Mr. & Mrs. Guy Andrus, Kitchener

422.   The provincial craftsman who made this clock
case preserved the basic line of the formal Chippendale
design and yet he produced a piece of work very different
in spirit. It is solid, firm, reliable. The decorative quality
relies on scale and the use of excellent fielded panel work;
but at the crown the traditional scroll work, evidently
unfamiliar to this maker, became in his hands a whimsical bit of confectionery. It has a set of "wooden works"
and a clock-face painted in the colourful provincial
German manner seen in much Pennsylvania work. The
case is made of pine and is painted and grained in yellow
ochre and brown. Lettered in ink on the inner surface
of its panelled door is "John Alberth   Clagmacher
Baden". The assumption is that Alberth's Baden is the
village of that name in Waterloo County.

1820–40

Jordan Historical Museum of the Twenty, Jordan

423. A very simple provincial clock case of cherry and walnut has a rudimentary pediment that probably was suggested to the maker by some Empire-style feature on an entirely different piece of furniture. The clock works, which like all long-case movements could be mounted on a wall and used without a case, were purchased, according to local tradition, by an Essex County woman about 1835. Tradition and style both suggest that the case was made locally at least ten years later.

1845–60

Hiram Walker Historical Museum, Windsor

424. A walnut clock case with a Niagara district tradition has a pediment which reflects classical-revival popularity in the early nineteenth century. Otherwise its case is much like others of the late-eighteenth- and early-nineteenth-century period. Curled maple is used effectively in accent features against the dark walnut; the vertical bands within the broad chamfers on the waist section are veneered. The moulded and bracketed base appears to be new.

1820–40

McFarland House, Niagara Parks Commission, Queenston

Tables

425. A kitchen or dining-table of black walnut which was almost certainly an import to the Niagara Peninsula is of an early-eighteenth-century provincial style familiar in the German communities of Pennsylvania. The flat box or outside stretchers joining the turned legs have been much worn by the feet of many generations who have sat at it. The drawers are lip-moulded and their bale brasses are original. Secondary wood is pine.

Niagara Historical Society, Niagara-on-the-Lake

426.   This is either a late-eighteenth-century table from
Pennsylvania or an early-nineteenth-century table made
by Pennsylvanians newly arrived in Lincoln County.
The wood is black walnut. The box stretchers, mounted
with board edge up, are of a later tradition than those
in the preceding table. Drawer faces are lip-moulded;
the wooden pulls are missing. Splines, the lateral pieces
projecting at each end of the frame, are mortise-joined
to the top boards. The top is fastened by two readily
removable pegs through each spline into the frame ends;
this device was used by Pennsylvania Germans in Ontario throughout the nineteenth century. The castors are
not original.

Jordan Historical Museum of the Twenty, Jordan

427.   Another eighteenth-century provincial table has
two sets of outside stretchers bracing the legs. The top of
pine is old but not necessarily the original. The turned
legs and stretchers are maple or birch and their earliest
coat of paint was blue. The table was found on the St.
Lawrence front in Stormont County.

Upper Canada Village, Morrisburg

428.   The style of turning used for the legs of this table was familiar in the late-eighteenth century but provincial ways change slowly and this is quite likely to be a product of the early-nineteenth century. The turned legs and the H-form stretcher-base are of ash; the rest is pine, and the over-all finish is red paint. The table was found in Simcoe County.

1800–30

Dr. & Mrs. Ralph Price, Port Perry

429. A large stretcher-base table, six feet long, has legs and end stretchers turned in rudimentary style. Narrow boards butt-jointed to each end of the top serve to resist warping of the long boards. Most common kitchen tables of this class have tops fastened to frames with nails; this one has a top fastened by wood screws from below, in the manner of better-quality tables. It came from the northern part of York County. Its present brown paint could be the original.

1820–50

Dundurn Castle, Hamilton

430.   The style of turning of this small stretcher-base table suggests a late-eighteenth-century origin, but the tradition of survival of older ways makes it just as likely a nineteenth-century piece. Small tables such as this today are rather indiscriminately called tavern tables, but they were, no doubt, as often as not made for household use. Turned components are of birch or maple, the rest is pine. This table was found in Stormont County and its original paint finish was red.

Mr. & Mrs. Blake McKendry, Elginburg

431.   Although turned legs for kitchen tables was an eighteenth-century tradition brought to Ontario, the general rule in the pioneering communities of the nineteenth century was squared legs, often tapered. Stretchers in an H-form were general, light in feeling in the earlier years, solidly heavy towards mid-century. This example from Lanark County is all pine and its frame retains old red paint. The top is a single board fifty inches by thirty-two. Table tops often went without finish; they were used as bread- and pastry-boards and were kept clean by regular scrubbing.

1820–40

Author's collection

432.   A larger country kitchen table, six feet long, has
the familiar H-form stretcher-base, square tapered legs,
and an apron which is decoratively shaped on one side
only. Found in Brant County, its wood is pine and its
original finish was red.

1820–50

Dr. & Mrs. Peter Bell, Sharbot Lake

434.   Only a little extra effort was required to raise this plain rectangular kitchen table out of the most ordinary class. Simple moulding applied to drawer faces and around the lower edge of the apron made one simple but effective modification. A slight outward curve at their lower ends gives the tapered legs considerable style. It is a Waterloo County table of pine and maple, having splines through which the top is pinned at each end to the frame.

1820–50

Mr. Robert Meiklejohn, Toronto

433.   A smaller example, the kind sometimes called a tavern table even though it may have come from an abstaining home, has legs suggesting a Sheraton inspiration. The top is bird's-eye maple, the front, including the drawer, curled maple. Sides and legs, stained to suggest cherry, are of maple or birch. It was found in Lanark County.

1825–40

Mr. & Mrs. M. F. Feheley, Toronto

435. Sawbuck is the name applied to tables with an X-frame supporting base. In Ontario the sawbuck is a type that more often than not is rooted in the Pennsylvania-German culture. This stout kitchen table from Waterloo County has a pine top six feet long. The frame beneath is all of ash and painted grey.

1820–50

Mr. & Mrs. R. L. Donaldson, Galt

436. A very crude sawbuck table found in Simcoe County is largely of pine with an ash stretcher. It was probably intended as a work-table and there are no signs that it was ever given a special finish. Utility tables of this pattern were simple to make and probably were once quite common.

1830–60

Mr. & Mrs. Azel Guest, Whitby

437.   From Grenville County, a country dining-table possibly of unique design has an elliptical top ninety-five inches long, supported by an elongated diamond frame with an oddly shaped but thoroughly satisfying scroll-sawn leg at each corner. The legs are of maple and the other parts ash.

1850–60

Mr. & Mrs. Blake McKendry, Elginburg

438.   A hutch table is one with some kind of box-base and a tilting top, usually circular. It falls into the pioneer furniture class and must have been developed as a space-saving device for small homes. The shaped pieces on which the upright sides rest are called shoes. This example was found in a Leeds County home; it is made entirely of pine and bears traces of brown and blue paints.

1800–25

Upper Canada Village, Morrisburg

439–440.   This is not a hutch table but a chair-table, a
type evidently more common than the former in old
Ontario. There is no storage-box section in this piece but
rather a platform which serves as a chair when the table
top is tilted to the vertical. Hutch is an old term meaning
box and one often incorrectly used in the antiques trade.
This chair-table from Hastings County is pine and was
originally finished with red paint.

1820–40

Mr. & Mrs. Thomas L. Riedel, Bath

441. The chair-table as such is essentially a seven-teenth-century development that appears to have been quite popular in nineteenth-century Ontario. This example with a distinct and unusual style of turning is a brown-stained maple and pine piece from Oxford County. Like most of its kind, it has a top which hinges on wooden pins.

1825–50

Dr. & Mrs. Peter Bell, Sharbot Lake

442. It didn't provide upholstered luxury but in this position a chair-table did make a rather special seat, almost throne-like in character. This example from Ontario County is of pine and ash. A wooden dowel or a pair of wooden pins has been replaced by a steel rod on which the top now hinges.

1820–40

Mr. & Mrs. Reginald Owen, Whitby

443. Chair-table from Ontario County is made of pine and ash and retains its original paint finish of brown with black accenting of the chamfered faces.

1820–40

Dr. & Mrs. Ralph Price, Port Perry

444.   A table with four fixed legs and two hinged leaves
which can be raised and secured by slides or wings in a
horizontal position was called a drop-leaf or even a fall-
leaf table by common folk, a Pembroke table by the
genteel or the aristocratic. The principle, probably dating
from the seventeenth century, is essentially a space-saving
one. This particular example in mahogany tends towards the formal and has legs and shaped leaves in a
Sheraton tradition. Castors with cup attachments are
original. It was found in Haldimand County.

1810–30

Mr. & Mrs. L. J. Ingolfsrud, Toronto

445.   A drop-leaf or Pembroke table largely of cherry
is of the same basic design as the preceding example but
the spirally shaped legs testify to the growing influence
of Empire ideas. This piece comes from a family long
resident in Lincoln County.

1820–40

Mr. & Mrs. John Harbinson, Agincourt

446. An eastern Ontario Pembroke table of bird's-eye and curled maple is designed in a continuing Sheraton style but the moulding profile around the top edge was more commonly used towards the mid-nineteenth century. The legs retain an earlier turned profile style.

1840–50

Upper Canada Village, Morrisburg

447. The spiral treatment of these graceful maple legs is rather more a Sheraton than an Empire style. The table top and apron ends are of curled maple.

1810–40

Mr. & Mrs. M. F. Feheley, Toronto

448. With its gracefully simple turned legs, this is as chastely designed a Sheraton-style drop-leaf table as is likely to be found in provincial Ontario. It is a walnut piece and was found in the Niagara Peninsula.

1820–40

Jordan Historical Museum of the Twenty, Jordan

449. The most familiar gate-leg table has a fixed leg at each of four corners plus two on hinged arms which swing to support each of the leaves. The hinged leaves are often as much as twice the width of those on Pembroke tables. This example of walnut, found in Wellington County, has quite fine legs, turned and reeded in a Sheraton style.

1810–30

Mr. & Mrs. John Harbinson, Agincourt

450.   A less familiar type of gate-leg table has two fixed legs at diagonally opposite corners and at the others two swing legs which are moved to support the hinged leaf sections. This example from the Niagara Peninsula is in the simplest of Chippendale styles. The square legs are chamfered on the inside corners in a Chippendale-survival style.

1810–30

Author's collection

451. A walnut gate-leg table found in Wellington County has turned legs that one is probably safe in labelling a modified Sheraton style. This familiar kind of leg-turning was retained by country furniture-makers right to the end of the nineteenth century.

1830–60

Mr. Barclay Holmes, Vineland

452. This diminutive drop-leaf table with the look of a colt which has yet to grow up to its legs was found in Prince Edward County and has maple legs with a curled maple top. The turned profile of the legs is one associated more with Empire than with continuing Sheraton tradition.

1830–50

Mr. & Mrs. Murray Copeland, Ottawa

453. The large sectional table for dining is evidently an English development and is today frequently called a banquet table. Furniture-makers in old Ontario referred to "a set of tables". The centre section of this cherry example is simply a gate-leg table; two separate sections, each with four fixed legs, are butted against and latched to the raised leaves of the gate-leg unit to make a table 102 inches long. The style is Empire.

1830–50

Royal Ontario Museum, Toronto

454.   In the years since they were made, many sets of
dining-tables have been separated. An older generation
often passed on the gate-leg centre table to one child, the
separable end sections to another. The D-ends, as the end
units came to be called, made convenient side tables,
and two D-ends together could sometimes serve as a
dining-table. Here is a semi-circular D-end of walnut in
a graceful Sheraton tradition; it was probably made in
Norfolk County.

1820–40

Norfolk Historical Society, Simcoe

455. This D-end from a set of dining-tables is of solid curled maple and is designed in the most basically simple of Hepplewhite styles. It was found in Leeds County.

1820–40

Dr. & Mrs. H. C. Burleigh, Bath

456. This D-end table found in Lanark County has an unusual bowed top in a shape somewhat similar to the leaves of some Pembroke tables (see Plate 444). The turned legs are of a countrified Sheraton style.

1830–50

Mr. & Mrs. Esmond Butler, Ottawa

457. A D-end table in a Sheraton style has a cherry
top and legs and an apron of bird's-eye maple veneered
over pine. The economy which resulted in a three-legged
version appears to have been ill advised. It came from
Lincoln County and its brass cup castors are original.

1820–50

Jordan Historical Museum of the Twenty, Jordan

458. Side tables evidently planned for use with the long
side against a wall are often indistinguishable from D-
ends except that they bear no evidence of having had
latches, dowel holes, or other devices used to secure them
to other table sections. Here is such a table in a late-
Sheraton style with top and apron of curled maple and
hardwood legs which have been ebonized.

1820–40

Upper Canada Village, Morrisburg

459. A provincial Sheraton-style side table acquired in Toronto is made of walnut and retains its original brass castors. The decorative design applied to the bowed apron is not inlay stringing but is actually done in paint.

1825–50

Mr. & Mrs. Howard Pain, Toronto

460.   The legs of this table are a finer than average rendering of Sheraton design in Ontario; the overall scale is most pleasing; the applied spirally shaped moulding is an excellent finishing detail, and the black walnut used is rich and particularly satisfying. It represents superior quality among Ontario provincial furniture. The table was acquired in Norfolk County and quite possibly came from the same workshop as the D-end in Plate 454.

1820–40

Mr. & Mrs. L. J. Ingolfsrud, Toronto

461.   The relatively fine proportions of this side table allow one perhaps to call it late Sheraton rather than Empire. The spiral shaping of the turned legs is well handled and the twist in each leg runs counter to that in the leg beside it. This is a city cabinet-maker's piece but it was found in a village in Wellington County. The woods are mahogany and mahogany veneer. The original pulls almost certainly were the mushroom-shaped brass variety, although the scars suggest that a pair of pressed-glass pulls have also been used.

1810–30

Mr. Barclay Holmes, Vineland

462.   The sofa table, a drop-leaf type so called because
it is frequently used behind a sofa, is seldom seen among
Ontario furniture. This Sheraton-style example is largely
of cherry; the drawers are of bird's-eye maple and the
surrounding frame of mahogany, both veneered over
pine. This piece is catalogued as originating in Napanee
and its cabinet standard is high among Ontario pieces.

1810–25

Royal Ontario Museum, Toronto

463. A very small curled maple table from Prince Edward County has greater decorative than utilitarian value. It is essentially an exercise in fretwork and might well be categorized a Victorian fancy. The lyre motif, still recognizable in the end supports, is one owing its popular revival to the Empire-style formulators.

1840–70

Dr. & Mrs. H. C. Burleigh, Bath

464. A pedestal candle-stand with a tripod base has a curled maple top in an eighteenth-century porringer shape. It is unusual, too, because it is adjustable in height; the centre post slides up or down in a kind of pedestal collar and can be secured with the top at any convenient height by a set-screw in that collar. It was found in Leeds County.

1800–30

Upper Canada Village, Morrisburg

465. This tripod-base pedestal table is of Chippendale style; the Chippendale tradition of the eighteenth century is best known in Ontario in this type of extremely useful and long-popular table. The snake foot and dish-shaped circular top are early design characteristics. Such pedestal tables, often used as candle- or lamp-stands, remained popular well into the nineteenth century. This one is largely birch with a brown stain finish.

1790–1830

Upper Canada Village, Morrisburg

466. Pedestal-base tables with small tops are frequently called candle-stands. More than any other piece of furniture, they perpetuated eighteenth-century English designs in nineteenth-century Ontario. The serpentine tripod-foot base and the turned pedestal, here of birch, are simple Chippendale types. The maple octagonal top is less familiar than circular and oval forms. It was acquired in Prince Edward County.

1790–1825

Mr. & Mrs. L. J. Ingolfsrud, Toronto

467.   In this eastern Ontario table of birch, the shaping of the pedestal with its spirally reeded urn feature is based on another Chippendale tradition. With a diameter of twenty-four inches it is larger than a candle-stand and very likely was regarded in period as a tea-table. The finish is brown stain.

1820–40

Author's collection

468. A Chippendale-style tilt-top pedestal table has the kind of foot some authorities call snake or snake-head; in this example found in Durham County this feature is more finely developed than in Plate 465. The hinged top is another feature associated with Chippendale's designs. Curled maple is the wood throughout this piece.

469. Detail photograph shows the blacksmith-made iron latch which secures the table top to the pedestal top when in horizontal position.

1790–1820

Mr. & Mrs. L. J. Ingolfsrud, Toronto

470. A thoroughly basic pedestal table found in Victoria County is designed in a manner suggesting the extremely simple and functional furniture of the Shaker communities in the United States. Pine with hardwood feet, it has been repainted recently to duplicate the original red.

1840–60

Dr. & Mrs. Ralph Price, Port Perry

471. A rather crude version of a pedestal table is a country-made piece from Lanark County. It is all pine and its four feet are scroll-sawn in a pattern indicating Empire influence.

1835–50

Mr. & Mrs. Blake McKendry, Elginburg

472. The Empire-period tradition is evident in the scrolled feet and the ponderously heavy turned pedestal of this quadrapod table found in Haldimand County. The rectangular top is of curled maple, the pedestal cherry, and the feet maple.

1835–50

Mr. & Mrs. L. J. Ingolfsrud, Toronto

473. This tilt-top pedestal table from Lanark County has feet of distinctly unusual design although the scroll form suggests the heavy-handed influence of the continuing Empire tradition. With its brown stain finish, the birch wood used looks more like walnut.

1835–50

Mr. & Mrs. Blake McKendry, Elginburg

474. Tripod feet of the earlier Chippendale patterns were usually modelled "in the round", but later provincial pieces based on a Sheraton tradition usually have feet of a constant thickness as cut from a board. The finial at the base of this maple pedestal, extending below the junction with the feet, is a characteristic little seen before mid-nineteenth century. The top and feet are of bird's-eye maple.

1840–60

Upper Canada Village, Morrisburg

475. A tilt-top pedestal table found in Durham County has a mahogany veneered top with an inlay feature of maple which was evidently inspired by eighteenth-century English work. The pedestal, however, is heavy and has a finial at its base, and the feet which appear a little inadequate for the superstructure are scroll-cut in the Empire-period way. The pedestal and the feet are maple.

1835–50

Mr. & Mrs. L. J. Ingolfsrud, Toronto

476. A pedestal table with an unusual and whimsical quadrapod base is a country-made piece from Lanark County. Its top is pine, the rest birch, and its original finish was evidently a brown stain.

1840–60

477. A fancifully modified pedestal table with four romantically shaped feet is an all-cherry country-craft product from western Ontario. Each pair of opposite feet is cut from one board; the two bow-shaped pieces are notched together and set into the pedestal base.

1830–60

Mr. & Mrs. Horace Dahmer, Guelph

478. This pedestal table entirely of pine might possibly be identified as the work of an ambitious whittler. The four feet betray some Empire influence but the pedestal, shaped to a near-hazardous wasp waist at one point, is probably original to the maker. It comes from eastern Ontario.

1840–60

Upper Canada Village, Morrisburg

479. A country table of special charm has a simple pedestal rising from a rustic crown formed by six bow-shaped pieces which serve as feet. Perhaps it should be called a hexapod base. The wood is all pine and its paint finish is black.

1840–60

Dundurn Castle, Hamilton

480. This Sheraton-style piece, frequently called a
drum table because the deep apron suggests that shape,
is an Ontario product in cherry. Reeding of the upper
edge of the feet, as in this example, is also familiar in
some of the more attractive early-Empire-period work.

1810–25

Royal Ontario Museum, Toronto

481. Heavier pedestal and scroll-shaped feet put this circular table in the Empire category. Providing an apron below a circular top was a means of increasing stability in tables of larger diameter; this one is forty inches across. Tables of this size were often used as a central feature in Upper Canada parlours. It has a birch top, walnut feet, curled maple pedestal, and walnut veneered apron.

1835–50

National Museum of Man, Ottawa

482. A large pedestal table with an apron which incorporates four drawers is particularly unusual in having a rotating top. Late Sheraton in a provincial manner is probably a safe way to classify it. It was found in Kingston. Butternut stained to suggest walnut is the principal wood. The brass pulls are not original.

1830–50

Mr. & Mrs. M. F. Feheley, Toronto

483. This is a pedestal table with a base one might call Empire, but it is really inspired by the English modified-Empire style called Regency. It is made entirely of butternut, stained to suggest walnut, and comes from Glengarry County.

1825–50

Author's collection

484. This late-Regency table is of a design derived from a French Empire model. The "triangular"-based pedestal table was very familiar in Britain. The base itself and the pedestal are largely dressed up with bird's-eye maple veneer, but the circular top is everyday pine. It was acquired from a York County family.

1835–45

National Museum of Man, Ottawa

485.   A large pedestal tilt-top table, forty-eight inches
in diameter, is that kind of piece in the English neo-
classical tradition that might be called Regency or
Empire or even late Sheraton. It is a transitional piece
of the mid-century period and probably was made in the
Hamilton area. The base is maple and the top is veneered
in bird's-eye maple.

1840–60

Dundurn Castle, Hamilton

486. This large tilt-top table is in the latest of the Empire styles, the kind associated with John Hall and his 1840 book, *The Cabinetmaker's Assistant*. Tables of this size, and this one is fifty-two inches in diameter, were often called breakfast-tables and certainly served sometimes as regular dining-tables. This example, which has a Toronto family history, is entirely veneered in mahogany. The secondary wood is oak.

1840–60

Mrs. J. R. Robinson, Waupoos

487. The designer of this odd piece began with a pedestal-table concept and then added four legs. The character of the turning suggests the table was made at the time of the Jenny Lind bed and the so-called Elizabethan revival. The underpinnings are made of maple, the top of curled maple. That top, essentially a square form but with four serpentine sides, is of a shape often used for mid-century parlour tables. This one comes from Lennox and Addington County.

1845–60

Mr. & Mrs. R. J. H. Roy, Ottawa

488.   The pedestal-base form was frequently used for sewing-tables, as in this example of late-Sheraton style. The canted corners were much used in the designs of both Sheraton and Hepplewhite. Drawers are divided into compartments for storage of sewing materials and tools. The pedestal and four feet are of bird's-eye maple; the upper frame is curled maple and rosewood veneered on pine. There is a "hidden" drawer in the upper right end. The original pulls were probably finer and a little more elaborate than the current replacements.

1825–40

Dr. & Mrs. J. D. L. Howson, Peterborough

489.   A walnut sewing-table retains some suggestion of Sheraton style but the quadrapod base is all Empire; the safe cataloguer would call it Regency. The top is hinged at the rear so that the case section is very much a shallow lift-top chest. Only the lower drawer is real. It was found in Ottawa but the underside of the drawer bears a Kingston address.

1830–45

Mr. & Mrs. M. F. Feheley, Toronto

490.   Probably intended as a sewing-table, this late-Empire piece is in the style most commonly associated with John Hall; the scrolled feet and the swelling pedestal are virtually trademark characteristics. Most flat areas are solid mahogany; all the curved surfaces and the drawer faces are veneered in figured mahogany. The pressed-glass pulls are probably the original.

1840–50

Upper Canada Village, Morrisburg

491.   A country version of the preceding table design was found in Northumberland County. It is almost entirely veneered in curled and bird's-eye maple; only the corner-post members of the upper frame are of solid figured maple. Secondary wood is butternut. The extended and pointed corner posts are probably a response to the kind of finial design seen in Plate 489.

1840–60

Mr. Paul Godfrey, Port Hope

492. An even more countrified treatment of John Hall table design is this thoroughly four-square product from Lennox and Addington County. Made all of pine, it has a painted and grained finish to simulate a finer mahogany piece, even to the conventional figured mahogany veneering of drawer faces.

1840–60

Mr. & Mrs. Mogens Philip, Markham

493. This sewing-table from western Ontario is Regency, the English modification of Empire style. The canted corners appeared in earlier British sewing-tables of Sheraton and Hepplewhite styles. The hinged lift-top is butternut which evidently was stained like walnut. The rest of the piece is bird's-eye maple, some solid, some veneered over pine. The linen-covered section below the upper frame is a deep well, providing storage space for sewing materials. When new it would have had a second covering of some more decorative fabric.

1820–40

Mr. & Mrs. L. J. Ingolfsrud, Toronto

494.   Small four-legged tables, most commonly with one drawer, sometimes as many as four, had many uses and may be called lamp-tables, candle-stands, bedside-tables and sewing- or work-tables. This example in walnut is one of several relatively fine tapered-leg tables which originated evidently in the Niagara Peninsula. Each of them has inlay stringing ornamenting the drawer face and sometimes, as in this case, the top edging.

1810–30

Mr. & Mrs. John Harbinson, Agincourt

495.   This sewing-table of cherry and bird's-eye maple veneered on pine was once the property of Mrs. John Beverley Robinson, wife of Upper Canada's first Chief Justice. It is a late-Sheraton-style piece and is clearly related in design terms to the tables in Plates 462 and 489. The mushroom-shaped brass pulls are the originals.

1825–40

Mr. & Mrs. G. Bagnani, Port Hope

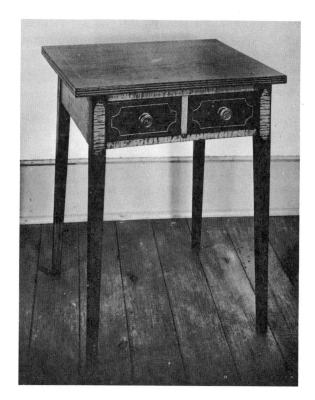

496. A more ambitious example of the design in Plate 494, which one could justifiably call provincial Hepplewhite, is a two-drawer table found in Brant County. The fine stringing work on drawer faces, top surface, and top edges may suggest a common origin with the preceding piece. Legs are cherry and the top and drawer faces are mahogany. Veneered panels and the drawer frame rails are curled maple. The original brasses bear a United States coat of arms but this does not necessarily mean that the table itself was not made in Ontario.

1810–30

Mr. & Mrs. R. L. Donaldson, Galt

497. Much less fine than the preceding example, a butternut table found in the Ottawa area still retains a Hepplewhite-survival character. Unusually tall, this table is thirty-six inches high; most in this group are about twenty-eight inches. The brasses are new but are similar in style to the original.

1820–40

Author's collection

498. A provincial **Hepplewhite**-style drop-leaf table has a bowed apron front and back, conforming to the curve of the top surface. It is all curled maple and was found in Prince Edward County.

1820–40

Mr. Paul Godfrey, Port Hope

499. Romantic bracketing of the apron adds considerable appeal to what is otherwise a plain and heavy table from Lanark County. Legs are of ash and the other parts pine; the original paint finish was red.

1820–40

Mr. William Brebner, Lanark

500. A small country table from Perth County has oddly shaped legs and that form of removable top familiar in larger tables made in a Pennsylvania-German tradition. The use of splines is the same as in the tables in Plates 426 and 434. It is entirely cherry, even to the pins which secure the top to the frame. The black ceramic pull is probably original.

1840–60

Mr. & Mrs. Horace Dahmer, Guelph

501. An unmistakably Sheraton-style cherry table from Northumberland County is much finer than the average in its old Ontario class. Turning and reeding of the legs is especially noteworthy. The wooden pulls, although suited to the period and evidently original, are coarse in contrast to the fine work on the legs.

1810–35

Dr. & Mrs. C. Stuart Munro, Unionville

502.   Another finer than average Sheraton-style table, this one from the Niagara Peninsula is even lighter in treatment than the preceding example. Again the legs are finely turned and reeded but an added refinement is the fine finishing moulding applied to the lower edge of the case. The wood is walnut and the present pressed-glass pull has replaced a larger circular brass pull.

1810–30

Royal Ontario Museum, Toronto

503.   A table of late-Sheraton style has more elaborate but less fine turning work than the two preceding examples. The scrolled rail below the drawers adds immensely to the appeal of this walnut and curled maple piece. Inlay bands in the drawer faces are mahogany. The glass pulls are not the originals.

1820–40

Royal Ontario Museum, Toronto

504. This table is unusual and therefore rare among Ontario furniture but it is not really beautiful. Late-Sheraton in style, it has legs in which the spirally carved sections are not well integrated with the turned sections; this failing would be less noticeable if the table had a larger top. It was found in Prince Edward County and is largely of curled maple. The drawer is of bird's-eye maple and mahogany veneered over the secondary butternut.

1825–40

Mr. & Mrs. H. Larsen, Sydenham

505. A mahogany table is in the Empire style as interpreted in the United States. The carving of the legs in a spiralled rendering of the old acanthus-leaf motif is characteristic. Figured mahogany veneer is used on drawer faces and the surrounding frame. The brass bale-type pulls are earlier in style than one would normally expect on a sophisticated piece of this period.

1810–30

Bellevue House, Kingston

506. An Ontario table of provincial-Sheraton style combines walnut top and sides with cherry legs. Bird's-eye maple veneer is used for inlay panels and drawer facings. Drawers are also bordered with strips of walnut veneer.

1825–40

Mr. & Mrs. M. F. Feheley, Toronto

507. Retaining some feeling of Sheraton tradition, this country table from Brant County is all butternut except for the drawer face of walnut. Turning is extremely simple but very fine and completely suited to this piece of provincial character.

1830–50

Mr. William Brebner, Lanark

508. Probably designed as a sewing-table, this Sheraton-style piece found in Frontenac County is of curled and bird's-eye maple. There are two drawers in the front and one in the right end; what appears to be a top drawer at the front is an immovable panel with useless pulls. The inset escutcheons are ivory. The edging of the top surface is reeded.

1820–40

Mr. & Mrs. J. E. Flanigan, Brockville

509. A three-drawer table found in Lanark County is in a simplified Sheraton style and is made of butternut and birch. It was probably stained originally to suggest walnut. The brass pulls and cup-castors are original. The kind of moulding around the top surface makes this piece probably ten or more years later than the preceding table.

1830–50

National Historic Sites Service, Ottawa

510. This later-Sheraton-style table comes with a family tradition that it was used in an officers' mess, possibly at Fort George on the Niagara River, in the 1830s. The principal wood is walnut; the three drawers have a curled maple veneer over pine. The brass pulls are the originals.

1825–40

Mr. & Mrs. Mogens Philip, Markham

511. Late-Sheraton table from eastern Ontario is of maple with curled maple drawers. Provincial furniture-makers continued to use Sheraton-style turning profiles through much of the nineteenth century, but legs became increasingly heavy with the passing years.

1830–50

Mr. & Mrs. Esmond Butler, Ottawa

512. A small table with its drop leaves shaped on a pattern familiar in more formal Pembroke tables was found in Lincoln County. Although no larger than the average candle- or lamp-table, this one has a drawer, necessarily shallow, at each end. The drawer faces are convex. The square section in the legs is out of the ordinary but by no means rare. Low-relief carving decorates the uppermost flat facing of each leg. The table is of cherry except for curled maple drawers.

1825–50

Mrs. Floyd Crabtree, St. Catharines

513. Its diminutive size makes it convenient to group this piece acquired in Peterborough County with the candle- and lamp-tables, but it is simply a shortened version of the familiar provincial Pembroke or drop-leaf table. The turning of the legs reflects Sheraton tradition, although it is unlikely that this cabinet-maker had ever heard the name of that English style-setter. The two leaves are of butternut, the rest walnut.

1830–50

Mr. & Mrs. John Matthews, Stoney Lake

514. The greatly increased size of the drawers makes this small table unusual if less graceful. It comes from Waterloo County and is all walnut. Panelled end construction is also out of the ordinary; in fact, the piece comes close to falling into the chest-of-drawers class.

1835–50

Author's collection

515. A mahogany card-table in Sheraton style is of a highly sophisticated standard compared to most surviving Ontario furniture. It was found in Glengarry County but its style suggests it may have originated in Montreal. The top is hinged at the centre so that the table can be used, half size, against a wall. Two legs at the rear swing to support the hinged leaf when the table is in use for games or at tea-time.

1810–30

Mr. & Mrs. M. F. Feheley, Toronto

516.   A duplicate of the preceding table acquired some years earlier appears to have come from the same home in Glengarry County.

1810–30

Royal Ontario Museum, Toronto

517.   A mahogany card-table in a classical-revival tradition associated with Sheraton belonged in the early years of the nineteenth century to the Baby family in the Detroit River settlement. The felt-covered top is hinged at the centre and can be folded to half size. It pivots ninety degrees then so that the reduced top is centred over the pedestal.

1815–30

Hiram Walker Historical Museum, Windsor

518.   An Empire-style mahogany card-table folds in the same manner as the preceding example. The carving of the pedestal and the base, incorporating classical-revival features with paw-type feet, is representative of the Empire style as popular about 1830. This table was found in Carleton County.

1825–40

Dundurn Castle, Hamilton

519–520.   Two card-tables in the rococo-revival style of the mid-nineteenth century are among the furniture made about 1860 especially for the official residence of Canada's Governor General. There are no labels or markings to distinguish the products of one furniture firm from another, nor is there any distinguishable difference in the quality of design or workmanship in the furniture of this class surviving at Rideau Hall. The Toronto partnership of Jacques and Hay is one of three Canadian firms known to have supplied that furniture, and it is quite likely that one, or even both, of these tables were made in its shops. The tables are well carved of black walnut and each has a hinged, felt-covered top.

Government House, Ottawa

Washstands

521. Washstands, or wash-hand-stands as they were generally called in the nineteenth century, are modified tables, sometimes even small cupboards but yet with a top surface about waist high. The primary purpose is to support a basin for wash-water; sometimes there is a circular hole in the top into which a basin fits. This example is of countrified Sheraton style and has a broken-arch pediment similar to that type frequently used on a tall-case clock.

1820–40

Upper Canada Village, Morrisburg

522. A rustic washstand, a simplified version of the preceding example, has a pediment suggesting an Empire derivation. It is an eastern Ontario piece of pine, retaining most of its old red paint.

1830–50

Mr. & Mrs. Blake McKendry, Elginburg

523. This is a provincial version of a fine Sheraton-style piece which would have been made in mahogany or walnut. This uncommon country version is made of pine and whitewood and appears to have been finished originally in a red-brown paint. The smaller hole in the top surface will hold a glass or perhaps a toothbrush-holder. The lower shelf might support a water ewer or even a slop-basin.

1825–40

Mrs. H. C. Walker, Toronto

524. A washstand from Durham or Ontario County in somewhat the same tradition as the preceding example is of pine and whitewood and was originally painted or stained. The bowed feet, which are continuations of the front stiles, are most unusual. The enclosed cupboard space might hold a ewer, slop-jar, or chamber-pot.

1830–50

Mr. & Mrs. Reginald Owen, Whitby

525. Countrified late Sheraton is the style classification for this cabinet washstand. The combination of three drawers is rather more odd than beautiful; the builder provided no easy way to open the two with convex fronts. The wood is mainly cherry; two door panels and the convex drawer fronts are bird's-eye maple.

1830–50

Black Creek Pioneer Village, Toronto

526. Painted and grained in a rather extreme kind of mahoganizing, this washstand is a flamboyant country-style Empire-period piece. Note that the turning of the front legs differs from that of the rear. It is mainly of pine and was found in Ottawa.

1830–50

National Historic Sites Service, Ottawa

527. A washstand with a trestle base and made entirely of curled maple is a piece of provincial work of late-Sheraton style. It was found in eastern Ontario.

1830–50

Mr. Paul Godfrey, Port Hope

528. This washstand of late-Empire style came from the same Lennox and Addington home and very likely the same maker as the table in Plate 492. The scrolled feet and the heavy-set pedestals are familiar features in that final wave of the classical revival before romantic rococo returned to favour. This piece is pine and was originally finished to simulate mahogany. The present finish is a yellow and brown graining of a type popular in the last twenty years of the nineteenth century.

1840–60

Mr. & Mrs. Mogens Philip, Markham

529. Washstands with towel-rails were little seen before 1840 but were the norm after 1850. This example from western Ontario is not a particularly handsome furniture design but it is interesting for the sake of its peasant-style decoration and for the Lilliputian looking-glass affixed to the pediment. In the case of washstands, of course, the word pediment might more realistically be rendered as splash-board. This piece is pine with a base coat of red, black or umber "finger" painting on the top and the shelf below, and stylized circular flower decorations in stencilled gold.

1845–60

Mr. & Mrs. Howard Pain, Toronto

530. Matching washstands all of walnut were made reputedly by a cabinet-maker in Hamilton as a wedding present for a prominent Dundas couple. With a kind of late Sheraton feeling, they are superior in quality to the average washstands of the period; note the gallery around each lower shelf. Identical in style, "his" is a little taller than "hers" and has a larger basin-hole in its top surface.

1850–65

Dundas Historical Society Museum, Dundas

531.   The style of turning in this piece suggests the mid-nineteenth-century Elizabethan revival. The wood is walnut. The workmanship and the shaping of the pediment is better than average, and the provision of two basin-holes suggests interestingly a certain intimacy at ablution time. It comes from Oxford County.

1850–70

Mr. & Mrs. Henry Dobson, Plattsville

532. Although bowed-front corner washstands were made in fine wood versions in Hepplewhite and Sheraton styles, this piece seems innocent of the manners and motifs most frequently associated with those worthy Georgians. Found in Northumberland County, it is a fine piece of provincial craft, made of a mixture of woods: butternut, whitewood, and pine. The relief carving may be of comparatively low grade in sophisticated company but it is evidence in provincial work of some aspiration to what at a later period were described as the better things of life.

1830–50

Mr. & Mrs. Mogens Philip, Markham

533. Representative of the common cabinet washstand, completely enclosed and incorporating one drawer, this eastern Ontario piece is outstanding for the sake of its unusual painted decoration. It is made of pine, whitewood, and butternut. The base colour is light brown and the free-hand designs are applied in green, red, dark brown, and white.

1840–60

Dr. & Mrs. Charles Danby, Kingston

534. The word commode has several valid meanings, and this commode or commode-stand is the one that is closely allied to the washstands and is that piece of furniture intended to sit beside a bed and to hide a chamberpot. This piece with its overhanging serpentine drawer suggests some recollection of Empire style and it was, no doubt, part of a matched set of "cottage" bedroom furniture, the kind of low-cost furniture much recommended in Downing's *Architecture of Country Houses*, published in New York in 1850. This piece, found in Grenville County, is largely of pine. Its base colour is pale green and the painted decoration is in pink, red, dark green, and gold.

1845–60

Mr. & Mrs. J. E. Flanigan, Brockville

535.   A cabinet washstand with a gallery verging on the fantastic is a country product from the Quinte shore of the County of Lennox and Addington. The wood is ash and pine and it appears at one time to have been painted black. The cast-iron spring latch is of a kind little known at 1850 but in general use before 1870.

1860–80

Dr. & Mrs. H. C. Burleigh, Bath

536.   A mahogany and mahogany veneer washstand has the overhanging drawer feature and the general neo-classical character which can be attributed either to Empire or to continuing Sheraton traditions. The use of marble tops, with serpentine edge to match that of the drawer front, was introduced about 1840 but became much more familiar in the 1850s and later.

1840–60

Dundurn Castle, Hamilton

537. This cherry washstand is a country version of the mahogany example preceding. The bracket base and serpentine drawer derive from the same traditions. This piece comes from Oxford County and all the wood showing, even the towel-rails, is cherry.

1850–70

Mr. & Mrs. Ronald O'Hara, St. Mary's

Looking-glasses

538. The fret-sawn frame of this mirror is a rococo style of the Chippendale period but one whose popularity may have persisted into the early years of the nineteenth century. Looking-glass rather than mirror was the familiar period term but whatever they were called they were precious, the kind of piece likely to have come with the settler's effects when heavier furniture could not be carried. Mahogany or walnut is the wood more frequently used for eighteenth-century frames of this particular style and the use of curled maple here makes it more possible that this one may have been made in Upper Canada. The frame is thirty-one inches high.

1780–1810

Upper Canada Village, Morrisburg

539. Another fretwork frame of Chippendale rococo style, this one found in a Lanark County home is of mahogany veneered on pine. The principal supporting part has a wide bevelled section, a feature which makes it unusual for the eighteenth century; it may or may not be an early-nineteenth-century Ontario product. The glass with crackled silvering, extremely precious when new, is probably the original.

1790–1820

Dr. & Mrs. Peter Bell, Sharbot Lake

540. Looking-glasses came in many variants of neo-classical style but the frames of most were decorated with devices of architectural origin. A very familiar type has a divided frame with a piece of mirror-glass filling the lower and larger area and painting on glass (in reverse) mounted in the upper area. Many came, as merchants' advertisements indicate, from the United States but others originated here. The original gilding over gesso, as in the case of this looking-glass found in Leeds County, has often been covered with later coats of cheap gold paint. The greater number of framed mirrors of this class surviving in Ontario can be classed with the American Empire style.

1810–30

Mr. & Mrs. Blake McKendry, Elginburg

541. A looking-glass found in Northumberland County has a frame of mahogany and mahogany veneer. The split-baluster pieces are turned and carved very much in American Empire style. Although some examples did appear originally with two mirror sections, it is difficult to be certain that an upper reflecting glass is not a substitute for a broken reverse painting.

1820–40

Mrs. Lenah Field-Fisher, Cobourg

542. A looking-glass from western Ontario has a mahogany frame holding a piece of mirror so much worn and flaked that it must be the original. Empire-style mirrors frequently appear with a split-baluster device below the cornice and the same material framing the glass.

1820–40

Dr. & Mrs. C. Stuart Munro, Unionville

543. A framed mirror of most forthright American Empire style came from a Leeds County home. The split-baluster framing is finished in contrasting black and gold. The inner frame is yellow. Corner medallions are moulded in gesso although often these features are in brass. Reverse-painting technique is always provincial and the subjects usually bucolic or sentimental.

1820–40

Mr. & Mrs. Blake McKendry, Elginburg

544. Basically very similar to the preceding example but a lighter version of it, this framed mirror was found in Prince Edward County. The split-baluster frame is black and gold; the gold for such work was usually gold leaf, whereas that used in stencilled decoration work was bronze powder. The primitive reverse painting is in blue, green, yellow, and red.

1820–40

Mr. William Brebner, Lanark

545. A looking-glass with bevelled mahogany veneer frame is a kind familiar in the same period as the common and more blatantly Empire-style black and gold framed mirrors.

1820–40

Upper Canada Village, Morrisburg

546. Over-mantel mirrors or chimney glasses are long enough to cover an entire mantel shelf; they were familiar in parlours or dining-rooms with fireplaces. The better known were of distinct neo-classical style with overhanging cornice, the entire frame inevitably finished in gold, and the mirror usually in three sections. It appears likely that most of them were of British or American origin. A contrasting example is this one made for his own home in what is now Toronto's High Park by John Howard. He makes mention of it in his diary in 1834. The wood is curled and bird's-eye maple with an inner mahogany frame.

Colborne Lodge, Toronto Historical Board

547. Representative of many dressing-glasses of the period is this mahogany stand with bevelled mahogany veneered frame from eastern Ontario. They were made in many different styles and patterns, were intended for use on dressing-tables or chests of drawers, and were frequently mentioned in the advertisements of Ontario cabinet-makers.

1830–50

Author's collection

548. This dressing-glass combines romantic and classical styles in a survival piece that might possibly be even as late as 1900. It is a Waterloo County piece entirely of cherry, featuring carved birds, a pineapple, and some geometric decoration, all motifs associated with the Pennsylvania-German tradition. The small oval mirror is mounted within a kind of organic lyre. The serpentine base is a box with hinged lid.

Author's collection

Miscellaneous furniture

549. A dough-box, dough-trough, or kneading-trough is a kitchen utility piece, a variety of chest known in every pioneer farm home. Although it may also serve as a flour bin, its primary function is to serve as a place to set bread dough to rise. Inside the box, of course, the dough is protected from draughts. The decorative relief carving, crude though it may be, makes this Leeds County box an unusual example. The handles are of smith-forged iron.

1830–60

Dr. & Mrs. Charles Danby, Kingston

551. The dough-box is usually a modified table that incorporates a chest or hutch section. This example is in a Pennsylvania-influenced style; note the splayed legs, the deeply overhanging top, and the splines through which the top can be pinned to the chest section. The cover is obviously a useful table-top, no doubt used to mix and knead the bread dough. The woods are white-wood and birch.

1830–50

550. A familiar style of dough-trough is this painted pine piece from eastern Ontario. Sides almost always taper. Earlier examples have dovetailed corner joints.

1840–60

Upper Canada Village, Morrisburg

552. A small functional kitchen or summer kitchen piece has cabinet space, a drawer, and a shelf probably intended to support a bucket of water just brought from the well. It is all pine, has a cast-iron spring latch probably of the third quarter of the nineteenth century, and was found in Waterloo County.

1850–80

Mr. & Mrs. F. M. Blayney, Waterloo

553. A Waterloo County piece that may have been made as early as 1860, this dry sink is earlier than most that have appeared on the antiques market in latter years. The dry sink, usually a low kitchen-cupboard structure, is so called because it has a trough in which dishes are washed in a dishpan. It may or may not have a drainage hole through which waste water can drip into a bucket below. Possibly very little known in the earlier settlements, dry sinks were mostly factory made after 1860; some of those surviving are twentieth-century pieces. It is a tradition most closely associated with Pennsylvania Germans. This one is of pine and white-wood. It has been repainted several times but the original coat appears to have been black.

1860–80

Mr. & Mrs. Walter Beevor, Stirling

555. This bucket-bench or bucket-stand is a utility piece of country-made furniture from Prince Edward County. It is all of pine and was once finished in that familiar red paint. For kitchen or summer kitchen use, it has two shelves, the upper one like a trough, suggesting that it may have been used as a dry sink.

1830–60

Mr. & Mrs. Thomas L. Riedel, Bath

554. A dry sink from Perth County has arched doors and an unusually decorative back piece, but it is probably no earlier than the preceding example. Made of pine and whitewood, it has traces of black and red paint and it probably once had a grained finish.

1860–80

Mr. & Mrs. John Harbinson, Agincourt

557. An out-of-the-ordinary clock-shelf is of a neo-classical style. It is forty inches tall and would be securely fastened to a wall by wood-screws through the flat vertical piece at the rear. It was found in Prince Edward County and is butternut with a brown stain finish; the drawer front is veneered in walnut.

1830–50

National Historic Sites Service, Ottawa

556. Simple clock-shelves were locally made in the early- and mid-nineteenth-century periods, scaled usually to the clocks which literally poured from New England factories to all settled parts of North America. The back board would be fastened by screws to a wall; the shelf itself was usually supported by a shaped bracket. This example is of pine, forty-two inches tall, and retains its old brown paint.

1830–60

Miss Patricia Lockwood, Ottawa

558. This spoon rack in birch is a simple but appealing fretwork product from eastern Ontario. As is frequently the case with such provincial pieces, the date of the brass drawer pull may be considerably earlier than that of the rack itself.

1820–40

Mr. & Mrs. J. E. Flanigan, Brockville

559. A simpler and cruder spoon rack of pine shows traces of old red finish. Like the preceding example, it has a shallow drawer and an open well-type shelf for storage of small kitchen items. This one comes from Frontenac or Lennox and Addington County.

1830–50

Mr. & Mrs. Thomas L. Riedel, Bath

560. A canterbury, a rack primarily for music but also used like later magazine-racks for periodicals and folio publications, is an English development, usually of early- to mid-nineteenth-century design. This Ontario version, which looks like a cradle with dividers, is a provincial piece of walnut, pine, and whitewood.

1850–60

Mrs. H. C. Walker, Toronto

561. One of the most familiar pieces of rural Ontario furniture must be the tiered plant stand which appears on so many country verandas. Here is a Glengarry County example of pine painted yellow and green. The tradition dates possibly from the 1830s but most examples surviving are no doubt of late-nineteenth- or even early-twentieth-century make.

Mr. & Mrs. Russell Harper, Alexandria

562. A hall tree of neo-classical influence incorporates an urn shape, scrolls, and lyre motif in a basically very simple rack of figured mahogany veneered on pine. Similar designs were illustrated in Loudon's *Encyclopaedia* and other style guides of the period. The box-like base is to support (and catch the drip from) umbrellas.

1830–50

Bellevue House, Kingston

Philip Shackleton

This superb, fully illustrated volume provides an authoritative guide to some of the most interesting furniture made in Ontario from the beginnings of settlement to 1860. From years of experience as a collector, dealer, and consultant, Philip Shackleton has selected nearly 600 pieces of the furniture of old Ontario. Each item is fully described with careful attention to the woods used, original finish, and outstanding details; and each is accompanied by a photograph, almost all of which were taken by the author especially for this volume.

The major concern of this book is with the many pieces most likely to be found by collectors today. But Mr. Shackleton has also included examples of the primitive, improvised furniture of the frontier, as well as later pieces of the more sophisticated variety, the refined work in choice material of skilled craftsmen. There are separate sections devoted to each major category: chairs, sofas and settees, bedsteads, cradles, chests, chests of drawers, desks and secretaries, cupboards, sideboards, clocks, tables, washstands, looking-glasses, and miscellaneous furniture. In his valuable introduction, Mr. Shackleton writes of the early settlers in Ontario and where they came from, the changing fashions in furniture, and the history of furniture-making in Ontario.

This beautiful book, presented here in a popularly priced edition, has been widely recognized as an outstanding work of reference, catalogue, and guide for collectors and for all those with an interest in the rich heritage of craftsmanship from old Ontario.

Philip Shackleton lives in Manotick, Ontario. A graduate of the University of Toronto, he is an authority on early Canadian furniture. For many years an active dealer in antiques, he now caters to special interests in the field. He was an advisor in the major restorations at Upper Canada Village and has been a consultant and supplier of period furniture for many of the important restoration projects in Canada.

"Beautiful, authoritative and comprehensive." *Toronto Star*

"In addition to being an expert on Canadian furniture, the author is a first-rate photographer. It is a combination of his expertise in both fields that makes the book so outstanding...an instant classic." *Hamilton Spectator*

Macmillan of Canada / Toronto   ISBN 0-7705-1665-3

The Furniture of Old Ontario